Advance Praise

"*Online by Choice* is a must-read from two well-known authors in the K–12 online education space. Prompted by the expanded use of online learning environments during the pandemic, Moore and Barbour describe how the 'not so perfect' experiences of untrained and unprepared teachers and students has led to further development of the online medium as part of a new and emergent educational ecosystem."

—**Dr. Randy LaBonte**, CEO, CANeLearn,
researcher, Vancouver Island University

"Do it this way! Moore and Barbour have expertly constructed a how-to (and why-to) book that is packed with practical, research-based guidance for designing flexible online learning solutions. Both newbies and seasoned pros will find tangible ideas and resources to help them understand community needs, design with intentionality, and support student success. It's a playbook you will keep coming back to."

—**Joseph R. Freidhoff, PhD**, vice president, Michigan Virtual

"*Online by Choice* gives educators on the frontlines and at the policy table all the tools they need to transcend fruitless fretting over emergency remote instruction and create the resilient, responsive learning ecosystems their students and communities deserve. Stephanie Moore and Michael Barbour put decades of hard-won expertise to work interrogating skewed assumptions about online learning while providing teachers and school leaders practical strategies for designing education environments that actually work—for today and tomorrow."

—**Mickey Revenaugh**, education innovator and
cofounder of Connections Academy

"The book we need in education right now! *Online by Choice* is not just about online learning, but about the education ecosystem. Exacerbated by the pandemic, online education has lacked a clear focus and strategic placement in traditional in-person education. Focusing on the key elements of resilient systems, *Online by Choice* is a roadmap for incorporating online learning into an engaging, consistent, and flexible educational system for all learners."

—**Colleen K. O'Neil, EdD**, P–12 education leader and teacher

"During COVID-19 lockdowns, most students, families, and teachers experienced some form of remote learning. Some found it not to their liking, but many discovered that they loved the flexibility of learning free of time and space constraints. Post-pandemic, many schools, districts, and national governments are creating online and hybrid schools for the first time. *Online by Choice* demonstrates the why, what, and how of online learning, whether you're a parent, teacher, or school or national leader."

—**John Watson**, founder, Digital Learning Collaborative

"*Online by Choice* is the go-to guide for educationalists looking to expand into online provision or rethink their current online offering. Underpinned throughout by research and case studies, Moore and Barbour guide you through the process of determining what excellent online offerings entail in your context. They then outline the practical steps required for you to convert your online design into an online educational ecosystem. A compulsory read for all involved in online schooling."

—**Heather Rhodes**, principal, Harrow School Online, trustee, Svitlo School

Online by Choice

Online by Choice

DESIGN OPTIONS FOR FLEXIBLE K–12 LEARNING

STEPHANIE L. MOORE
and MICHAEL K. BARBOUR

Norton Professional Books

An Imprint of W. W. Norton & Company
Celebrating a Century of Independent Publishing

Note to Readers: This book is intended as a general information resource for professionals practicing in the field of education. It is not a substitute for appropriate training. No technique or recommendation is guaranteed to be effective in all circumstances, and neither the publisher nor the author can guarantee the complete accuracy, efficacy, or appropriateness of any recommendation in every respect.

Any URLs displayed in this book link or refer to websites that existed as of press time. The publisher is not responsible for, and should not be deemed to endorse or recommend, any website, app, or other content that it did not create. The author, also, is not responsible for any third-party material.

This is dedicated to all the teachers who had just days or weeks to try to adapt their classes to online formats; we hope that future efforts around online learning are more carefully planned to give teachers and students real opportunities to shine and succeed.

Contents

Foreword

I have been eagerly awaiting the publication of this book, and I am thrilled to see it ready for readers. Technology has revolutionized traditional classrooms, providing opportunities and possibilities for students, educators, and parents. The COVID-19 pandemic forced many educators to rethink how they deliver instruction, and introduced families to online learning. For some, the pandemic-related online learning experiences were less than ideal, but as Moore and Barbour astutely state in Chapter 1, ". . . declaring that [online learning] did not work during the pandemic turns out to be an oversimplification that can cost educational systems opportunities and future resilience." Online learning offers several benefits, including greater flexibility for students and families, and increased access to a range of courses and resources that may not be available in their local schools or communities. Many educators and parents are now embracing online learning as their desired modality for teaching and learning. While there are still challenges to be addressed, such as ensuring that all students have access to the technology and bandwidth they need, online learning has the potential to transform K–12 education for the better. Additionally, while we all hope it will be a very long time before the next event that forces a global interruption of schools, being prepared for more local events requiring online solutions for continuity of instruction is prudent.

As we navigate the ever-evolving educational landscape, it is crucial to have a reliable guide that illuminates the path ahead and empowers us to make informed choices. The book you are reading, *Online by Choice: Design Options for Flexible K–12 Learning*, serves as a compass for all those who seek to understand, embrace, and excel in designing online schools. Authored by two internationally-known online learning experts, Stephanie L. Moore and Michael K. Barbour, this book showcases their knowledge, experience, and mastery of the research related to online learning. With their collective expertise spanning years of dedicated study and practice, they have witnessed online education's growth, evolution, and impact firsthand. Their insights, perspectives, and practical advice have been distilled into twelve comprehensive chapters, each meticulously crafted to address critical aspects of K–12 online learning.

This book covers a wide range of topics, from laying the foundations of effective online education to exploring innovative designs, from building online communities to understanding effective instructional strategies and assessments for online learning. Its pages offer a wealth of knowledge that seamlessly blends theoretical frameworks with practical insights, equipping readers with the necessary understanding and tools to succeed in the online classroom.

The twelve chapters cover many topics that will seem familiar to educators. For example, you will see topics like student engagement, instructional strategies, and formative and summative assessments. These topics, however, are presented in the specific context of online learning so that the reader can carefully consider the nuances of this format. In addition to familiar topics, the authors include critical concepts such as online learning communities, the presentation of digital content, and online course organization that may be new to many educators.

Complementing the enlightening chapters, this book also includes three invaluable appendices. These appendices serve as rich resources, and contain a checklist for successful online learning, a gap analysis worksheet, and information on ethical online learning, among others. The resources the authors provide empower readers with tangible tools for implementation and foster an environment of continuous growth and improvement.

While most of the book is about quality online learning, Moore and Barbour bring attention to the system-level decisions and leadership required to ensure that quality online learning is possible. Without the proper tools, time, policies, and incentives, educators (whether teaching online or not) will struggle to succeed or sustain the successes they achieve. Moore and Barbour provide several essential questions and checklists concerning school and district-level leadership for online learning that can significantly enhance the effectiveness and success of online learning initiatives.

Choosing to offer quality K–12 online learning requires one to embrace the transformative potential it offers. It can transcend geographical limitations, provide flexibility, and create global communities of learners. The authors of this book invite you to embark on this journey with an open mind and a willingness to embrace change. They provide information and resources that can guide you through the complexities of K–12 online learning, empowering you to make informed choices and to be an agent of positive transformation in education, leveraging the benefits of K–12 online learning.

In a world of constant change, staying informed, being adaptable and being committed to providing high-quality education is paramount. *Online by Choice* is not just a book; it is a beacon of knowledge and inspiration that will illuminate your path, enabling you to navigate the future of education with confidence and purpose.

Charles B. Hodges, PhD
professor of instructional technology
Georgia Southern University
Statesboro, GA
https://about.me/hodges.chuck
June 2023

Online by Choice

Chapter 1

Online as Part of the New Educational Ecosystem

Online learning has historically been a niche area of practice in primary and secondary education in the United States. However, it has become more mainstream as a result of emergency remote teaching during the early stages of the COVID-19 pandemic, and it is a common cornerstone in academic continuity plans for disruptions and disaster preparedness. After the first year of online teaching during the pandemic, school districts around the United States reported that an unexpectedly large number of parents and students requested the ability to continue learning via the online modality as a permanent option. Now, many of those districts are preparing for ongoing delivery of online learning as an option for families. In February 2021, the *Dallas Morning News* reported that the school district in Denton, Texas, decided to create an online academy and that the Dallas Independent School District already had plans for a hybrid virtual and in-person school that they were accelerating (Donaldson, 2021; Richman, 2021). Two months later, *The New York Times* reported that "online schools are here to stay" and documented several hundred districts in the United States that have established virtual schools with the intention of offering them as permanent solutions (Singer, 2021). The story reports soaring demand with districts across multiple states creating virtual academies and anticipating significant numbers of enrollments. In a RAND Corporation report titled "Remote Learning Is Here to Stay," Schwartz et al. (2020, para. 1) reported survey results indicating that 20% of school districts "have already adopted, plan to adopt, or are considering adopting virtual schools as part of their district portfolio after the end of the

COVID-19 pandemic." This is a significant increase in the number of full-time, permanent online learning solutions in primary and secondary education.

Although online may not have been an original modality of choice for most, many parents, students, and school systems are now choosing online. Lehrer-Small (2022, para. 8) reported that even virtual academies that had been open for decades experienced "a well-documented enrollment explosion" during the pandemic and, importantly, maintained enrollment gains even after school buildings reopening. In many instances, they even added seats after schools reopened. The report features one family story that captures this change: Kristy, a mom of three, watched her two younger children in particular flourish in their learning during the forced shift to online learning; her family decided to keep the two younger children in online learning, believing that to be the best for them academically. They weren't alone—reports from several state departments of education indicate that virtual learning is more than a temporary option during a crisis (Lehrer-Small, 2022). States across the nation, including Arkansas, Florida, Iowa, Massachusetts, Michigan, Minnesota, North Carolina, Oregon, Wisconsin, and Wyoming, have seen dramatic increases in enrollments. In a few instances enrollments dipped a little in the 2021–2022 school year but did not recede to prepandemic levels.

However, online learning is not—and is not intended to be—a replacement for the entirety of an educational system. Rather, it is helpful to think of educational systems as educational *ecosystems*. Ecological ecosystems are a good analogy to help envision what an educational ecosystem is and why it is important. A healthy and resilient ecological ecosystem has a variety of different species and processes, all interacting and creating an essential richness of diversity. Cleland (2011) describes how biodiversity in an ecological ecosystem is essential to that system's flexibility and resilience over time. Dominance by any one species can create serious imbalances during more normal times and can make an ecological system brittle in the face of more challenging times. Resilient ecological systems have more biologically diverse communities, enabling these ecosystems to flourish. In difficult circumstances, such as hurricanes or other disruptions, biodiversity enables ecological systems to adapt and be flexible as it weathers the difficulty and recovers. Rather than relying on a single modality of instruction, such as in-person, to serve all needs for all learners in all situations, having a range of options contributes to a more flexible system that supports learners in identifying the options that best meet their diverse needs. That flexibility and richness of options in normal circumstances can offer an essential form of resilience during more difficult circumstances and disruptions.

Despite many lessons learned during the pandemic, most school leaders and teachers are still in the early stages of adopting and implementing online learning as they find themselves transitioning from a rushed process to a more planned approach for online learning. In this book, we aim to support educators and educational decision makers by providing research-anchored insights on effective online teaching and instruction, as well as effective system-level planning and leadership for online programs. Throughout, we feature both research-supported ideas for instruction and system-level planning, and vignettes and examples of practice from online educators and virtual school leaders. We also explore how planning and development processes can foster alignment between instruction-level needs and system-level planning and infrastructure, to lead to a comprehensive plan for quality online learning.

Building a Resilient Educational Ecosystem

In conversations and planning discussions for education post-COVID-19, *resilience* is a word and idea that comes up time and time again. For example, Moore and Hill (2020) argued that education should be thinking about online learning and face-to-face learning as both-and, not either-or, approaches to create a more resilient educational system. They state, "A false dichotomy robs us of options and agency" (para. 6), arguing further that bias against online learning as an option in the educational ecosystem is strategic short-sightedness that is "potentially the greatest threat to institutional resilience" (para. 7). Thinking of online learning as an additional option, as a subset of possibilities, rather than a competing modality, affords educators and educational leaders the ability to consider how online learning can fit within the larger arrangement of learning options and modalities. Weaving online learning into educational planning and ecosystems can help make our educational systems both more resilient in the face of future disruptions or challenges and more flexible for meeting different needs for diverse learners. Rather than thinking of online learning as a competing option or idea, it should and can be part of the educational portfolio.

What Is Resilience?

Resilience has been defined in a number of ways. Common definitions tend to emphasize a system's or organization's ability to bounce back from a challenge or respond to threats or opportunities. In the context of educational systems, authors describe resilience as the ability to maintain academic continuity despite disruptions and "being able to return previously to a good condition after facing disruptions" (Bartuseviciene et al., 2021, para. 5). However, many resilience researchers suggest that system or organizational resilience is much more than simply "bouncing back." Resilience can be viewed as happening in three phases—resilience during a crisis or emergency, resilience immediately after, and resilience as longer-term revisioning for future success. We have termed these *Coping*, *Returning*, and *Learning* (see Figure 1.1).

In the Coping phase, a system is in the middle of a disruption or unexpected event and focuses primarily on coping and surviving as the disruption or event is unfolding. Much like an individual in a tornado or a hurricane, the focus is sharply on making it through, as it should be. Ideally, over time, any Coping phase feeds into a Learning phase through a feedback loop of analysis and ongoing improvement in disaster preparedness and planning.

Once the immediate disruption or danger is past, a healthy system quickly turns to figuring out how to return to its precrisis state: the Returning phase. Sometimes, simply returning to the previous state makes sense as an objective. If one's house is destroyed during a tornado or hurricane, one naturally wants to return to a state of having a house. However, there are some dangers in staying stuck at the Returning phase. In the example of a tornado, perhaps rebuilding the

Figure 1.1 Three stages of system resilience: coping, returning, and learning.

house as it was doesn't take into the account the risks just experienced or plan for ways to experience less disruption in the future. In Oklahoma, for example, newer homes and rebuilt homes often include a safe room with concrete walls (Patton, 2013). As another example in recent U.S. history, the levee system protecting the city of New Orleans was designed to withstand a Category 3 hurricane, but in 2005 the city experienced a direct hit from Hurricane Katrina—a Category 5 hurricane. The levee system design was insufficient, leading to widespread system failures that resulted in substantial flooding, loss of life, displacement, and property damage. In rebuilding the levee system post-Katrina, the agencies that worked to redesign the levee system did not simply return to pre-Katrina standards. Instead, they designed the system for 100-year storm events, by increasing the size and scope of the seawalls and improving the pumping system around the city, along with other improved designs and reinforcements (McQuate, 2021). Staying stuck in the Returning phase would have proven catastrophic for New Orleans. In 2021, Hurricane Ida struck New Orleans as a Category 4 hurricane. Because of the lessons learned and improvements made from Hurricane Katrina, the city experienced much less flooding and other consequences from the event (Fisher & Root, 2021).

The post-Katrina Learning phase is an excellent case study in why "returning to normal" is rarely, if ever, the ideal way to define resilience. After Katrina, the U.S. Army Corps of Engineers, one of the key agencies involved in the original levee system design, conducted a failure analysis. Their report led to changes both in the New Orleans levee system design and in practices and standards for civil engineers in any project going forward. This ability to learn from difficulties and failures is essential to future resilience.

Resilient Systems Learn and Evolve

In studying when systems work well and when they do not, Meadows (2008) explains that one common characteristic of systems that work well is resilience. She states that the goal is not stability and illustrates how stability and resilience are not synonymous ideas using one of Aesop's fables, "The Tree and the Reed" (or "The Oak and the Reed" in some translations). The story opens with the tree mocking the reeds as they bend and wave even in the slightest of breezes. The tree admonishes the reeds that they should be more like the tree, able to stand firm and mighty and resist any winds. Then a strong storm comes, described as a violent storm or a hurricane, depending on the translation. After the storm passes, the tree's many branches are broken and scattered about. The tree's rigidity, which seemed like strength in lighter winds, had become a weakness in the storm, making the tree's system brittle. But the reeds were able to bend and flex even with the strongest of winds, so after the storm passed they remained largely undamaged. Often, resilience is defined as stability—as the ability to resist and withstand—when it should be approached as the ability to be flexible and adaptable. Meadows (2008) describes resilience as stemming from a rich infrastructure, with two key features central to building more resilient educational ecosystems: (1) the ability to learn and adapt or evolve, and (2) the biodiversity (or ecodiversity) to provide this rich infrastructure.

Evolving, Not Just Rebuilding

Meadows explains that resilience in a system stems from *feedback loops*, which feed information about the system back into the system. Sometimes they provide good information that helps with decision-making, and they do so in a timely manner, in which case the system is working well and is able to make good decisions based on quality information it gets quickly enough. Other times, the system either has poor information (focuses on the wrong things, lacks information, relies on perceptions rather than actual data, etc.), or the right people do not get that information in a timely enough manner to act on it, or both. In this case, the system is working poorly. A system that gets and uses bad information or doesn't get information in a timely enough manner has difficulty learning and evolving because it doesn't know what it should learn and it can't adapt because it doesn't know why or what to adapt from or to. A system that does get good information in a timely enough manner, in contrast, can identify important lessons to be learned and take action based on that information and those lessons learned.

Thus, Meadows explains, having feedback loops in a system is necessary, but not sufficient. The presence of feedback loops is a sign of a strong system. And having feedback loops that help the system restore and rebuild is even stronger. But the strongest systems have feedback loops that are designed and used to help the system learn, create or design new possibilities, and evolve (see Figure 1.2). This ability to learn from situations and evolve (through creating new possibilities or redesigning existing infrastructure) is essential to future resilience. This involves analyzing what happened that worked well and did not work well during a moment of crisis and identifying areas of improvement.

For online learning, declaring that it did not work during the pandemic turns out to be an oversimplification that can cost educational systems opportunities and

Figure 1.2 Strongest systems are those with feedback loops that help them learn, create, design, and evolve.

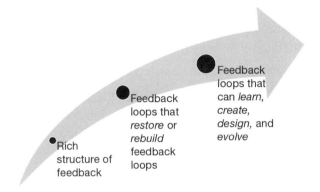

future resilience. In an analysis of how well educational institutions weathered the pandemic, Hill (2021) observed that while no single variable can explain which institutions thrived, it was clear that those with previous investments in online education and that had embedded it such that it was mainstream experienced far less disruption during the COVID-19 pandemic. Two ideas are key here: (a) online learning played an important role in institutional flexibility, and (b) online learning that was well established and deeply embedded into an educational system was key to resilience. Those that fared better featured online learning that was integrated and established and had been supported and institutionalized over time. Simply shifting to online quickly when it was not otherwise embedded in important ways was not sufficient. In such a case, learners and educators do not have well-developed habits and practices that they can more easily shift to or turn on when they need to rely on that modality more than usual. Such preliminary postmortem analyses of school performance during the pandemic suggest that weaving online learning into the fabric as part of a "new normal" for everyone is an important way to create resilience and flexibility in learning systems (Moore, 2022).

Thus, the acts of integrating online learning into an educational ecosystem and seeking to better understand how to do it well (quality) and how to institutionalize it (supports) are important ways we can learn lessons from recent disruptions and challenges and adapt and evolve based on those lessons learned. This leads us to the second feature of resilient systems identified by Meadows: biodiversity in the system.

Resilient Systems Are Diverse

Ecological ecosystems offer us a metaphor for how we can think about the educational ecosystems we design and build. Biodiversity has long been understood as an important feature of ecological ecosystems that are resilient over time. For example, Cleland (2011) explains how a biodiverse community is essential to an ecosystem's ability to adapt and fluctuate over time. Different organisms in the system are often better or less adapting to fluctuations in the environment. Some organisms may thrive better in warmer years but struggle in colder years, for example, while other organisms may thrive better in colder years but struggle in warmer years. In other ecosystems, certain species play a central role in helping systems rebuild after a major disaster. In forest and mountain biomes, for example, aspen trees are quick to grow into bare or sparse areas after wildfires and help the biome retain soil and regrow organic material quickly that can feed further long-term regrowth. A forest or mountain biome that features only pine trees might struggle to rebound after a forest fire, but the presence of alternative species like aspens helps the biome recover.

When too much damage occurs over time and causes a species to disappear from a biome or ecosystem, that ecosystem can become destabilized and have trouble recovering from disasters. For example, as climate change, pollution, and overfishing lead to warmer waters and loss of habitat for species in some coastal and marine biomes, that cascades into loss of biodiversity, which creates systems that struggle to survive in such difficult conditions (Kennedy et al., 2002). As illustrated in Figure 1.3, Species 1 may flourish in warm years ("above average") but struggles in cold years ("below average"); conversely, Species 2 may struggle in warm years but flourish in cold years. If a system is dominated by either species alone, the system will struggle through these fluctuations. However, if both species are present in the ecosystem, that system will remain relatively stable over time even if the overall balance across the two species fluctuates under the differing conditions.

In landscape architecture, Holmes (2021) explores how biodiversity is critical for "designing for change" and anticipating changing conditions. He describes how professionals in their field are increasingly asked to design landscapes that are more resilient to rapid changes and unpredictable extreme events. A key principle he advances as "designing for change" is multilayered diversity: genetic diversity within species diversity within ecological diversity. Professionals in education are similarly increasingly asked to design *educational landscapes* that are more resilient

Figure 1.3 Biodiversity in an ecological ecosystem as conditions change.

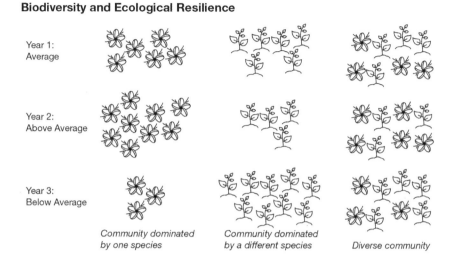

Biodiversity and Ecological Resilience

Year 1:
Average

Year 2:
Above Average

Year 3:
Below Average

*Community dominated
by one species*

*Community dominated
by a different species*

Diverse community

to rapid changes and unpredictable or more extreme events. Using these insights and analogies from ecological and natural sciences can help us think about how classroom learning and online learning can and should coexist as different species in a more diverse—and therefore more resilient—educational ecosystem.

Rather than relying purely on one modality (or one educational "species") in the educational ecosystem, integrating online learning in meaningful ways during average years can create better resilience in the system over time. In years or situations when it may become necessary to lean more on online learning, having it already established as an option in the system makes it easier to rely on (Coping) and then shift back to relying on it less as conditions change (Returning) and lessons are applied (Learning). Having zero presence of online learning, however, contributes to a more brittle system that is more likely to crack or break under the pressures of challenging circumstances. This happened in many educational systems during the pandemic, as visualized in Figure 1.4.

Online Learning Ecosystems as Educational Resilience

As noted earlier, the educational systems that fared better during the pandemic were those that had already incorporated and established online learning. The presence of this second modality, a sort of second "species" in the system, created flexibility,

Figure 1.4 Reliance on one modality—in-person learning—created a brittle system that struggled under the pressure of the pandemic.

Community
dominated by
one modality
(in-person)

Year 1:
Average year

Year 2:
Exceptional year

Year 3:
Pandemic

affording the ability to shift to it more seamlessly. As we discuss in Chapter 4, emergency measures to move to online learning are not the same as an established online infrastructure. Emergency measures lack the rich infrastructure, habits, and practices that make it a truly robust alternative learning modality. Imagine if, in an extremely cold or hot year, biologists suddenly introduced a new species into an ecosystem. Organisms that aren't well established need time to build their habitats—to truly take root and become established. Similarly, introducing new modalities *in the middle of the emergency or crisis* is not a recipe for success. Instead, more meaningful and intentional integration of the new modality during more average times is a better way to prep the soils and sow the seeds for success when more challenging conditions do arise.

Educational systems have the choice and the opportunity to envision what's next: returning to in-person modality (Figure 1.4), or learning to develop an educational ecosystem with diverse modalities, creating the rich infrastructure that characterizes resilient systems (Figure 1.5), with possibilities of in-person and online modalities coexisting, and even blended learning playing a key role in stitching them together. Developing a robust online and blended learning infrastructure for any district is an integral part of disaster preparedness and planning. While an online academy may serve a smaller portion of learners during normal conditions,

Figure 1.5 Imagining what is next: diverse modalities creating a more resilient system that meets different needs.

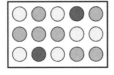

Learning ecosystem with
diverse modalities

Diverse modalities meeting
different needs

that infrastructure can be a real asset during a disruption. So we encourage schools to consider developing online and blended learning as part of their larger educational ecosystem. Often the discourse around online learning or, really, any new technology is that of replacement or displacement. But what we see throughout the history of educational technology developments is that, rather than displacing or replacing traditional education or teachers, they provide *additional* options that augment systems and provide new opportunities for learning.

Questions About the Effectiveness of Online Learning

As the saying goes, anything worth doing is worth doing well. If we are to serve our learners well, this maxim certainly applies to integrating online learning into the educational ecosystem. Many experienced a low-quality version of online learning during the pandemic that understandably raised many questions and concerns. As you consider and plan permanent online learning options, you may be wondering about common assertions made about online learning, such as whether it is effective, whether it leads to learning loss, and whether it has a negative impact on students' psychological and/or emotional well-being. Here we offer a summary of the research on these important questions. Throughout the book, we provide more detailed treatment on these topics, as well as research-anchored design decisions and strategies to help mitigate concerns about effectiveness or negative impacts. The content presented throughout this book offers a research-grounded approach to online learning and the various elements and design decisions that contribute to effective, supportive learning in the online and remote learning environment.

Is Online Learning Effective?

While there is quite a bit of bias against online learning—and indeed, many instances of emergency remote instruction offered during the pandemic were not high quality— research shows that online learning is as effective as or even more effective than face-to-face learning. Online learning was not invented during the pandemic; rather, it is a well-established modality of instruction that has been extensively studied for over two decades, building on a richer history of research and development on distance education using various modalities. There is enough research on online learning that several meta-analyses (statistical summaries of research data across multiple studies) have been conducted over the years (Bernard et al., 2004; Zhao et al., 2005). This includes a meta-analysis by the U.S. Department of Education (2009), which noted that few rigorous research studies at that time had been published on the effectiveness of online learning for K–12 students. However, those few studies found that students who took all or part of their classes online performed better (on average) than those taking the same courses through traditional in-person instruction. They also found that students in online learning spent more time on instructional tasks and that differences between online or in-person modalities were larger when researchers observed differences between the design of online and the design of face-to-face instruction (such as different instructional approaches). This analysis echoes research findings in online learning across many studies over time (Means et al., 2014). In fact, the educational technology research community has stopped conducting these "media comparison studies" (Lockee et al., 2001; Surry & Ensminger, 2001) because they were generating no new insights and were not helpful in identifying what variables specifically contribute to a quality online learning experience.

The picture that these studies do paint is that the effectiveness of *any* learning environment depends greatly on myriad instructional decisions, as well as presence or absence of systemic supports. In short, the mode of instruction (in-person, online, or blended) does not affect the quality or the outcomes, but the design of instruction in any modality does. More extensive research also shows that key strategic decisions and planning around online learning makes a significant difference in the outcomes and satisfaction levels. Rather than the choice simply being online or in-person, many choices need to be made, each contributing to or detracting from a quality learning experience online.

This may be easier to understand if one stops to ponder in-person learning and supports. The mere presence of four walls is not the only determining factor in whether an in-person class is effective. We have all had in-person learning experiences that were high quality, and we have all had in-person learning experiences that were not as great. Many different factors and decision points affect quality learning online, just as is the case for classroom-based learning: from the strategies that a teacher uses to the nature and degree of interactions between learners with teachers and with other learners, as well as more systemic factors such as how well resourced the learning environment is (or is not) and whether any policies motivate behaviors or performance that actually detracts from quality and effectiveness.

Based on this research—and because of this research—as well as our own experiences designing and teaching online for more than twenty years, we have structured this book to focus on the various design choices and systemic supports that enable effective online learning.

Does Online Learning Lead to Learning Loss?

While *learning loss* as a term existed prior to the pandemic, the more than two decades of research into online learning prior to the pandemic found no evidence of learning loss. Some opinion pieces and studies from researchers have inferred a causal relationship between online learning and learning loss during the pandemic, but those pieces have been criticized for poor methodologies and unsubstantiated inferences (correlation does not equal causation), especially as they fail to account for the effects of the pandemic itself as a factor overriding modality, or effects of other educational decisions that can be decided differently. Careful analyses of research on learning loss and online learning suggest that the underlying condition of the pandemic itself was the causal agent of learning loss, as students missed school because of their own illnesses or major life changes during the pandemic due to their caretakers' illness, loss of life, or job changes (Apgar & Cadmus, 2021; Moore et al., 2022). Learning losses are not attributable to any mode of instruction but, instead, to disruptions to the learning process, such as time away from the educational environment or loss of access to resources. For example, Becker et al. (2020) found that students with ADHD struggled more in emergency remote instruction, but this study's findings are complicated by the fact that 21% of students in the study received *no* remote or online learning access during the pandemic, and participants in low-income families were significantly more likely to not even receive emergency remote instruction. Furthermore, Becker et al. found that only 59% of school services received prior to COVID-19 were maintained during emergency remote learning, only 35% of study participants continued receiving substantive supports such as remote school counseling, and only 39% continued receiving remote tutoring. The main support continued for students with ADHD during emergency remote learning was extra time for tests—a necessary support, but insufficient. A full 25% of families participating in the study did not even receive materials to support remote learning, affecting families with lower income at higher rates.

These all result from *explicit design and resourcing decisions* made by schools and districts that could have been decided or designed differently. To the extent that learning loss was attributable to emergency remote teaching during the pandemic, those studies document instances of teachers lacking the necessary resources and supports for quality online instruction, poor internet infrastructure interfering with online access, and dedicating little to no time to planning, designing, and developing quality online instruction. Learning loss in a different modality of instruction was not evident in any research conducted before the pandemic, strongly indicating that the pandemic and the emergency nature of the circumstances that led to rushed decision-making, as well as ad hoc and uneven implementation of interventions, account for learning loss during the pandemic.

Thus, what is less effective is *emergency remote teaching*, a term Hodges et al. (2020) use to describe as the different set of teaching circumstances during emergencies or crises, such as school shutdowns during the COVID-19 pandemic. They state that "in contrast to experiences that are planned from the beginning and designed to be online, emergency remote teaching . . . is a temporary shift of instructional delivery to an alternate delivery mode due to crisis circumstances" (para. 13). They observe that the primary objective of emergency remote teaching, in contrast to online learning, is "not to recreate a robust educational ecosystem but rather to provide temporary access to instruction and instructional supports in a manner that is quick to set up and reliably available during an emergency or crisis" (para. 13). Emergency remote teaching can also involve different technologies, including the use of radio, mobile learning, public television, print materials and mail, and other infrastructures. Educational continuity and learning are different during an emergency or crisis than in noncrisis or nonemergency contexts.

Stepping through the Becker et al. (2020) study alone, decision points that could contribute to higher-quality learning and better outcomes, as well as decision points that can further exacerbate inequities and learning barriers, can readily be identified. In the decision to move online, there are myriad choices that leaders and teachers can make to design and drive online learning toward different outcomes. In the Becker et al. (2020) study, for example, we see the importance of supporting learners not just with online classes but support services as well. These services are provided to in-person learners and are part of the educational ecosystem that helps make in-person learning more effective. Removing these supports for any learners, in any modality, logically impacts their learning and their outcomes. Thus, we want to design *intentional educational ecosystems*, not simply courses and curricula.

Of course, research typically looks at and compares averages, and finding no evidence of learning loss attributable to online learning does not mean that it works for all learners all the time in all circumstances. In fact, the story of *design* that the research tells would caution against sweeping assertions one way or the other about either online learning or classroom learning. Some students or families may find the structure, resources, and supports provided by in-person learning to be much more valuable, even necessary, whereas others may find it limiting. A key take-away from the research is not that every learner should be learning online but that we need not worry about online learning as a substandard option in part because there are so many ways design it as a great learning option. We hope this book shows both teachers and educational leaders and planners the range of options and solutions they have—and we should not start with assumptions about what is or is not possible or for whom. Many schools and educators have devised surprising and creative solutions for content areas or learner populations that one may have assumed are "too difficult" for online. Throughout the book we explore real-life case studies of these examples.

Does Online Learning Have a Negative Impact on Students' Emotional or Psychological Well-Being?

There are anecdotal stories that students learning online during the pandemic experienced significant stress. There are also anecdotal studies of students who reported feeling less stress as a result of remote learning during the pandemic. More systematic research on this question presents a very mixed picture. While some studies documented an increase in stress or anxiety, the percentage of students reporting those increases was still relatively low. For example, Asanov et al. (2021) reported only 16% of students had mental health scores indicative of depression, whereas 68% reported being happy during remote learning and attributed stress to typical educational stresses (learning and performance on tests), as well as social isolation and household finances. These sorts of trends persisted across studies on pandemic learning, where for instance 62% of students rated emergency online learning as average or excellent (Chaturvedi et al., 2021). Some studies even documented decreased stress in students after the move to online learning (e.g., Gusman et al., 2021), similar to the story about Kristy and her younger children at the beginning of this chapter. However, we must underscore that nearly all of the research on the relationship between mental health and online learning was conducted during the pandemic. In our review of that body of research (Moore et al., 2022), we could identify only one study that predated the pandemic, and that focused on mothers in graduate online programs. Furthermore, every study during the pandemic measured *perceptions* of online learning, not actual learning outcomes. Perceptions of learning are a problematic proxy for learning outcomes, as students rarely prefer the strategies that are most effective. Think of dietary preferences: We may prefer ice cream, but vegetables are healthier.

Despite significant challenges with the quality and rigor of the studies conducted on online learning and mental health, there are some trends in the data worth observing and considering for online planning and design. There are some indications in the research that learners with severe depression, severe anxiety, or ADHD may struggle more in online learning environments. Students with mild or even moderate depression or anxiety did not exhibit statistically significant differences in perceptions or mental health impacts, but those with severe forms of each did (Biber et al., 2020; Racine et al., 2021). The available data on ADHD is complicated, as discussed earlier, because the only studies of ADHD and online were conducted during the pandemic, when many learner supports were removed. Our conclusion to date from the available research is that students with ADHD can thrive in online learning *if* they receive the same adequate supports offered in classroom-based instruction. However, we would also urge that schools and teachers remain attentive to individual circumstances, which will naturally vary, and evaluate interventions to ensure they are working for every learner with ADHD. (Chapter 4 discusses online learners and their needs in more detail.)

Additional Considerations: Solution Sets, Self-Regulation, and Structure

Studies during the pandemic show a common trend we have seen in online research prior to the pandemic as well. Students expressed clear preferences for either online in-person learning, or a mix of both for a variety of reasons. As we noted earlier, measuring student preferences is not the same as measuring efficacy. Even if online is just as effective, different students will prefer different instructional modalities, and those differences can inform system-level planning. Rather than focusing on preferences expressed by a few students or a subset of families, stepping back to view the range of preferences is a helpful way to think about how a system might meet varied needs and interests. The idea of the educational ecosystem can be a helpful organizing concept for envisioning multiple pathways for students afforded by different modalities (classroom, online, and blended). Creating a richer array of learning options and modalities allows learners to opt for the modality, or mix of modalities, that works best for them. All of these form a *solution set* rather than relying on a single solution to solve all problems for all learners. For each of those pathways, we want to build a model of learning that is effective for each of the learners who want to pursue that pathway.

Some other common questions that arise relate to younger learners or those who struggle with self-regulation. Many learners, especially younger ones, benefit greatly from more structured learning environments, and self-regulation is a key factor in learners' success in online learning. Both structure and self-regulation can be intentionally designed and planned for in both classroom and online learning (Blau et al., 2020; Moore, 2021b; Zimmerman, 2002; for details on how to design online learning to support self-regulation, see Chapter 4; see also Moore, 2021b, Chap. 2). Neither of these are static features of the learning environment or in learners. In online learning environments, these needs for structure and self-regulation can be addressed by providing better-structured online learning environments and integrating more development of self-regulation strategies for all learners regardless of learning environment. An interesting theme across the research on mental health and online learning is how different design decisions in online learning can proactively support learners' mental health. For example, Biber et al. (2020, p. 3) suggest that "infusing positive emotional skills techniques into a required curriculum, such as health, wellness or physical activity course, may help to reach all students," to bolster mental health and well-being. During the pandemic, the major destabilizing factors were losses: losses of routines (eating, sleeping, exercise), losses of health due to COVID, losses of loved ones, and losses of family stability (e.g., job loss or relocation) (Biber et al., 2020). If you are considering how to integrate social and emotional learning (SEL) and mindfulness into online/distance learning offerings, Stephanie's book *SEL at a Distance* (Moore, 2021b) offers detailed strategies and examples for how student mental health and well-being can be supported through intentional design.

What You Will Find in This Book

Choosing online instruction is very different from rushing to remote learning in an emergency (Hodges et al., 2020). Once schools and districts make a choice to deliver fully online learning options, they face myriad system-level planning and instructional decisions. While other resources for designing online learning tend to focus on tactical decisions and lead with technology, here we incorporate more insights for leadership of online learning initiatives, and we reposition pedagogical decisions as primary informants for technological decisions.

In this book we provide support for teachers and school leaders seeking online education solutions. Systemic and leadership-level considerations serve as book ends to our organization of chapters. In Chapters 2 and 3, we explore the initial choice of whether to offer fully online learning options and how learning gaps and diverse learners' needs can and should inform the choice to offer online options. We offer a variety of front-end analyses to use for decision-making that provide important early insights for a host of subsequent decisions, including design, development, technology selection, implementation, and evaluation. From there, we explore different varieties of online learning and how to determine which are best suited to the needs of your students and district.

Chapters 4–10 take a deep dive into quality online teaching and learning, with insights from practice and research about the ingredients that contribute to effective online teaching and learning. These chapters cover effective strategies to help online teachers

- facilitate learning and interaction online,
- build online learning communities,
- address motivation and self-regulation with online learners,
- use formative and summative assessment methods that can be employed online, and
- organize and deliver their courses.

The final two chapters of the book returns to important systemic supports and planning, covering organizational planning and performance supports that are essential to quality online offerings. Chapter 11 covers infrastructural details to tend to, such as resources and tools, skill development, policies, job definitions and expectations, and other organizational aspects of supporting any effective online learning initiative. It also covers characteristics of excellence in online schools and programs that have been identified in case studies from around the United States, exploring system supports such as a community of practice, alignment with strategic vision and mission, aligned policies, and other features of successful online programs. Chapter 12 addresses coordination between instructional decisions and school- or district-level planning to help leaders and educators crosswalk tactical needs with operational and strategic planning.

We also have incorporated several appendices with additional supports for online learning initiatives. In Appendix A, we provide a summary of main ideas from the book as a "Checklist for Successful Online Learning" that can serve as a quick reference during planning and design meetings or processes. In Appendix B, we provide a Root Cause Analysis Worksheet to help you identify barriers to or supports for online learning in your district so you can design a better support system. In Appendix C, we provide a starter set of references and resources for ethical and legal considerations for online learning, such as privacy and security, accessibility, and other topics.

In the chapters that follow, we'll use the example of a fictitious school district, which we've called Applewood, to illustrate some of the common questions and concerns that arise as schools make decisions about online learning. The Applewood School District is not unlike many school districts in the United States prior to 2020. It could be located in a state that has a statewide virtual school. Across the United States there were 21–27 states that had these statewide supplemental online programs in recent years (Digital Learning Collaborative, 2020). Maybe Applewood School District is located in a state that has one or two statewide cyber charter schools that were probably operated by corporate educational management organizations (EMOs), or maybe there are a lot of cyber charter school options – some being operated by EMOs and others being operated by neighboring or competing school districts. There were 32 states that had statewide full-time online schools in recent years (Digital Learning Collaborative, 2020). It may even be possible that Applewood School District is located in one of the 16 states that had both supplemental online programs and full-time online schools operating statewide. In fact, prior to the pandemic there were only nine states that didn't have some form of statewide online learning available to students—but maybe the Applewood School District was located in one of those nine states. Regardless, like most other school districts across the United States, schools in the Applewood School District made the temporary transition to remote learning during certain period through the pandemic. Throughout the book, we'll follow Applewood's journey, using that journey and the questions commonly raised at different stages and for different tasks, to help structure online learning choices.

Ways You Can Use This Book

We have envisioned this book as a support for all different people playing various roles in our educational systems. School leaders will likely be more engaged by

Chapters 1–4 and 11, and teachers who are actively working with students or getting ready to teach online may find Chapters 5–10 more useful. However, our book reflects a philosophy that effective online learning begins with careful planning and that instructional decisions and systemic planning should inform each other—like yin and yang, working together for a unified whole. Instructional needs should inform technology evaluation and procurement. A district's vision for online, the particular needs of learners in your district, and standards for excellence should inform instruction. Thus, we advance a cooperative vision of online learning where planning, decision-making, and instructional decisions interact with and inform one another in which this book could be used by leaders and educators to work together towards a vision for online learning.

If a school district is looking to add online learning or improve its current offerings, this book could be used for administrators and educators to work and plan together. Some chapters of this book could be used specifically for administrative or leadership planning meetings; other chapters could be used specifically for educators planning meetings.

Throughout the book and in Chapter 12, we also have incorporated *handshakes* between these two levels of planning, educational and administrative, to identify where and how these two levels can inform each other. These moments also present opportunities for joint meetings when educators and leadership can work on aligning instructional needs and design decisions with infrastructure and supports. You will also find many checklists to help you, as well as *activities, idea sparks, job aids*, , and *worksheets* to help with design and planning processes. There is also a free and open planning guide, developed by Stephanie and available through her university (http://digitalrepository.unm.edu/ulls_fsp/154), that has the same worksheets as in this book—you may find it useful to download that PDF file and print and fill out some of the worksheets during planning sessions. And we emphasize that, at every turn, we have attempted to anchor everything in practices that show repeated promise in research.

We also envision colleges or education may use this book to offer a class or part of a class on online learning for preservice or in-service teachers. Additional readings can be identified through the bibliography, and many of the activities and job aids in the book can be turned into class discussions, assignments, or activities. Much of the structure and content for this book stems from Stephanie's class on online instructional procedures for K–12 that she taught at the University of

Virginia—it is envisioned as the book she wishes she had had been able to provide to her students. While it presents research and research-anchored frameworks, we have endeavored here to translate that research into practical, applicable information, supports, and ideas for educators and leaders. The book features activities and *idea sparks* that can be used as class activities and examples, and the references at the end provide a rich list of resources that can be mined for additional class readings. Stephanie has also published a "design case" that describes the design of that course and provides examples of course materials, organization, and a virtual practicum structure (Moore and Hong, 2022). She is happy to share her syllabus for the course to help you kick-start your journey in designing a course to support online educators and leaders.

Chapter 2

Choosing Online Options

Originally, the Applewood School District offered some alternative schooling options for students who participated in Olympic sports or other activities that made it difficult for those students to attend class regularly. Lately, however—and especially since the pandemic—they've received more requests from parents seeking online learning options for their children for a variety of reasons. They had disconnected requests and needed a way to bring everything together into a more coherent plan. What was the scope of the problem? What were the various needs and reasons underlying these requests? Were these limited to middle and high school, or did they have requests at the elementary level as well? Were these requests sufficient to warrant creating a permanent online option? Furthermore, they needed a way to assess the viability of a permanent online option and develop a plan that was responsive to the needs expressed by the families in their district, but also realistic based on available infrastructure both in the district and in the community. In short, they needed a needs analysis, learner analysis, and context analysis with an environment and infrastructure scan to help them decide whether online made sense and, if so, what the shape of it would be. How could they expand from offering a few one-off solutions to a permanent, robust option that would serve a growing number of online learners well?

There are many reasons that schools decide to offer online learning and that parents and students choose to pursue online options. It is helpful to think about online learning as a type of solution that is best suited to meeting particular needs. Making the decision to offer online learning should be informed by front-end analyses of gaps and needs that can help decision makers choose not only whether online learning makes sense but also what mix of which type of approaches will best meet their specific needs. In this chapter, we start with the idea that online learning is one among a suite of educational options, situated in a larger learning ecosystem of options for learners and families. Choosing online instruction requires careful consideration of what will best fit the needs of learners, caretakers, the school, and the community.

Why Online?

Often people begin planning for online learning by selecting technologies and a learning management system. However, decades of research on the use of technologies for learning repeatedly suggest that successful efforts start with a clear understanding of *why* a new intervention may be helpful, or even necessary. This includes understanding the nature of what needs or gaps may be motivating the choice to move online, as well as how an online learning initiative fits within the larger vision and mission for any given school district. Beginning with *why* focuses on clearly aligning technology solutions with the problems they are trying to solve (rather than implementing solutions in search of problems).

Figure 2.1 presents a general decision-making process for choosing online. Once the *why* questions have been answered, decision-making regarding *what* technologies and systems to use should then be informed by a clear understanding of different varieties or forms of online learning, so that careful decision-making can proceed. For example, in a meeting with a vendor who is pitching a tool that promotes "personalized learning," it's important to know what personalized learning is, whether this tool is truly enabling personalized learning, whether personalized learning is what your school or district really wants, and if so, how you intend that to fit into your district's or school's larger learning ecosystem. Once both the *why* and the *what* are clear, the tactical decisions around the *how* are much better informed by and aligned to support desired outcomes and impacts.

In this chapter, we will work through the *why* using three specific types of front-end analysis that are important to informing the decision to offer online learning: gap/needs analysis, learner analysis, contextual analysis that includes environmental and infrastructure scan. Chapter 3 works through the *what*, exploring three types of online learning—social, individualized, and personalized—as well as blended learning. The subsequent chapters in the book delve into the *how*. Figure 2.2 sum-

Figure 2.1 General decision-making process for choosing online: from *why* to *what* to *how*.

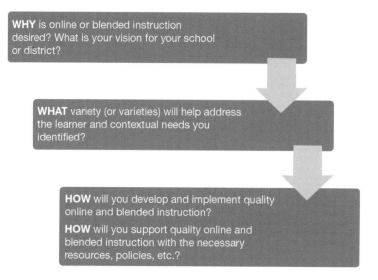

Figure 2.2 Planning architecture for online learning decision-making, design, and support: *why, what,* and *how*.

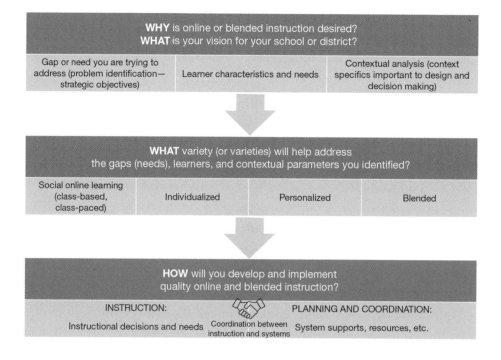

marizes a planning architecture to work through the decision to develop online options and deliver effective online learning experiences and opportunities.

To help structure the planning process, we have created several *job aids* that are integrated throughout and are available altogether in the planning guide that Stephanie developed. Job aids are tools that can be used while you work on tasks to help people remember important details or considerations. They usually prompt action, such as detailing plans or ideas for something or completing a required task (one example would be a start-up guide for a new phone or device). For this book, the job aids are intended as scaffolding for the planning process at all three stages depicted in Figure 2.2. They have also been designed to facilitate the "handshake" between instructional planning and system-level planning.

Figure 2.3 Articulating the *why* for online learning.

WHY is online or blended instruction desired? WHAT is your vision for your school or district?		
Gap or need you are trying to address (problem identification—strategic objectives)	Learner characteristics and needs	Contextual analysis (context specifics important to design and decision making)

The rest of this chapter focuses on the first part—the *why* (see Figure 2.3). For this first step in the process, the job aid in Table 2.1 includes some important questions related to needs analysis, learner analysis, and contextual analysis, including an environmental scan. Each of the questions for each of these types of analysis is discussed in detail below. We have designed this series of analyses to be completed quickly, but the section below detailing gap/needs analysis offers additional ideas for more comprehensive analyses that may be helpful as well. In the space provided in Table 2.1, note responses to the questions. Questions can also be added—again, these are prompts, or scaffolds you can adapt to suit your district's or team's planning process. Some of these questions inform system-level planning, while some inform instructional planning, and many inform both.

Table 2.1 Job Aid: Rapid Front-End Analysis (adapted from Hodges et al., 2021)

Rapid front-end analysis: Surveys or focus groups can be very helpful to gather information and insights for many of these questions.	
Needs analysis: • What are the critical instructional needs? • What are critical noninstructional needs, including ethical and legal considerations (e.g., health, safety, security, privacy)? • What learner needs or families' expressed preferences seem to be primary drivers for considering online learning options? • How many and who are expressing what needs or preferences for fully online? For blended online and in-person options? What is the nature of these expressed needs or preferences? • Why are families or learners expressing needs or preferences for online or blended learning? How can better understanding of their underlying motivations or needs inform instruction, technology selection, policies, processes, and other aspects of instructional and systems planning?	
Learner analysis: • What are important personal and social characteristics of your learners to take into account? • What specific preferences or needs are learners or their families conveying, such as flexible schedules or particular resources or supports? • How many learners will experience accessibility barriers, and what are the barriers and solutions that can be anticipated? • How can these understandings of learners' needs and characteristics inform instruction, technology selection, policies, processes, and other aspects of instructional and systems planning?	
Contextual analysis: • What is the status of internet connectivity and availability in your local neighborhoods and district? • How many families or learners who prefer online options have and plan to use internet access? How reliable is that access? How many have and plan to use mobile devices and networks? How can you ensure can equally access content, media, interactions, etc.? • How can policies and plans for technologies include considerations of learners' living environments to inform expectations on availability, schedule, willingness to share video, etc.?	

Environmental scan/infrastructure analysis:	
• What infrastructure will students have access to? • What different education and communications infrastructures can you tap into? For example, does it make sense to partner with a local public radio or television station as well, to integrate some nononline options? • What backup systems and infrastructure are considered alternatives in case of disruptions? For example, if mobile is more reliable, how can your plan incorporate mobile flexibility from the beginning?	

We have adapted the questions in Table 2.1 from Hodges et al. (2021), with the aim to incorporate resilience as a part of your systems planning process. Hodges et al. created a rapid front-end analysis for emergency remote teaching that better addresses disruptions and emergency situations. It may be worth reviewing some of those considerations as well, to consider how you can include more resilience in your front-end planning.

Gap/Need Analysis: What Gap or Need Will Be Addressed?

The first part of Table 2.1 focuses on needs. We think of needs as gaps. Kaufman (2000b) defined a need as a gap between current results and desired results. In other words, it's useful to start with questions around what online learning will help address and why online learning in particular is best suited to bridging that gap. A gap or needs analysis not only can help planners or designers identify gaps or needs but also can help describe a desired end state and identify metrics for success that can inform evaluation and progress. It is good to start by questioning assumptions around whether online learning is indeed the right solution for addressing the need. During COVID-19, part of the problem that arose around online learning was it was often quickly selected as a solution when in fact critical variables suggested other solutions might have been better under the circumstances. As we witnessed, not all learners had reliable access to internet connections. Solutions that relied on these connections failed to bridge actual needs. Some districts installed internet hotspots on buses and parked them around their areas. Others relied more heavily instead on solutions that could be delivered via mobile phones and tablets using a cellular network. Others still identified a suite of solutions that included public television, public radio, and print/mailings.

We recommend starting first with a sound understanding of why online learning is desirable. This means identifying the felt needs or preferences that learners and their families are expressing, as well as mapping out both instructional and noninstructional needs that should be addressed.

What are the critical instructional needs?

Is the need for a few classes, so you can pool enrollments across different schools? Or is the need for an entire curriculum or even for multiple grades, or to address demand from families and students for a full-time online option? Start first by identifying the educational goals and gaps online learning will meet, and then identify what learning objectives and content areas will need to be covered. Note anything that comes to mind on types of activities as well, such as labs or field experiments for science classes or physical activities for phys ed.

What are critical noninstructional needs, including ethical and legal considerations?

Considerations that must be incorporated into the planning process that are not solely about learning outcomes include such concerns as health, safety, security, privacy, and accessibility, which should all greatly inform decision-making. For example, how will students' data be protected in any of the technology systems that you select for online offerings? How will parents and students be informed about data collection and use and be able to consent or opt out? Generate a list of specific concerns—both legal and ethical—that you want to ensure are addressed as you evaluate tools, platforms, and activities, so you can incorporate these considerations into evaluation and procurement processes. This front-end analysis should form the basis for any policies that you develop, as well as technology evaluation and selection criteria.

What learner needs or families' expressed preferences seem to be primary drivers for considering online learning options?

If you have not already done so, surveying and meeting with families through open houses or focus groups to learn more about what their preferences are relative to online can be helpful. Try to focus on inviting those who are interested in online options so the conversation is not distracted by those who only wish for in-person learning. By engaging those who are interested in online learning, you can better understand their specific reasons and motivations for their interest, which can allow you to better tailor the online system to those who will actually use it.

How many and who are expressing needs or preferences for fully online? How many and who are expressing what needs or preferences for partially online? For blended and in-person options? What is the nature of these expressed needs or preferences?

Sometimes a few loud voices can obscure how many people are actually interested in a given option. Consider surveying students and families for their interests or needs that would suggest fully online. For such surveys, interest can be surveyed directly (e.g., "Would you like to have some online options?" or "Describe for us the types of online learning options you would like to see") as well as indirectly ("Do you experience schedule conflicts that we can help deconflict?" or "What are some learning opportunities or experiences you wish were available?"). Questions that are not specifically about online learning can be a great way to identify specific opportunities without assuming online learning as the default solution.

Why are families or learners expressing needs or preferences for online or blended learning? How can better understanding their underlying motivations or needs inform instructional and systems planning?

Questions that are not specifically about online learning can be a great way to identify why learners or their families are interested in online learning, and this can inform instruction, technology selection, policies, processes, and other aspects of planning at both the instructional and systems levels. Often, we hear about schedule conflicts or family needs where a more flexible modality allows a family to better manage their needs, whether it's related to health issues or job-related for a parent or caretaker. During the pandemic, we also heard many instances of learners who preferred online because they experienced less bullying, racism, or other forms of discrimination in online environments. Some of these underlying motivations may suggest that online learning is helpful. Others may reveal school climate issues that should be addressed regardless of the medium of instruction. It may also be important to observe trends in who selects online and who does not, to identify when and how possible diversity and equity issues are affecting learning and decision-making. While indirect questions can illuminate some of the whys, direct questions may also be useful (e.g., "Why is online learning an appealing option to you?" or "What specific needs or problems do you believe online learning will help you address?" or "What specific opportunities do you believe online learning could create for your educational journey?").

Learner Analysis: Learner Needs or Characteristics That Should Inform Decisions

Most learning analysis focuses on understanding what your learners already know. This is a microlevel focus. For choosing online learning, we want to zoom out to more macrolevel understandings of learners to inform online learning choices and design decisions.

What are important personal and social characteristics of your learners to take into account?

As we witnessed during the pandemic, characteristics of students personal and social lives greatly influenced their ability to participate in online learning. For example, students whose families had lower incomes were less likely to have an adult who could work from home and also less likely to have reliable internet access. Some students also have home lives that are much more fraught with tension than the school environment, making online learning at home an extremely stressful proposition. Conversely, some students had good support networks at home and reliable internet access. Others also experienced less stressful learning environments at home than at school. Better understanding your learners can challenge assumptions. Teachers may be in a particularly helpful position to provide insights about what they hear or observe. As with all of the other considerations, the key here is to not overinterpret observations, comments, or survey results to presume that what's best or preferable for one is best or preferable for all. Where and how does learner diversity surface as you seek to better understand learners' personal and social characteristics, and what does that suggest for an educational ecosystem design to better serve diverse needs and learners?

What specific preferences or needs are learners or their families conveying, such as flexible schedules or particular resources or supports?

You may gather quite a bit of this during your needs analysis, especially if you incorporate learner/family analysis into a comprehensive needs analysis process. As you develop needs assessment surveys, town halls, or focus groups, consider how you can drill down to understand specific needs that families are trying to convey. It may be helpful to categorize these or preferences, such as flexible schedules, new or different learning opportunities, and learner differences (e.g., ADHD or accessibility needs). One way to frame questions to gather specific insights can be to ask about barriers or issues experienced with in-person learning and why or how an individual believes online learning can help overcome those barriers or difficulties. This may suggest not just different modalities but different strategies or different instructional approaches altogether, as well as improvements to in-person learning.

How many learners will experience accessibility barriers, and what are the barriers and solutions that can be anticipated?

Accessibility and other equity issues are much harder to address at the point of fixing or reengineering a system or an environment. Rather than waiting for issues to crop up, how can you anticipate these needs from the beginning? Accessibility needs are not an automatic determinant that online learning will not be successful; indeed, some students with disabilities express that online learning is a more desirable or more equitable learning environment. Some learners with accessibility needs will likely select online learning, or select online options as part of a blended solution, if given the chance. Who are those students in your school or district who would choose online and also have accessibility needs? How can you then incorporate accessibility considerations into criteria for technology evaluation and procurement? What are supports or resources that should be made available at a distance to support these learners? The following summary of a study on accessibility practices during emergency remote teaching may provide some ideas.

Idea Sparks: Accessible Online Learning Designs

Although some schools cut or ceased accommodations and accessibility supports during the pandemic, many educators and leaders made different decisions. Rice (2022) shared examples from teachers of students with disabilities in kindergarten, Grade 3, Grade 6, and Grade 10 who made different choices to ensure their students would still benefit instructionally from various technologies and changing modalities. They shared how they reflected on and reconsidered their technology choices and uses and adapted their practices to create more accessible and inclusive learning environments. For example, at first they appreciated the ability to mute students but then changed their use of that feature to give students more voice and power in their online classes. Another shared that she initially turned off chat features but then realized that created barriers to learning and connecting that were very important for students. By changing her use of chat, she made her online class more inclusive and less exclusive. Another teacher shared an instance where she was initially excited to use surveillance software that her district had purchased. She thought this would help her keep her students on task, but in one instance she stopped a student with autism from playing a learning game, and the student reacted intensely and negatively to this. She realized the features were disempowering her learners, so she rethought her practices to emphasize more structure and integrate warnings and student consent.

Teachers in Rice's (2022) study also used educational technologies for more than just instruction. They used learning technologies to support students with educational needs by working closely with families and other specialists such as counselors or therapists. They reported using a range of communications strategies and technologies like email and phones to stay in touch with families and experts so they could monitor students' learning as well as their social and emotional well-being. Educators also used video to conference with parent meetings, which contributed to increased parent access and decreased parent discomfort compared to in-person meetings in schools where parents often felt overpowered.

How can these understandings of learners' needs and characteristics inform instructional and systems planning?

Once you identify various characteristics, be sure to explicitly map out implications for decisions regarding instruction, technology selection, policies, processes, and other aspects of instructional and systems planning, such as instructional strategies, infrastructure needs, and supports and resources. Before we delve into instructional details and systemic supports, during the initial planning process it is helpful to create a map of instructional implications and system support implications and to brainstorm how insights from your needs, learner, and context analysis influence both instructional decisions and system decisions. This can be used during key processes such as technology evaluation and procurement processes, as we've noted above. Generate a list of questions based on your needs, learner, and context analysis that you can incorporate into evaluation criteria and ask these of vendors as part of your procurement process. These processes are key leverage points that schools, districts, and states have in driving technology developers to create solutions that meet these needs.

Idea Sparks: Meeting Different Learner and Learning Needs

Students and their families choose online learning for a variety of different reasons. The **Texas Tech University K–12** online public school system serves U.S. students, global students through international partnerships, and adults seeking to complete their high school diplomas. They identify four different populations in particular whom they serve: full-time students who want a fully virtual/remote program; international students who want to participate in a dual-diploma program; credit-seeking part-time students who want to make up lost credits; and advanced part-time students who want advanced classes that aren't available in their local districts.

In contrast, **Gem Prep Online** focuses on supporting students in a specific geographic region, in this case the U.S. state of Idaho. Gem Prep is unique from others by focusing on college readiness and having a more college preparation emphasis in its vision and design. While is it a K–12 public charter school, students can earn 18 college credits and even graduate with a two-year associate degree. Students at Gem Prep who live near a bricks-and-mortar school can participate in face-to-face activities like extracurriculars and field trips and even take periodic face-to-face classes. They also feature such wrap-around supports as tutoring and supports for students with Individualized Education Plans (IEPs) or 504 plans. Another interesting design feature of Gem Prep is its "learning societies" environment: As part of a learning society, students can access their online classes with other Gem Prep students from a community space such as a church building, recreation or community center, or a family's home. Under this model, students work with a trained paraeducator employed by Gem Prep. You can readily see how Gem Prep's model for online reflects a particular vision, is designed to meet specific needs, and is integrated with contextual infrastructure and resources.

Learning Accelerator (https://learningaccelerator.org) has curated a number of examples of virtual academies that vary in their mission and scope and the learner/learning needs they seek to serve. Its website includes vignettes from many online programs, links to those programs, and artifacts and resources shared by each program, such as videos on the strategies they use, rubrics, and study plans.

Contextual Analysis: Contextual Details That Should Inform Decisions

Table 2.1 separates contextual analysis into a general contextual analysis and an environmental scan with infrastructure analysis—both are key components to understanding what is feasible and what most learners and their families will have access to. As with the other forms of analysis, these are interconnected with felt needs or preferences and learner characteristics, so these may arise as you assess needs and learner characteristics. Still, it is good to explicitly ensure information is being gathered on these considerations and that they are used to inform decision-making.

General Contextual Analysis:

What is the status of internet connectivity and availability, and of mobile access and networks, in your local neighborhoods and district?
These days the difference between online and mobile connectivity and learning is quite blurry. While internet access may be less pervasive or reliable, cell phone access may be widespread even in very rural areas. Some carriers may also offer connectivity and devices for free to those who qualify. In New Mexico, for example, Assurance Wireless provides both devices and service throughout rural areas and in urban centers for those who qualify. Even if network or device availability may be low, this may be a good opportunity to identify possible partners for solutions that would increase both access to learning and access to other services and sup-

ports. At a minimum, this contextual analysis will help you better understand the nature and degree of connectivity in your district or state. Service providers can be a good source of information on coverage, or perhaps the district or state has already conducted a review of connectivity and access that you can consult for planning.

How many families or learners who prefer online options have and plan to use internet access? How reliable is that access? How many have and plan to use mobile devices and networks? How can you ensure they can equally access content, media, interactions, etc.?

These questions focus more on better understanding exactly how different learners or families plan to participate in online learning. For example, you may find that most plan to use high-speed internet; or perhaps a majority plan to use mobile devices and cell phone networks. This is important to understand because, as different platforms and technologies are evaluated for use or considered for instructional activities, you may note that some tools may not have mobile-friendly versions or have a less optimal mobile-friendly version with fewer features or are harder to read or use.

How can policies and plans for technologies include considerations of learners' living environments to inform expectations on availability, schedule, willingness to share video, etc.?

Requiring video to be turned on for synchronous discussion, or even requiring other software like proctoring software that records environments and learners' eye movements and expressions, have significant legal and ethical implications. These were very hot topics for debate during the pandemic as use of such software and policies requiring cameras on became more pervasive. Some students felt this was intrusive, while others expressed concern or shame for how their home environments would be on display. Rather than tripping into a very sticky legal situation, try to involve learners and families who wish to learn online as stakeholders in these sorts of policies. Identify possible solutions that teachers could employ in their classes to help mitigate concerns, and consider what kind of learning culture is created based on the technologies selected and the policies designed that shape their implementation. This question in particular can be reframed to ask what type of learning culture you want to create in your online classes or virtual academy, and how a given technology choice or policy decision contributes to or detracts from that desired learning culture.

· · ·

It is also wise to be aware of the current status of legal and ethical challenges to some of these technologies. For example, a student at Cleveland State University recently won a federal lawsuit in the United States against the university for breach of Fourth Amendment rights when the university used the student's webcam to conduct a room scan prior to an online test (Sapolin, 2022). Rather than using technologies that could be invasive or may discriminate against students with darker skin or learning disabilities (e.g., students who may move more due to neurological disorders or ADHD or some other underlying characteristic) and thus introduce unnecessary legal or ethical issues, concerns over cheating and other academic considerations are better addressed through instructional and assessment design decisions. Front-end analysis that helps you articulate policies and decision constraints can greatly inform decisions down the line, as well as the unintended impacts of those decisions.

Environmental Scan/Infrastructure Analysis:

What infrastructure will students have access to?
In addition to internet or cell phone infrastructure, what are other key aspects of the local environment or supports and resources that students will or will not have access to? This could include access to outdoor activity spaces for walking or running as part of remote physical education or access to natural environments or parks where students could conduct field experiments or science observations. Thinking through nononline or nonmobile infrastructure can also be a great way to generate ideas that students can still do remotely but that don't require them to be in front of a computer or tablet screen all day, contributing to a better balance that includes noninstructional needs such as health and well-being. For older students, local businesses or farms that could potentially partner for internships or co-ops could be great ways to create new opportunities for learners that better scaffold them for their career interests while also affording flexible options that are part of an online or blended learning ecosystem. Your community is your infrastructure— what options does it enable?

What different education and communications infrastructures can you tap into? What are backup systems and infrastructure to consider as alternatives in case of disruptions?
Both of these questions circle the planning process back to questioning an over-reliance on online infrastructure alone as the sole solution for enacting distance education. For example, does it make sense to partner with a local public radio or television station as well, to integrate some non-online options? If there are some strong public local television or radio stations, they may be eager partners who can help provide some interesting variety in the educational ecosystem. It's also important to understand backup systems and infrastructure that may be more reliable in case of major disruptions, such as flooding, tornadoes, or hurricanes. For example, if mobile is more reliable, how can your plan incorporate mobile flexibility from the beginning? Local emergency planning personnel likely are an excellent source for better understanding that infrastructure and what they have assessed to be more or less reliable in the community. An hour or two in a meeting with these local experts could provide key information for designing a more flexible, resilient learning system.

Framing Choices: Accessibility, Data Privacy, and Other Ethical Considerations

Svihla (2020) defines problem framing as a process of taking ownership of a problem, explaining that designers and planners do not just produce different solutions but actually solve different problems because they have framed even what seems like the same problem quite differently. She also describes how problem framing can be a shared process where stakeholders are involved in helping envision both the problem and the solution. Educators and planners make a series of decisions as they frame the instructional and educational problems they work on, for instance, whether or not to include such issues as justice and equity, data rights and privacy, and other considerations that are a part of the problem they are trying to solve (Moore, 2021a; Moore & Tillberg-Webb, 2023).

Increasingly, ethical and social considerations are being integrated into design, decision-making, and planning processes. Moore and Tillberg-Webb (2023) explore how different considerations may be incorporated into front-end analysis—a key place where we define and frame the problems we are trying to solve. Moore and

Tillberg-Webb recommend starting the process for educational technology planning and design with articulating commitments to certain values or ethical perspectives that will frame the project or effort and identifying specific ways from the beginning to incorporate perspectives of stakeholders (e.g., parents, students, community members, teachers). Designers and planners take a variety of approaches, from gathering input at different stages to codesign (participatory design) or communal design (for an excellent example of communal design for rebuilding a school in New Orleans post-Katrina, see Beabout, 2014). Decide up front how you want to engage stakeholders and what sort of process you want to engage in for your online learning initiative. Participatory or communal design can be particularly useful in contexts where sharing agency with marginalized communities may be a specific concern or commitment.

Moore and Tillberg-Webb (2023) also describe Kaufman's (2000a, 2000b) strategic planning model for any initiative or organization, which starts with desired societal and organizational impact. This can include, for example, articulating desirable impacts on educational access, health and well-being of students, and accessibility and inclusiveness of the online program. Your district could articulate desirable impacts on the community, such as increasing education and graduation rates and thereby impacting employment and community stability. When these outcomes are treated as explicit objectives, you can more readily align resources and decisions that contribute to those desired outcomes. While this doesn't guarantee a perfect plan or design (no plan or design is perfect), failing to consider these impacts during plan otherwise contributes to undesirable unintended consequences. It helps for your planning team to incorporate these considerations as explicit constraints that inform operational and tactical decisions. For example, what are potential impacts on health and safety for learners? What are your desired impacts, and how can you drive your decisions toward desired impacts? What are potential impacts on discrimination or access? Articulate strategic objectives related to these ethical considerations much as you would any other type of objective or technical specification. Many if not all of these types of considerations can also be identified and addressed through sufficient contextual and environmental analyses.

Activity: Framing the Online Learning Initiative

During a team meeting, one good activity would be to work together to frame the problem you are endeavoring to address in your school or district. Doing so can help you establish clear strategic objectives and evaluation criteria for technology selection, as well as implementation choices. Start by generating questions centered on instruction, learners, technology, your community, and ethical or legal considerations. Table 2.2 is one way to help organize a conversation and responses as you gather input from various stakeholders. This activity should help you begin to articulate the strategic objectives and school/district/organizational vision.

Table 2.2 Questions to Prompt Problem Framing and Reflection-in-Action for Online Learning Initiatives

Instructional considerations	Technical considerations	Ethical and legal considerations
What are specific instructional needs and opportunities? (You may have addressed this already in your front-end analysis, described earlier.)	• What are specific technical considerations, including desirable and undesirable features? • How do environmental and contextual factors shape your technical considerations? • What other factors, such as usability and interoperability, should influence technology selection?	What specific ethical and legal considerations reflect the values of your school/district and a commitment from the team to better serve learners and comply with legal requirements? Considerations include accessibility, data rights and privacy, student mental health, health and safety, and diversity and equity.

Summary

In this chapter, we have discussed specifics for a rapid front-end analysis that includes needs analysis, learner analysis, contextual analysis, and an environmental scan/infrastructure analysis. These analyses are key to ensuring that the choice to move to online learning is a solution that clearly maps to a well-defined need or gap. One of the most significant decision points for any educational technology is ensuring the technology actually meets gaps identified as part of a clearly framed problem or need. Choosing online learning starts with understanding the choice to develop online learning: understanding what needs and what learners are being served and how you can best serve those learners; asking questions that help you identify both instructional and noninstructional (or additional) needs and impacts of learning technologies and systems; considering ethical and legal implications of decisions that help you frame the problems you're solving and the solutions you select, such as accessibility, data rights and privacy, equity, and access issues. Questions for front-end analysis as well as process recommendations in this chapter can help you identify important considerations that will cascade down into every other decision you make around online learning.

Chapter 3 covers additional considerations that should help you develop your strategic objectives and vision for online learning and start connecting your rapid front-end analysis to strategic and operational decision points, by fleshing out the different varieties of online learning for a better decision-making schema. Then, with a better understanding of the needs, learners, and context, and clear strategic objectives and vision, decision-making can turn to selecting solutions: the *how* of online learning covered in Chapters 4–10.

Chapter 3

Understanding Different Options

The Applewood School District had made the decision to develop a robust, permanent online option. The demand was clearly present, and they had sufficient infrastructure. But the world of online learning and different technologies felt dizzying and confusing. Personalized sounded good—should they offer personalized learning? What if students felt isolated? Was it even possible for online learning to be social? Did it make sense to think about a blended option? Every vendor presentation or brochure seemed to have either big ideas or some specific tool for a small subset of needs. Plus, they knew they wanted to offer a mix of learning options for students with online classes as the main option, but they didn't have a way of organizing their thoughts that could inform what possible tools or design decisions supported the various possibilities for online learning. At first, they thought they knew what online learning looked like, but now the idea seemed difficult to define, and therefore difficult to plan. How could they clarify their vision and ensure that they built online learning that emphasized students learning together in classes?

While we tend to talk about online learning in a monolithic manner, there are vastly different conceptions of and approaches to online learning. Just as not all classrooms look the same, not all online courses or online programs look the same. In this chapter, we explore differences between online learning based on social learning theory, which is class-based and class-paced, and online learning that emphasizes either individualized or personalized learning. We include definitions of each of these online learning options and explore when and why you might choose to

Figure 3.1 Articulate what approach to online learning makes the most sense for your school or district.

WHAT variety (or varieties) will help address the gaps (needs), learners, and contextual parameters you identified?			
Social online learning (class-based, class-paced)	Individualized	Personalized	Blended

implement one of these varieties or some mix of them. We also include a research-based definition of blended instruction and a brief discussion on when blended might make more sense as a choice versus fully in-person or fully online education. The remainder of the book focuses on a social approach to online learning, with emphasis on class-based, class-paced designs and ideas, which we describe in this chapter, with a discussion of why we encourage this approach as a primary strategy for online learning initiatives. However, you may wish to consider other varieties in your online learning ecosystem to meet a range of different needs. Understanding these differences can provide greater clarity as you consider different technologies or instructional decisions and what variety of online learning those technologies and decisions do and do not afford to address your particular needs, learners, and context. This is the second part of the planning process introduced in Chapter 2 (see Figure 2.2): better understanding *what* you seek to build and offer (Figure 3.1), so that you can articulate clear strategic objectives and a clear vision for your online offerings, and then better evaluate technology and design options to achieve your goals.

Some Slippery Terms

The language of online learning can be quite dizzying, especially as vendors try to develop ways to distinguish their products from others on the market. Underlying different terms are fundamentally different visions for online learning. This chapter works through commonly used terms to provide clarity and to unpack the underlying visions of online learning that gave rise to different varieties of online learning. Better understanding these different visions is critical to making clear decisions about what varieties make sense to meet learner needs and expressed preferences. As you plan for system-level infrastructure or instruction, you may find that one variety of online learning makes most sense for some needs or preferences, whereas for others a different variety makes most sense. A clarified vocabulary can also be helpful in evaluating vendor pitches and products. Even if vendors use language differently from the definitions we provide here—and they inevitably will—having a schema for different online varieties can help you start to cut through the confusion to identify *what* type of learning would be engaged in by your learners if you adopted one tool versus another, so you can better ask which tool better aligns with your desired outcomes or options.

To clarify these terms, we draw from the body of research on online and blended learning in which researchers have spent more time than most of us can devote to considering distinctions between terms and ideas.

Online, Blended, and Tech-Enabled

Before we present definitions of each of these online varieties, we would like you to pause for a moment, take out a sheet of paper or a digital notepad, and write a brief definition for what you think each of these terms mean. How would you distinguish among *online learning*, *blended* (or *hybrid*) *learning*, and *tech-enabled learning*?

One comment we hear frequently when we work with teachers on this topic is confusion in particular over blended learning. You may also often hear the term *hybrid* instead of or in contrast to *blended*. For our purposes, we treat *hybrid* and *blended* as interchangeable or synonymous terms, so in this book we use the term *blended* for simplicity. In their attempts to define blended (or hybrid) learning, several organizations have developed percentages as a way to define these categories. Using percentages, however, ends up being rather time-consuming and impractical for teachers or administrators to measure or track. While it may be one way to think about differences, exact percentages are generally not worth investing a lot of effort. Additionally, using percentages as a way to categorize doesn't help clarify instructional quality or rationale for instructional or systems planning decisions. Means et al. (2014) suggest instead definitions that are anchored in the nature of *interactions*. (We cover types of interactions in much more detail in Chapter 6.) Here we consider where interactions take place. Many folks may focus on the nature of content delivery (e.g., is it digital/offered via an online tool?). However, consider the distinctions summarized in Table 3.1 that focus instead on where and how interactions occur.

Table 3.1 Online, Blended, and Tech-Enabled Instruction
(adapted from Means et al., 2014)

Instruction style	Description
Online	All instruction and interactions are carried out via the internet.
Blended	Some of the interactions between learners and with the instructor occur online; some interactions occur in an in-person setting.
Tech-enabled	All interactions between learners and with the instructor occur in the classroom; online tools are for information, resources, or practice activities that students use either together in class or independently outside of class, without interacting with others.

To understand the differences, some examples may be helpful. If your class meets entirely in a classroom but you assign students activities or homework that they work in outside of class in a tool they access online, that is not online or blended learning—that is *tech-enabled learning*. If, however, you design your class so that students are meeting and working together both in a classroom and virtually outside of a class for group work, that falls more under *blended learning*. If you as the educator are also interacting with those learners both in a classroom and outside of class, such as providing asynchronous feedback on their work in Google Docs, viewing a video presentation and providing recorded feedback, or engaging with students in a discussion board, that is also blended learning. Tech-enabled instruction merely uses technology for some aspect of an otherwise in-person learning experience. Blended learning means learners engage with one another and the instructor both in physical and in virtual learning spaces. Some courses may be blended on a day-to-day basis; others may be structured differently. For example, a course may meet in person on certain days or weeks and then meet online other days or weeks. This could be particularly useful if you want students to spend some time out in the field, such as field experiments, internships, observations, or co-ops: they can still document and discuss while they are in the field, but you can routinely bring them back together for further reflection and planning. In *online learning*, all of these interactions happen virtually. Without getting bogged down in percentages, as soon as you mix together in-person and virtual interactions, you have a blended learning design.

Blending can happen within a given course, across a curriculum, or both, so it may make sense to keep some classes in an in-person format and offer other classes in an online or blended format. This is an especially great approach for creating a range of different learning opportunities for students across the curriculum. Blending across the curriculum is a key way to strategically leverage online learning systems and options for many or all learners to create a more robust learning ecosystem, not just used as a separate stand-alone option for a subset of your students.

At this point, it is important to note that none of these options is better than the others. As we discussed in Chapter 1, the research does not suggest any one of these options delivers better learning outcomes. Rather, choosing among these options is a matter of matching the options with the learning objectives and learner needs, based on your needs, learner, and context analyses from Chapter 2. Choosing blended or online instruction means that some of the interactions need to be or are better conducted at different places rather than at the same place, perhaps even at different times for learners rather than all at the same time. Using the same examples of field experiments or internships, perhaps learners need to be outside the classroom to gather observations and data from the field or conduct interviews with experts.

Choosing a Modality Based on Needs & Opportunities

What learner needs or learning objectives might suggest that blended learning is a better option?

What needs or objectives might suggest that online learning is a better option?

What are some new opportunities you might be able to create for learners by leveraging online or blended options?

Students can also report their data from somewhere other than the classroom and collaborate with peers in a group either through video or chat or by putting together a group presentation on their findings. The whole class can then reconvene either in a classroom for a blended learning experience or online as part of a fully online class. High school learners in particular may also benefit from being able to spend time interning at a local business or facility, learning about jobs they may be interested in pursuing. To provide flexibility to make such an opportunity happen, a class or school could mix remote days, when students are active at a different location and report in, submit work, or participate in discussions online, and classroom days, when those same students reconvene to engage in a guided reflection activity. Or perhaps your school opts to enable opportunities for students around the state or in another country for some period of time, in which case a fully online internship or co-op experience affords learners a unique opportunity.

Idea Sparks: Offering Online and Blended

None of the options presented in this book are *either/or* ideas. Rather, they are best thought of potential *ands*. Centennial School District in Warminster, Pennsylvania, is a good example of this. They created two different pathways for learners in their districts, leveraging online learning and blended learning.

1. The first pathway features an asynchronous, virtual learning academy in which students schedule synchronous meeting times with their online teachers. They specifically selected *asynchronous* (different place and different time) because their learners and families conveyed a need for a solution that helped them resolve scheduling difficulties. Students in the online pathway are still connected to their school buildings and can participate in sports, school dances, graduation ceremonies, and other in-person events—a nice example of online learning woven into the fabric of the educational system.

2. The second pathway features a blended credit recovery program. As part of this program, students spend part of their week taking online classes and part of their time taking in-person classes in the school building.

Now that we've provided definitions for each of these learning modalities, anchored in types of interaction that occur in learning environments, have a look at the definitions you wrote down at the beginning of this section. Did your original definition focus more on content, on interactions, or on something else? How would you revise those definitions now? Using interaction-anchored definitions, how would you (re)classify your current, previous, and future teaching experiences?

Personalized, Individualized, and Differentiated

Another set of terms that get confused regularly are *personalized*, *individualized*, and *differentiated*. While these terms may sound similar, they are in fact different approaches to learning. As with the first set of terms, pause for a moment and write a brief definition for what you think *personalized*, *individualized*, and *differentiated* mean.

Perhaps no set of terms are used more frequently in vendor marketing descriptions than *personalized* and *individualized*. They connote that you are paying attention to the individual learner, and who doesn't want to do that? However, research can help provide important distinctions between these two terms. You will most certainly hear these terms used differently and even interchangeably by vendors, but as with *blended*, *online*, and *technology-enabled*, we want to provide some research-anchored definitions that will allow you to readily categorize the type of instruction being proposed or envisioned by a vendor as you review options, regardless of what language they use for marketing.

Individualized instruction is instruction where an expert establishes the objectives and the content to be covered, and then a learner takes an individualized path through the content to demonstrate mastery of that content. The emphasis with individualized instruction is mastery learning. The pacing and sequencing may vary to adapt to individual learners' paths, but the desired learning outcomes and definition of *mastery* are the same for all learners, established by someone external to the learner. A synonymous term for individualized instruction is *self-paced*, and that's a helpful way to distinguish between class-based online learning that is class-paced and individualized online learning that is self-paced. If the pacing for an individual learner varies, then you are probably delivering individualized online instruction.

Personalized learning is also self-paced, but the learner is the one who determines the objectives, the content, and the desired level of mastery. Consider your own history as an example of personalized learning. Throughout your life, you may have identified new things you want to learn more about, such as raised bed gardening, a new language, a particular type of cooking, or how to change the oil on a lawn mower. Nobody is telling you that you should learn any of these things—you decide for yourself. You also choose exactly how much you learn, what you learn next, and when you consider yourself done with the learning. Perhaps you conclude that you don't want to learn much more. Perhaps you keep going, searching for videos on YouTube, seeking out learning communities, looking for books in the bookstore, and so on. When the learner is directing all aspects of learning, that is *personalized* learning, which varies not just in pacing and sequencing but also in the focus, objectives, and content. A synonym for personalized learning is *self-directed*, and this is a good way to distinguish personalized learning from individualized learning: Who is directing the learning, who is choosing the content, and who is deciding when the learning is complete and whether the learning outcomes are sufficient?

It may be easy to assume that learning in a school context is always class-based learning, but there may be opportunities for students to engage in individualized instruction and even personalized learning at various points in their education. For example, independent studies or directed studies are a common form of individualized or even personalized learning. If a needs assessment generates felt needs or preferences from learners or families for more options where learners can customize their processes and foci, then creating options where students take an independent or directed study as part of their curriculum could be a good solution. These don't necessarily have to be completed in person, either. These course options could be designed as blended or online learning opportunities either where an instructor provides a structure and assesses a final product or where the learners direct their learning and can choose objectives, content (readings/videos), and deliverables. For example, perhaps a learner who is interested in agriculture and food science could choose to learn how to build a hydroponic garden, and that learner then directs their own learning to identify resources such as local experts, online videos, and books and to select a final deliverable that evidences learning, such as a hydroponic setup. Other learners might take the same class but choose an entirely different focus, content, and final deliverable.

Many online learning systems and products focus on either individualized or personalized instruction. Especially in instances where a vendor uses such terms as *adaptive learning*, this is an individualized or personalized model of instruction. This is very different from class-based and class-paced learning. Again, you may want to consider individualized or personalized online learning as options within an educational ecosystem. For example, your schools or district may identify highly standardized content that you want every student to learn but decide it makes more sense for students to be able to work at their own pace through the content until they reach mastery. For example, if some students in your district are behind on literacy and reading, perhaps an adaptive learning system that supports individualized instruction on literacy can make sense for learners who can complete activities and assessments on their own time and at their own pace as a supplement to the curriculum. Or perhaps you want to integrate some mental health and well-being or library-related instruction into the curriculum for all students but be able to use that content in a modular way where students can be assigned to complete the learning on their own time within a certain deadline, or as support material in their classes or class schedules. In addition to class-based, class-paced online learning that is social, you may also identify some needs where individualized or even personalized learning is a good part of your solution set.

These are not the same as *differentiated instruction*, which often focuses on instruction within a class-paced learning environment, although it's probably most helpful to think of differentiation as something that happens within a class, across a curriculum, or even across the instructional system. In fact, individualized and personalized instruction are two strategies that can be used to differentiate instruction for learners within a class, across a curriculum or across the educational system. Table 3.2 summarizes individualized instruction, personalized learning, and differentiation.

Table 3.2 Individualized, Personalized, and Differentiated Learning

Individualized instruction	Personalized learning	Differentiated instruction
• *Self-paced*: Learner takes an individualized path through content to demonstrate mastery of an established objective. • Focus is mastery learning, usually cognitive outcomes (understanding and retention), maybe near transfer (ability to apply knowledge to a new problem). • Varies in pacing; may vary in sequencing (adaptive).	• *Self-directed*: The learner determines the objectives and the content: "I want to learn about X." • Varies in focus, content, sequencing, pacing, etc., based on the learner's choices.	• Learners work toward the same learning objectives at the same time; flexibility and adaptation is achieved by varying students' examples, assessment methods, modes of representation, etc. • There may be some variation in pacing.

Our walk through these definitions helps highlight the different underlying philosophies that inform these options and infuse different technology systems and tool designs. Some designs and options emphasize learning as individualized, or self-paced, whereas others emphasize learning as social, taking place in a community of learners (see Table 3.3). These differences are very important to understand, because they frame very different possible technologies and options. The terms are not simply different words—they are very different views of education and learning. With a better understanding of these differences, you can better shape your class, school, district, or state strategy for online and the infrastructure to support that vision for online.

Table 3.3 Learning as Individualized versus Learning as Social

Learning as individualized philosophy	Learning as social philosophy
• Value in individual needs and background knowledge • Primarily focuses on cognitive learning objectives • Facilitates mastery learning and individual progress through the content	• Value in interactions/community • Objectives in addition to cognitive learning (e.g., affective objectives, collaboration/participation valued or expected)

A key decision point is whether your vision for online learning focuses more on individualizing instruction for students, so they can pursue or access self-paced options in their studies, or whether you want learners to interact with teachers and with fellow students (in their classes, districts, or even across the state or with students in other states or other countries). Or, do you want to do both as part of a learning ecosystem, leveraging each for different reasons and different learning experiences? This has significant implications for the types of technologies to procure and implement and requires careful system-level planning for which learning opportunities leverage which tools and how those options get communicated to learners and their families.

One of the most common concerns we hear educators and decision makers voice is that online learning is "not social." Your team may be hearing about or reviewing tools and systems that are oriented more around individualized (self-paced) or personalized (self-directed) learning, and those indeed are not anchored in a social definition or philosophy of learning. However, the most common form of online learning is actually social online learning, where students are in the same class together and all go through the learning experience at the same pace (even if that pace is daily or weekly). One of the reasons social online learning is so pervasive is that many educators and learners value the social interactions. In social online learning, students are in a class with other learners and have a high degree of interaction with other students and the instructor, as well as with the content. Social online learning can be asynchronous, synchronous, or both, but regardless of synchronicity it places a high value on human interactions as integral to the learning process. Most of the remainder of our book focuses on social online learning, since this is by far the most common form of online learning that both educators and learners wish to participate in, and the evidence base suggests this is the most effective approach. To facilitate decision-making, Table 3.4 compares and contrasts the major varieties of online and blended learning.

Table 3.4 Varieties of Online and Blended Learning

Social Online Learning (class-based, class-paced)	Individualized (self-paced)	Personalized (self-directed)	Blended
• Most common approach. • Students are in a class with other learners, working and learning at the same pace and often working together in some manner. • High degree of interaction with content, students, and instructor. • Asynchronous, synchronous, or both.	• Instructor/ expert establishes the objectives and content. • Learner determines pacing, may impact the sequencing. • Learner takes an individual path through content to demonstrate mastery. • Objectives usually retention and comprehension.	• Learner determines the objectives and the content: "I want to learn about X." • Varies in focus, content, sequencing, pacing, etc.	• Some interactions between learners and with the instructor occur online/ at a distance, and some occur in a face-to-face setting. • Requires consideration of geographic context (which may also have implications for affordability and flexibility).

Idea Sparks: Self-Directed Online in Georgia

Most virtual and hybrid academies feature class-based, class-paced learning. However, some focus more on a self-directed learning model. The Forest School Online in Georgia is designed around what they call *signature learning experiences*. These include maker challenges, storytelling challenges, real-world apprenticeship, quests, and other learning experiences that learners are active in directing. You can learn more at https://online.theforest.school.

Translating Definitions into a Vision and a Plan

At the front-end of your process for choosing online, you are also choosing what variety or varieties of online learning you want to integrate into your school's or district's educational system or into your curriculum or class planning. In planning guide that Stephanie created (http://digitalrepository.unm.edu/ulls_fsp/154), the process starts with articulating and aligning standards and strategic objectives. All other decisions cascade from these decisions on standards and strategic objectives. For that alignment to happen, you must articulate your strategic objectives and standards, so let's focus on these planning elements and how the varieties of online learning fit within both of these.

In Chapter 2, we started with the *why* with two questions: why is online or blended instruction desired, and what is your vision for your school or district? The rest of Chapter 2 walked you through analyses for answering the first question; now it's time to articulate your vision.

Activity: Strategic Objectives and Vision for Online

Chapter 2 walked you through front-end analyses to help you identify why online or blended instruction is desired. Summarize your findings from your analyses into strategic objectives and a vision for online learning. Then, consider whether you will also leverage online learning for additional online or blended opportunities for all learners. Articulate this part of your vision and incorporate it into your vision and strategic objectives. Below we provide an imagined vision and strategic objectives for the Applewood School District that you can readily adapt to suit your district.

Example Vision: Applewood School District

As families and students in our district seek new learning opportunities and express a need for more flexible options, our district endeavors to create an educational eco-system that better meets these needs and provides for better stability in the event of a disruption to standard operations. To accomplish this vision, we have identified the following strategic objectives that will drive instructional planning and systems planning, such as technology selection and procurement, policies, and resourcing:

- *Strategic Objective 1:* The Applewood School District will establish a fully online learning option that is anchored in promising practices from research for online learning. This option will feature class-based, class-paced instruction intentionally designed to facilitate meaningful interactions between our students and the content, with their fellow learners, and with their teachers. Our vision for online learning emphasizes active learning, not "sit and get" video sessions, where students are learning and applying their knowledge and skills to relevant, authentic topics and problems.

- *Strategic Objective 2:* To support these learners, we seek to build not simply a suite of courses or curriculum but a robust online education system that connects students with resources and supports such as the library, guidance counseling, personal counseling and mental health resources, accessibility resources, and other features of an educational infrastructure necessary for supporting learning and learner flourishing.

- *Strategic Objective 3:* We are committed to building a safe, secure, and accessible learning environment for Applewood District learners and their families. To this end, evaluation of technology options and district policies will include specific criteria for accessibility, data rights and privacy, security of data and communications, and learner dignity as values that should be embodied in our systems, both human and technological.

Establishing Standards for Online and Blended Instruction

One significant way to translate your vision for online learning into actual practice and application is through an articulation of standards for online instruction. The planning guide developed by Stephanie that you can use as a companion to this book (available at http://digitalrepository.unm.edu/ulls_fsp/154) reflects research-anchored practices, helping you more readily incorporate standards for quality that reflect most sets of standards available today. By working your way through the planning process in that guide and throughout this book, you will in effect be establishing standards for online and blended instruction. Nonetheless, anyone responsible for planning and evaluation of the online system may also wish to review the different standards and rubrics that exist today and decide to either adopt or adapt these for their districts or use them as a basis for developing one more customized to the district's priorities, infrastructure, and values. Here, we provide a set of standards your district could choose to adopt along with a summary of different standards (open and proprietary), should your district wish to adopt a more formal process.

Cornerstones of Quality Online Education

For effective online learning, the instructional design process starts with clearly defined learning and performance objectives and articulates readings/course content, activities or exercises, assignments, and assessments. Strong instructional designs help ensure a cohesive instructional and assessment strategy throughout the course that weaves together the activities, assignments, and assessment (we cover this in detail in Chapter 7). Online courses should be designed to facilitate student interaction based on research into types of interaction (Bernard et al., 2009): interaction with content, with students, and with the instructor (we cover these in detail in Chapter 6). Instructor interactions with students should be frequent, consistent, and timely. Student interactions with content should be facilitated by instructional strategies that are consistent with theories and evidence in human learning research. In other words, students interact with content beyond just reading or viewing (consuming) and are asked to engage in higher-order learning as well, such as analysis, application, and evaluation. The range of options for instructional strategies varies widely, and a strong online program reflects varied uses of strategies that are well aligned to the learning and performance objectives.

Student interactions with other students should also be intentionally facilitated both through course design and structure, as well as through affordances of the learning platform and larger technology ecosystem. Additionally, course content should be up-to-date, with regular updates.

Learner diversity can be prioritized through an instructor's willingness to differentiate instruction and/or assessment and employing principles from Universal Design for Learning (Rose & Meyer, 2002, 2013), as well as attempts to make learning materials and environments accessible for learners with varying needs or disabilities. For example, any PDFs or Word documents provided in class should go through an accessibility check, and videos used in class should have closed captioning in accordance with Section 508 of the Rehabilitation Act. Where possible, any course content presented to students, such as videos or PowerPoint slides, should be designed based on principles of how humans process visual and auditory information. Richard E. Mayer's work on multimedia learning (Mayer, 2008, 2020; Clark & Mayer, 2016) provides a well-tested set of principles for designing learning materials to facilitate comprehension and near transfer (ability to apply knowledge to a new problem). Lohr's (2007) book on creating graphics for learning and performance is also an excellent reference for how graphics and interface facilitate cognitive schema development (based on cognitive principles of learning). Any investments in multimedia content should strategically emphasize key course concepts that students should retain long past the end of the course as a way to help decision makers balance the scope of any multimedia development with budget constraints.

Finally, courses and programs should be evaluated on an ongoing basis using evaluation methods that address reliability and quality and that provide students an opportunity to give meaningful, useful feedback that can be used for ongoing course or program revisions. Evaluation does not consist of "media comparison studies" that result in the well-established no-significant-difference phenomenon. Instead, they focus on instructional effectiveness, which can be summarized in three basic questions: (1) what is working and what is not, (2) when it works and when does it not, and (3) how it works when it's working well (Clark & Mayer, 2016).

Table 3.5 translates these well-established, research-anchored standards into a set of rubrics that can be used both to inform design at the front end of the process and to evaluate effectiveness over time. They can also be used to inform technology procurement, to determine whether a platform, tool, or suite of materials contributes to or detracts from these standards. If your district wants to use scores as a way to track improvement over time, we offer a simple Likert-type scale as well, which can be used for longitudinal comparison.

Table 3.5   Rubrics to Inform Design and Evaluation of Quality Online Learning

0 = No evidence   1 = Needs improvement   2 = Proficient   3 = Exemplary

Design and planning Instruction has been designed and developed following an instructional design process that starts with clearly defined learning and performance objectives and articulates readings/course content, activities or exercises, assignments and assessments. Strong instructional designs reflect a cohesive instructional and assessment strategy throughout the course that weaves together the activities, assignments, and assessment.	
Course objectives are clearly articulated and reflect a generally greater emphasis of higher-order learning objectives, such as application, evaluation, analysis, and synthesis.	
Content (readings, videos, support tools, etc.) align with the objectives and facilitate learners' ability to achieve the stated objectives.	
Course activities, exercises, and assignments measure learning or performance in alignment with the stated objectives.	
Course evidences a clear attention to alignment and details throughout to create a cohesive course.	
Interaction and engagement Courses are design to facilitate student interaction based on types of interaction research (Bernard et al., 2009): interaction with content, with students, and with the instructor.	
Clear evidence of intentional student–instructor interaction, such as discussion in forums where students and instructor are active, virtual office hours or virtual class sessions, and timely feedback to whole class and individual students.	
Students have opportunities to interact with their classmates regularly or even to collaborate on work through forums, group projects, small-group activities, peer review of individual work, and/or virtual class sessions.	

Course employs engaging or creative instructional strategies that facilitate meaningful interaction with the content consistent with research on effective learning strategies (e.g., application, analysis, development). Course provides more than just content and weekly discussions but features assignments and activities—individual or group—in which students must apply course content. Examples might include simulations, modeling and demonstration (cognitive apprenticeship), reflection and articulation activities, and applied assignments.

Content
Course content is up-to-date and updated regularly. Videos and multimedia content used in the course are consistent with principles of multimedia learning content identified in research (Mayer, 2008, 2020; Clark & Mayer, 2016).

Course content is up-to-date and updated regularly to reflect the most recent work in the domain. Any course content that is not a "recent" publication is clearly relevant to the instruction and objectives (e.g., historical perspectives or understanding how a particular theory evolved over time) or is considered a seminal piece of work students should know.
Multimedia content (e.g., videos) supports primary learning objectives (i.e., not simply because a cool video exists). Multimedia tools are not "talking heads" but present visual content with audio narration, chunk the content into manageable sizes, and focus on core concepts without extraneous or distracting information/visuals.
Content is accessible for learners with disabilities. For example, any PDFs, Word documents, PowerPoint slides, or videos have gone through accessibility checks and have alt tags for images, captioning, transcripts, etc. in accordance with Section 508 of the Rehabilitation Act.

Learner experience
Learner diversity is a clear priority, demonstrated by a teacher's willingness to differentiate instruction and/or assessment and to employ principles from Universal Design for Learning (Rose & Meyer, 2002, 2013), as well as attempts to make learning materials and environments accessible and flexible for learners with varying needs. Learners receive timely feedback and responses and perceive the class learning environment to be supportive and welcoming of diverse perspectives, experiences, and circumstances.

Teachers are responsive, answering emails and questions in a timely manner with a clear policy communicated to students on expected turnaround times for emails, grading, etc. Teachers provide regular interaction with students in discussion forums each week and formative and summative feedback to students on their activities and assignments.

Course communications and policies convey a learning climate that values diversity and welcomes diverse perspectives, experiences, and life circumstances that every student brings to the learning environment.	
Course learning environment and materials are accessible and do not introduce barriers to learning or barriers to accessing learning activities or content. Educators and support staff make every effort to identify and eliminate or reduce barriers—technical, physical, or otherwise—that may prevent students from fully participating in an online class.	
Ongoing evaluation and improvement Courses and programs are evaluated on an ongoing basis using evaluation methods that address reliability and quality and provide students an opportunity to give meaningful, useful feedback that can be used for ongoing course or program revisions. Evaluation does not consist of "media comparison studies" that result in the well-established no-significant difference phenomenon but rather focuses on instructional effectiveness that can be summarized in three basic questions: what works, when does it work, and how does it work (Clark & Mayer, 2016).	
A plan is developed for ongoing evaluation.	
The evaluation plan includes opportunities for students to provide feedback on both courses and the program, as well as other institutional supports and systemic aspects.	
Evaluation focuses on instructional features specifically for online offerings and aims to address what is working and what is not, when it is working and when does it not, and how does it work when it works well, rather than focusing only on comparing online or blended courses to in-person courses (Clark & Mayer, 2016).	

If your district thinks it might be more interested in a competency-based approach to online learning, the Aurora Institute has published *Quality Principles for Competency-Based Education* (Sturgis & Casey, 2018). Their principles are grounded in research and standards for traditional online learning—Aurora Institute was previously iNACOL, which established the first set of standards for online learning in K–12 in 2008. Many of the same principles from their standards for quality online programs are present in their principles for competency-based education as well. Because these are copyrighted documents and materials, they are not reproduced here, but they can be located easily through a web search. These documents are similar in their emphasis on basing school design and pedagogy in the learning sciences (as we explore throughout the rest of this book), creating active learning environments, designing for interaction and feedback to students, aligning the elements of system and instructional planning and design, and increasing organizational flexibility. They include a standards document with a rubric that can be used to support instructional development, professional development of teachers, and evaluation of competency-based online learning. Their principles document is a statement of principles and beliefs about education and educational systems, with some exploration of how these principles may lead to substantive changes in how an educational system is reconceived or redesigned. Some may find the rubric format easier to understand and to readily apply or adapt for social online learning. Even if your district or state chooses to implement a variety of online learning options, you may still find the rubrics helpful in course design and online teaching for any variety of online learning, or at least as a starting point.

Additional Resources for Competency-Based Online Learning

Recently, some schools have adopted a competency-based approach to online learning (Thackaberry, 2017). This approach is similar to individualized (self-paced) learning: learners do not determine the objectives or the content but move through the material at their own pace. Before they can move on in the curricular sequence, they must show proficiency—which they can do at a faster or slower pace than other learners. Reigeluth (1993) was one of the earliest proponents for a paradigm change in education that moves from age-based grouping to competency-based grouping. He has worked with districts over the years to make this sort of shift (Reigeluth & Stinson, 2007) and more recently published a book that details competency-based education (Reigeluth et al., 2020). If you are considering a competency-based approach, these resources would be helpful, as would looking at examples such as Laurel Springs School (https://laurelsprings.com).

There are other proprietary standards as well, such as the Quality Scorecard from the Online Learning Consortium (OLC) and the Quality Matters (QM) rubric.

Although both of these are proprietary, they are grounded in current research and are maintained and revised based on user input. They both also offer a lot of support materials, including rubrics that help structure the course design process and rubrics that help design and evaluate systemic supports for online. All of these proprietary options also have user communities where people in your district can connect and share ideas. The one downside we have observed with nearly any rubric is that for some schools or institutions they can reinforce more of a cookie-cutter approach to online course design, taking out a lot of creativity and flexible ideas or options. Often, though, this results more from how the rubrics are applied than from the rubrics themselves. We also have observed situations where educators felt that the rubric we provide above better articulates a vision for online learning that is aspirational while flexible, and that the rubrics from OLC or QM provided more detailed scaffolding on how to accomplish that vision. In one meeting with educators designing online, during an activity reviewing our rubric along with those from OLC and QM, the team adopted the rubric we've shared here as their vision and mission definitions and then cut the OLC and QM rubrics to rearrange elements to help achieve that vision and to add items they felt were missing or underdeveloped (e.g., Universal Design for Learning) or to remove pieces they found less helpful. As you plan, you may want to consider conducting a similar activity with educators, support staff, and administrators as a way to create a shared vision for online learning in your district and make the most of a host of existing resources.

 Instruction and Planning Handshake

Establishing standards of quality for online learning is an important element for aligning online instructional design and plans with school and district planning. Standards should flow down into instructional features of online classes and should flow outward into the district vision for online learning, criteria for procurement, policies, resources, and other system-level planning points (see Figure 3.2). In Chapter 12, we cover in more detail specific ways that instructional needs and standards can inform each other and create a firm handshake between micro- and macroplanning.

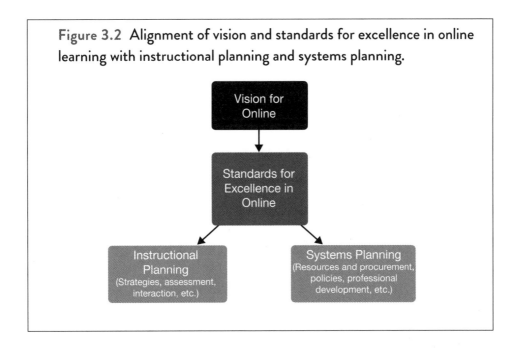

Figure 3.2 Alignment of vision and standards for excellence in online learning with instructional planning and systems planning.

Summary

In this chapter, we enriched the possibilities for a vision for online learning by covering a range of online learning varieties. A strong vision starts from the point of understanding the different options and clarifying language and approaches in a way that can better inform planning, design, and technology selection. Specifically, clarifying whether your district seeks to implement social online learning, individualized online learning, personalized online learning, or some mix that better targets different needs can help you establish a clear plan and make the design and technology choices that help you accomplish that vision. A sample vision and an example from a virtual school are included to help you develop a vision that best fits your district.

Additionally, we covered standards for online and blended learning that are anchored in research but articulated as a rubric. Rubrics can be helpful tools both as front-end inputs that guide design and decisions and back-end tools for evaluation and continuous improvement. The rubric we provide in this book features standards for design and planning, interaction and engagement, content, the learner experience, and ongoing evaluation and improvement that are all grounded in frameworks and concepts for online learning that have repeatedly shown positive outcomes in online and distance learning.

Chapter 4

Meeting Learner Needs Through Curriculum and Course Decisions

The team leading the effort to establish an online initiative at the Applewood School District was feeling much more clear and focused on what type of online learning opportunities they wanted to build for their learners. But they were still worried about whether those learners were truly going to succeed in an online learning environment. They had heard that some students just don't do well online, and that online learners needed greater skill in managing their own learning. They also wanted to design online learning to meet the needs of diverse learners, just as they do for place-based learning. It was time to start drilling down to specifics and focus on how they could best meet learners' needs. Maybe they should question certain assumptions about which learners succeed online, since some learners with various characteristics and needs were asking for online solutions. How could they support learners in successfully managing their online learning experiences? Should they weed out those who weren't ready, or could this be an opportunity to help students develop important self-regulation skills that would be useful throughout life? What were some key strategies for providing students a more structured learning environment that was still interactive?

So far in this book we have focused on a broader set of needs—shared needs across a community and varying needs across learners in a district. The goal is to identify individual needs that add up to collective needs, which can then be addressed through systems planning and infrastructure. In this chapter, we scale down the focus to individual learners and how their needs can be addressed through curriculum and course design.

Imagining Possibilities

Let's start first with an activity to help frame the process of design to think about what is possible (design possibilities) and what you can do as leaders and educators (agency in the process). To kick off this activity, consider a statement we recently heard from an individual that in online learning it is up to the students to learn the material on their own. This is a theory of how learning happens online. It isn't the soundest theory, as there's no evidence to support it, but it is this person's operational theory of how learning happens in online environments: only as a result of what the students themselves do. To be fair, there may be some instances when this is indeed the case, as in personalized (self-directed) learning (see Table 3.2). However, even for individualized learning situated in a larger formal learning structure (e.g., an independent study option within a curriculum), the teacher still provides quite a lot of structure to facilitate the learning process.

So let's start our curriculum and course design process by articulating an inspiring, sound theory of how learning happens online. You may feel that theorizing is something researchers and academics do, but in truth people do it all the time concerning all aspects of our lives. These theories inform how we understand, view, and approach the world and our actions. And these beliefs or theories about how things work get embedded into everything we design or create. For example, a writing instrument that does not have an eraser reflects a particular view of humans and how they work, theorizing a space where no mistakes happen, or if they do, one can simply throw it out and start over, or perhaps it reflects the idea that humans put to paper a perfectly formed idea. Conversely, a writing instrument that does have an eraser reflects a different view of humans and how they work, theorizing a space where humans make mistakes and are likely to modify their work in some way or may want to rethink an idea or written artifact over time. When you ask students to use something with an eraser instead of something without an eraser, you're theorizing the type of learning that will take place during the activity or assignment. We may not often pause to unpack these theories, but for online learning in particular doing so can be helpful because a lot of inaccurate theories are shaping ineffective practices.

In Table 4.1, we pose questions about key parts of online course design and delivery aimed to help elicit your operational theory for how online learning happens and perhaps prompt some further brainstorming. For each question, write (or type) your answer for both practices you currently use ("Do") and those you could improve on ("Could"). If you have not designed or taught online before, you can leave the "Do" column blank; we will focus primarily on the "Could" column. Take time to fill out this table, either individually or together as a group, as the answers here will start to shape course and curriculum designs. (As you read more throughout future chapters in the book, we encourage you to revisit your answers and revise your "Could" column in particular, so perhaps use a pencil with an eraser or a document on your computer to record your answers.)

Table 4.1. Activity: Theorizing a Quality Online Learning Experience

Question	"Do"	"Could"
How do or could any objectives or standards for your online class impact or facilitate student learning?		
How do or could any materials you post online for students facilitate their learning?		
How do or could any of your online assignments, activities, or discussions impact student learning?		
How do or could any of your online interactions with students impact their learning?		
How do or could students' online interactions with other students impact their learning?		

If you have any answers at all in either the "Do" or "Could" column, then you have an operational theory of how learning happens online. And, part of that theory includes a role for professional educators (yourself or your team) in making it so. This sense of agency is central to designing effective online instruction. Throughout this book and even for the title of the book, we emphasize the theme of choice as a reflection of the agency we have when designing online learning systems. Too often, learners and educators alike can feel like this is something that is done *to* them, or perhaps they take the view, as illustrated above, that in online learning a teacher merely posts things online and the real learning process is regulated entirely by students. It is important to flip this script and identify all the different places where in fact we exert agency and professional knowledge to make online learning systems and experiences what we want them to be.

Each of the questions in the activity in Table 4.1 reflects major categories of the decision points when designing any instruction. You may recall from Chapter 1 the discussion on whether online learning is effective. The research suggests that numerous factors impact the effectiveness of online learning, and design and technology choices reflect these factors. In short, both the presence of a design process and certain design decisions impact whether or not online learning is effective. Those choices are made by someone, somewhere. These are decision points and choices we can harness more intentionally and explicitly to exercise agency and create effective learning experiences and systems.

Design Thinking for Online Learning

Educational design is the process of harnessing decision points and choices to exercise agency and construct effective learning experiences and systems. Design has existed long before the current emphasis on "design thinking." In his work "On Fire and the Origins of Architecture," Vitruvius retells the beginning of humanity to describe design—a form of constant human yearning to continuously develop and improve upon conditions and society that leads to all manner of developments, including fire, shelter, language, and deliberative assembly (Pérez-Gómez & Parcell, 2011). Design as an origin story for humanity is a lovely way to envision how innate it is for human beings to engage in design. When we build systems, when we design classes (and in other aspects of our lives and work), we engage in design quite naturally.

Design is also imbued with ideals, such as imagining possibilities, changing futures, fulfilling human needs, recognizing that perfection is a false objective, embracing continual improvement—all ideals that serve many human endeavors well, including how we imagine ecosystems of learning and online education. Consider the following samples of historical definitions of *design* and how they might inspire what we as designers and architects of online learning attempt, envision, and enact:

- Design is the initiation of change in man-made things. (Jones, 1966)
- A purposeful activity, design is directed toward the goal of fulfilling human needs. (Asimow, 1962)
- Design is an imaginative jump from present facts to future possibilities. (Page, 1966)

- The designer . . . designs whatever purpose [they] have in [their] mind and devises a scheme to accomplish this purpose. (Rittel & Webber, 1973)
- Design is concerned with how things ought to be. The designer devises a course of action aimed at changing existing situations into preferred ones. (Simon, 1969)
- The entire activity from the stage of realization of a need to change to translating the image of the future system into reality is termed design. (Mathur, 1978)

If you are here, reading this book, in any role, you are engaged in design. We are not focusing on how things were during the pandemic or as part of an online initiative where teachers had no prior training in online teaching. Instead, here we are concerned with how things *ought* to be, with how we can make things better. This has imaginative potential for the work you and your team are doing for online learning. For example, whereas online learning may have been something foisted upon you and your students because the pandemic version was less than ideal, through design you are devising a course of action aimed at changing an existing situation into a preferred one. Inherent in these definitions are practices such as identifying or recognizing a need and responding to that need by creating a solution directed at having a more desired impact.

Imagining the possible impact your instructional choices could have on learners and imbuing that with a sense of imagination and creativity inherent in design is a great starting point for thinking about the people in and impacted by the system being designed, particularly our learners. With some ideas about what could be, let's discuss learners who are learning online and how we can best design for their needs.

Online Learners' Contexts, Needs, and Learning Strategies

One of the major insights from research on online learning is that starting first with clarity around your learners and their needs makes a big difference in the instruction's effectiveness. This section discusses important considerations of learners' contexts and needs that influence their ability to be effective online learners. We also explore characteristics of learners that contribute to positive outcomes in online learning, such as their ability to self-regulate and their motivation. Before any specific instructional decisions are made, we want to start by understanding our learners, their needs, and their learning systems and then plan instruction accordingly.

Context and Needs

In most formal instructional design models, learner analysis focuses on their age and prior knowledge. These are important considerations for any design—this is why curriculum sequencing is so important. However, other learner characteristics are equally important to consider, especially for online learning. In particular, an understanding of learners' social and personal characteristics should inform such decisions as technology and strategy choices. For learners who learn at home, the educational system has less control over whether they have access to a supportive learning environment or even stable shelter or food supply throughout the day. If there are concerns about whether a student has the necessary supports or will experience distractions at home, it may be important or even necessary to have a delicate conversation with the student's caretaker(s) to encourage in-person learning. Some students may thrive more with in-person learning because of their access to meals and ability to focus in a quiet environment where they can shut out other worries for a few hours. For many students, however, some knowledge and strategies for arranging their home environments can help them create a context more conducive for learning online. Many of these approaches relate to helping students develop specific self-regulation strategies and regulate their learning environments and processes, which we cover in the next section on self-regulation.

Additionally, students will naturally have diverse needs that should inform instructional planning. Some students will have learning disabilities such as dyslexia or ADHD, or they may have a visual, hearing, motor, or other impairment. As we discussed in Chapter 1, the answer to the question of whether online learning is the right fit for a particular learner will depend on a range of factors and family preferences. Some students and/or their families may find that online learning is better for them for any number of reasons: they can pace activities differently, they experience less bullying and discrimination, which lessens their emotional loads and allows them to concentrate on learning better; they have more supports at home; and so on. Conversely, some students and/or their families may believe they have better access to resources and supports in the physical school space, have fewer distractions, and so forth. There is no simple answer for whether a student with a visible disability, invisible disability, or any other particular need will prefer online or perform better with online or in-person learning. There is some evidence to suggest that students with ADHD, severe depression, and severe anxiety may perform better and experience lower impacts on mental health with in-person learning. And some with those same conditions in those same studies report that in-person learning environments can present more distractions or less opportunity to adjust the environment to their needs, or even feature situations that exacerbate their depression or anxiety (such as bullying or discrimination). Even as the research suggests that more students with these particular needs are likely to benefit from in-person learning, it also nonetheless shows that a sizeable minority of students with these characteristics perform fine in online learning with no differences in impacts on learning or mental health, and in some cases may perform slightly better.

A good approach for learners with these characteristics, if they are expressing interest in online learning, is to work with them and their caretakers to determine whether online makes sense, to understand why an individual learner or family prefers online, and then to further understand how they can be supported in their online learning. It is also okay to approach this as a process of experimentation for a student. Some districts require a student who opts for online to stay in the online option, but a more flexible policy will better allow educators, students, and their families to assess what does and does not work for an individual learner and then adjust accordingly.

Additionally, as discussed in Chapters 1–3, the school or district should assume learner diversity and diverse needs as a default characteristic of all learner populations, including those in the online modality. Thus, the school or district should, as a default practice, identify necessary supports for learners that will be offered in all modalities for all learners. In Chapter 1, we shared data from one study where families of students with ADHD noted that during emergency remote learning they were receiving only 59% of services they received prior to COVID-19, and nearly 25% did not receive any materials to support remote learning. We must ask questions here about whether ADHD was the real predictor of student performance. The research on students with ADHD learning online is extremely limited and is all situated in the context of the pandemic, which was an exacerbating context for learning in a number of ways (Moore et al., 2022). Obviously, if students and parents are not receiving any materials, then learning will not occur. If they are receiving materials but only a fraction of the supports they had before, then that will have a clear impact on not just learning but frustration, mental health, and other outcomes as well. Putting any learner in a learning environment where they do not actually receive instruction or supports puts them at an immediate disadvantage, regardless of any learning disability.

Building an Online Learning Ecosystem to Support Learners

Putting our design thinking hats on, we can unpack these statistics and issues to identify specific ways we can design an educational ecosystem that better supports learners. This starts by intentionally conceiving of online learning not just as courses or curricula but as an educational ecosystem—just as we do already for in-person learning (Moore & Piety, 2022). The reason these supports exist for in-person learning is because we already recognize how important they are for learners' success. That doesn't change just because learning takes place in a different modality. In other words, we can do better than the conditions described in the research: we can ensure all families receive materials to support their learning, and we can aim for equity of support services regardless of modality.

The *educational ecosystem* is a particularly useful framework for identifying where and how you can support diverse learner needs. For example, in addition to courses and curricula, a quality online learning initiative should include access for students to support services like remote school counseling and remote tutoring—for students with ADHD and for all other students. In addition to setting up these services and ensuring they are part of the expectations for the staff that provide those services, integrate access to those services in places where students and their families can easily locate them and immediately access them. Build a system of support around the curriculum to create an *online* educational ecosystem, and integrate links to those parts of the system into the learning management system and other sites or resources that online learners will use. Figure 4.1 depicts an online educational ecosystem where various support services and entities are included in the planning for the system. These are essential to supporting diverse learner needs and for ensuring online learners are connected to social and informal parts of their education as well as the formal learning opportunities. You may also identify other parts of your system that should be offered to all students regardless of their learning modality. Start by identifying what supports for learners are provided for in-person learning in addition classes. This will help you map the educational ecosystem to which all learners should have access. Your final map may look different from Figure 4.1, with different entities, offices, and resources, but this should help with envisioning the difference between individual online learning offerings and an integrated online educational ecosystem.

Activity: Mapping an Educational Ecosystem

If you do not already have one, create a diagram of all the staff offices and rooms in your physical school or district buildings that are *not* classrooms. What services/supports and entities do these offices and rooms represent? Work with each team to develop a plan for how they will support online students and integrate their presence into the online learning system and related websites. For example, many libraries now offer "Ask a Librarian" chat features. Ensure online students can access that as well. Perhaps other teams can offer similar live chat support or windows to schedule video meetings.

Next, identify the different groups in your school or district that do not have physical spaces. These might be student groups, academic groups, or other social or informal learning groups. Work with them to identify options for engaging online students, and integrate their presence into the online learning system and websites.

Based on the above information, generate a visual map of your educational ecosystem (Figure 4.1 is our example). Be sure to depict the noninstructional parts of your school or district system that support learners in some way. Beside each on your map, create an empty box. When you meet with these teams (or using notes from meetings you've already had), make notes in these boxes on how each team will reach online learners as well.

Figure 4.1 Support services and entities that should be available online to provide a comprehensive online educational ecosystem.

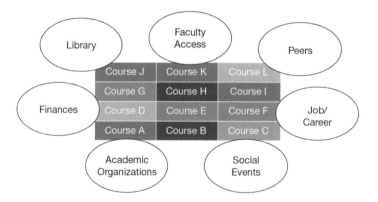

☀ Idea Sparks: Supporting Special Education Online

Too often, we hear instances of people saying certain students cannot be taught online. And yet, we see inspiring stories and examples where others are thinking and designing differently. One case in point is the Greater Commonwealth Virtual School and their approach to supporting special education online. They have selected tools and assembled an ecosystem that enables them to fully support learners with Individualized Education Programs and Section 504 plans. Learner resources are an intentional, robust part of their online learning ecosystem. They have integrated specialized learning tools into their online platforms, such as line reader tools, text to speech, accommodations for response, highlighting, ability to change background and font colors, and magnifiers. They provide teachers and students with such tools as *Read Aloud* (speech-to-text and text-to-speech), *EquatIO* (allows students to write, type, or speak mathematical expressions), and adaptive lessons in IXL to support accessibility and differentiated instruction. You can learn more at https://gcvs.org/special-education-technology/.

Structure as Strategy for Supporting Online Learners

For all online learners, the structure of the learning environment is a critical element for their success, although we must also be careful that online learning is not overstructured, as that can increase a learner's sense of distance and isolation. In studying effective distance learning, Moore (1990) identified three general strategies in online course design that impact learning outcomes and learners' sense of distance or isolation: structure, dialogue, and autonomy.

Structure relates to how you design and organize your online course, and it is necessary for learning to occur. Any course should have a good degree of structure and organization. In online learning, when courses and curricula are well organized and clearly communicated to students, students will experience less frustration with learning and the system and will have better clarity on what is expected of them and what they need to do when. Organization and clarity are common factors that students cite when describing satisfaction or dissatisfaction in online learning. That is why for online learning we usually recommend a more extended lead time for designing and developing courses before they are delivered; this allows the teacher to map out the course structure in as much detail as possible and then to communicate that structure to students even in the first messages sent to them. *Structure in a course* means having clear expectations that are communicated explicitly to students, perhaps in more detail than you may be used to. Structure also means having a consistent, reliable rhythm to the course design—daily and weekly rhythms.

However, online course structure should be balanced with dialogue and student autonomy in classes as well. While structure helps create what is known as "teaching presence" in online learning (Moore, 1989; Garrison et al., 2000)—meaning learners have a sense that a teacher is present and helping guide their learning—too much structure can actually exacerbate students' sense of distance. This is because structure can start to feel rigid and inflexible—or inhuman. Young learners or novice learners require more structure in their learning, so if you are designing for these populations in particular, you will want to ensure they are highly structured. But we can balance even highly structured learning with the other two strategies—dialogue and autonomy—to reduce psychological and emotional distances in class, to create connections with our learners, and to encourage connections among our students. Chapters 5 and 6 provide much more detail on strategies for bridging distances and creating presence. Here we emphasize the general design strategy—structure, dialogue, and autonomy—as keys to how we support online learners and their needs.

Dialogue is a design strategy that focuses on how much interaction you foster with your students—both with you and among the students themselves. The degree of dialogue in a course impacts their sense of distance: the more dialogue and interaction a course features, the lower a student's sense of distance. Our goal is to increase interactions in a class and intentionally create opportunities for interactions (discussions, feedback loops, office hours, informal live class meetings, etc.).

Autonomy is the degree of input and control learners have in their learning. This does not mean students have to engage in self-directed learning, but it does mean that we want to create opportunities for students to provide input. Our goal is to provide an increasing sense of autonomy for learners (in cases where perhaps you need to scaffold that autonomy more, e.g., with younger learners) or to design courses with either a moderate or a high degree of autonomy, depending on developmental stages of learners and their background knowledge. For example, facilitate a discussion with students at the start of on online class on what makes for a good online learning experience and what their rules as a class should be for learning together. Encourage them to generate ideas and expectations. This creates an opportunity for some student input into class rules and expectations and also helps foster early dialogue (and expectations of dialogue) for students. We want online learners to have as much a sense of ownership in their online classes as we want in the classroom. By identifying opportunities students have to shape the class, lead discussions, identify topics of interest, or pursue a tangent of their choosing along with the main class content, you can create opportunities for autonomy that facilitate shared ownership in the class and learning process.

Table 4.2 summarizes these three key design strategies that work in tandem for online learning to help meet learners' needs while also yielding a more flexible learning environment that is responsive to their needs and inputs. Table 4.3 structures these strategies into a planning activity. Complete Table 4.3 either on your own or as a team to generate ideas for how you can apply each of these strategies in your online course design and development. If you have ideas for specific activities, go ahead and draft those as well, so you can readily integrate them into your course planning.

Table 4.2 Structure, Dialogue, and Autonomy as Key Strategies for Supporting Online Learners

Structure	Dialogue	Autonomy
The degree to which an online class is organized, has a reliable rhythm, and has expectations that are clearly communicated.	*The degree of dialogue you foster with your students (with you and among students themselves).*	*Opportunities for students to provide input into the class or direct some aspect of their learning.*
↑ Structure = ↑ Distance	↑ Dialogue = ↓ Distance	↑ Autonomy = ↓ Distance
The more inflexible the structure (less responsive to learner needs and inputs), the greater sense of distance learners perceive, but structure is also necessary for learning.	Facilitating dialogue (as a group, individually, in small groups) can lessen the sense of distance.	Some degree of learner input and control is desirable. Identify opportunities where your students can inform the class design or lead the learning.
Goal: Balance structure with dialogue and autonomy.	**Goal:** Increase interactions.	**Goal:** Provide increasing or moderate to high degree of learner autonomy, depending on developmental stage and background knowledge.

Table 4.3 Activity: Identifying Opportunities for Structure, Dialogue, and Autonomy

Strategy Questions to Prompt Ideas	Your plan
Structure: How can you create and communicate a course structure (e.g., a course schedule that is a table with weekly dates, readings, etc.)? What is the daily and/or weekly rhythm you want to create for class? What are class expectations (standards/outcomes, etc.), and what different ways can you communicate those? When will you communicate with students (e.g., a welcome email one week before class, a kick-off email on Day 1, etc.)?	
Dialogue: What opportunities for dialogue does your online class offer? What dialogue do you want to facilitate between you and students—whole class or individually? What dialogue to want to facilitate among students? How will you help students feel they can reach out to you and talk to you? How can you create habits of dialogue so students see interactions as a class norm?	
Autonomy: What opportunities for student input does your online class offer? How can you facilitate that input? What activities or discussions can you design (and what tools or features do you want to use) to foster input and collaboration?	

Self-Regulation: Helping Learners Develop Key Strategies for Succeeding Online

Self-regulation is a key characteristic of learners who perform better in online learning compared to those who do not. However, self-regulation is not a static characteristic—it is dynamic and changeable. In fact, many common educational strategies, especially with younger learners, help students develop more self-regulation of their learning processes and environments. For online learning, developing these skills is essential. Students who do not self-regulate well will struggle more in online learning (Cho & Shen, 2013; Lynch & Dembo, 2004).

Self-regulation is a learner's ability and efforts to manage their learning process intentionally in order to achieve their learning goals (Zimmerman & Schunk,

2011). Zimmerman (2002) explains that self-regulation is not a static or innate characteristic of individuals but, rather, is something learners can develop and improve over time. Thus, we can help students develop their skills and competencies for self-regulation by providing them instructional and other types of support or scaffolding for self-regulation online. Because this ties to social and emotional learning (SEL) online as well, Stephanie's book *SEL at a Distance* (Moore, 2021b) covers this in-depth for distance learning. That book can serve as a useful companion to this book. Here, we want to summarize some ideas for how to support students in their self-regulation of online learning.

Regulating the Learning Environment: Creating a Conducive Context for Online Learning

Blau et al. (2020, p. 2) define regulation of the learning environment as "an effort to build an environment that will facilitate the completion of learning tasks." In many instances caretakers may not understand how to better support their children in online learning, but with some supportive training and tips they can easily make the home environment more conducive. In most instances, challenges related to online learners' surroundings can be addressed through training and support for their caretakers. Knowledge and ideas around how to do this increased during the pandemic, and many of those strategies are still applicable for full-time online or remote learning. Students should have a space that is designated for learning where they can access a tablet or computer with a camera and microphone and with space to spread out papers or projects. Parents could even consider options such as adjustable-height desks that allow students to stand or sit throughout the day. That space ideally should be away from disruptions where students do not have to worry as much about the family pet, doorbells, others walking by or in the background, and other common home disruptions.

Educators can help learners develop strategies for regulating their learning environment through explicit instruction. Discuss with students regulation of their learning environments as online learners, perhaps even during Day 1 or Week 1 of your online class. Ask students to generate ideas and strategies for how they can regulate their learning environment. LaToya Sapp, a teacher at Northside Independent School District in San Antonio, Texas, uses an activity in Padlet where she shares a picture of her best learning spot at home and discusses why it's a good learning spot (Moore, 2021b). She then asks students to share their best learning spot at home in the Padlet activity and to include pictures if they feel comfortable. This simple activity facilitates learner reflection on what makes a good spot and helps them get situated early. You could similarly extend this exercise by asking students to share what resources they do or should have near them to support their learning throughout the day and share pictures of their workspaces if they choose to.

As in the classroom, it is also important to consider how we can encourage students to get up and move and to get outside during the day, not just sit at a desk or computer all day. Many PE activities can be conducted away from the computer, either by simply stepping away to build a fort or do some exercises somewhere else in the home, even on cold or bad weather days, or by going out into the yard. Nearby parks, sidewalks, trails, nature areas, and other outdoor options can also become part of their learning context as well and can be intentionally integrated into daily and weekly plans. For science and physical education in particular, these are good options for having learners conduct field experiments or complete a physical activity. They can also visit local resources like libraries, interview people in different jobs or community roles, or visit a farm, restaurant, or other sort of business to integrate remote learning that is not necessarily at the computer. This helps students view the community as their learning environment and helps online students continue building important community connections.

Regulating Behaviors: Managing the Online Learning Process

It is important for students to manage their time and determine how to meet deadlines in online learning. Rather than treating this as prior knowledge students already have or should have, this can and should be baked into the online class to support students in developing their self-regulation capacity. Regulation of behaviors online typically focuses on their ability to manage and complete tasks. This is different from regulating their own learning, involving more of the management side of work and learning. These are highly transferable skills for learners to use outside any learning context, so explicitly scaffolding their development of these behavior regulation tasks will serve them well throughout life.

As with regulating their environment, you can support self-regulation of behaviors through explicit activities in which you talk with students and get them to generate ideas on how they can plan for tasks and deadlines that are part of the class. Identify periodic spots—including in Week 1—when you can work with students to walk through important class tasks and deadlines. You can have them develop an activity plan for the class or put together a calendar with reminders or a board in their room with stickies as reminders. As another example of an activity that supports learners' regulation behaviors, from *SEL at a Distance* (Moore, 2021b), Dr. Teomara Rutherford uses Padlet to ask her students to share ideas on how they can support their own success in the online learning environment. As part of that activity, she also asks them to brainstorm together how their peers and the instructor can support their learning. These types of activities are great kick-offs for early class sessions to help students generate ideas and solutions early on.

Regulating Learning: Choosing and Using Strategies That Work

Strategies for self-regulation of learning means that students are able to choose and use "a variety of cognitive strategies for memorizing, learning, thinking and problem solving" (Blau et al., 2020, p. 2). Helping learners regulate their learning involves *metacognition*, in which students are prompted to think about how they think and learn. Again, explicit instruction is helpful in getting students to talk about the strategies they use and to develop more effective learning strategies. Start by asking students to identify what learning strategies they use—either individually or in small groups. You can even have them keep a learning journal or log to reflect on what is working for them and what isn't. Feedback from you on their journal or log can focus on suggestions for what they can do instead in instances where their strategies aren't working. Self-assessment is a great tool in learners' ability to self-regulate, so helping them develop their ability to self-assess is great scaffolding for learners. Another approach could be to ask learners to develop a learning plan at the start of your class. You can provide them preliminary feedback early on, and then partway through the class ask students to pull out their plans and reflect on them. They can submit revisions with reflections to you for further iteration and feedback. You can also incorporate periodic small-group discussions on learning plans to facilitate their articulation and reflection on students' learning.

Additional types of self-regulation, such as regulating emotions and regulating interactions with others, are covered in more detail in *SEL at a Distance* (Moore, 2021b). As you work through this book considering how you can support all learners in their ability to self-regulate their learning in the online environment, you may find that book to be good instructional planning companion.

Summary

We started this chapter by articulating a theory of how learning happens in the online learning environment. Rather than assuming that learning happens only as a result of what the student does, we explored how learning online is a result of many design decisions made by the online educator. We also explored how using design thinking to approach our work as online educators helps us imagine possibilities and move from weak examples toward more desirable online learning designs.

One way we can design differently is to start with considerations of online learners and their needs. To address diverse learner needs, we discussed the *online learning ecosystem*: a suite of supports and services to support learners that extends beyond the basic building blocks of courses and curricula. For learners to be successful online, they require a suite of resources just like those we provide for in-person learners. These include such supports as library access, school counseling supports, access to social events, career services supports, and other forms of supports commonly provided to students in scaffolding them toward success. Thus, our goal with online learning is to build an online learning ecosystem, not just a collection of courses. Because special education learners are often cited as examples of learners whose needs cannot be met online, we provided an example from one online school that supports learners who have IEPs or 504 plans.

We also covered structure as an important feature for learner success in online learning. Structure relates to how you design and organize your online course. The more organized an online course is and the more this is communicated clearly to learners, the more the course supports their ability to succeed online. We also discussed how too much structure can create a sense of distance and isolation, so it should be balanced with dialogue and autonomy. Together these three ideas—structure, dialogue, and autonomy—form a design triad that provides a solid foundation for designing online learning that meets online learners' needs.

Finally, we discussed a learner characteristic that is very important in online learning: self-regulation. Learners who are able to regulate their learning are more successful in an online learning environment. However, instead of treating self-regulation as a static characteristic—as something a learner does or does not have—it should be treated as a dynamic characteristic, something a learner can develop over time. Developing self-regulation serves learners well throughout their learning journey and their lives and careers beyond school, so investing time in helping them develop their self-regulation pays dividends. We explored three specific types of self-regulation—regulating the learning environment, regulating behaviors, and regulating learning—with ideas for activities teachers can integrate to support students in developing their self-regulation and self-assessment capabilities.

Chapter 5

Building an Online
Learning Community

The Applewood team was feeling confident and excited now about building an online option in their district that was well-justified with a clear vision. They felt they had a better understanding of how they could support students to succeed in the online learning environment. Now it was time to drill down to specifics and focus on the instructional details. Teachers were raising questions as well. Isn't online learning less social and less interactive? Did research have any insights to offer on whether learners could build a sense of community online? Where there some good practical ideas that the research could offer? Building a sense of community seemed so easy in a classroom, and much harder to do in the online environment. The teachers also wanted their students to feel like teachers were "there" for them, and they wanted students to engage with each other. Was that even possible online? If so, how could they build a rich online learning experience?

Chapter 4 introduced design strategies structure, dialogue, and autonomy that support online learners' success and can help decrease their sense of isolation in online learning. These three variables were originally conceived of by distance learning researcher Michael G. Moore as he developed his theory of *transactional distance*, or the psychological distance between the learner and the teacher. Moore (1983, p. 155) stated:

> There is now a distance between learner and teacher which is not merely geographic, but educational and psychological as well. It is a distance in the relationship of the two partners in the educational enterprise. It is a transactional distance.

This transactional or psychological distance was based on the potential for misunderstandings between learners and teachers due to the physical space and time gap in their communication (Moore & Kearsley, 1996). The basic assumption of Moore's theory of transactional distance is that reducing the perceived psychological distance (or sense of isolation) between the learner and the teacher will increase motivation, satisfaction, and persistence—all of which will increase engagement of the online learner and thus the amount of learning that is happening. Over time, Moore's theory of transactional distance and the impacts of designing to reduce transactional distance have stood up very well (Bernard et al., 2009).

Stephanie's book *SEL at a Distance* (Moore, 2021b) explains that this helps us think about how we can bridge different types of distances: We bridge physical or geographic distances with technology, but we bridge transactional distances with strategies. This chapter and the next explore some key frameworks that have been developed to aid in the design of online learning communities and interactions that bridge transactional distances and reduce learners' sense of isolation. This chapter focuses on the overarching idea of building an online learning community, and the next drills down to focus on different types of interaction that support learning and sense of connectedness online.

Community of Inquiry

Chapter 3 discussed different views of learning and how that leads to different approaches to designing online learning. A significant difference is whether your desire is to have learning options where learners pursue individualized learning paths or whether your vision for online learning values interactions and community as a central feature of the learning experience. If you choose to design for a social online learning experience, where students are learning together, then you will want to use a framework for design that helps you emphasize design decisions that create social learning and foster interactions. One of the most common models associated with social and interactive online learning is the Community of Inquiry (CoI) framework. The CoI is a concept that deep and meaningful learning will occur when there is interaction among three essential constructs: social presence, cognitive presence, and teacher presence (Garrison et al., 2000).

The basic idea is that these three constructs work together to create a community that facilitates inquiry. Notice how engagement is a core feature of the CoI module shown in Figure 5.1. The belief is that the stronger each type of presence is within that learning community, the greater the educational experience becomes.

Figure 5.1 Imagining what is next: diverse modalities creating a more resilient system that meets different needs. Image used with permission from the Community of Inquiry website and licensed under the CC-BY-SA International 4.0 license (https://creativecommons.org/licenses/by-sa/4.0/). The original image is located at https://www.thecommunityofinquiry.org/framework.

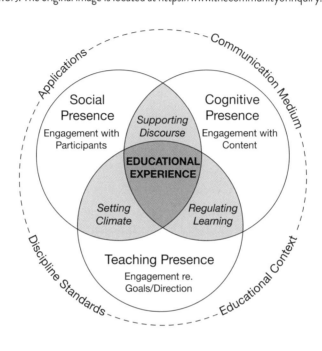

And you can imagine these circles as dynamic, not just static circles on the page: the larger each circle representing a type of interaction becomes, the more the overlap between any two presences and the larger the space at the center. Conversely, the less investment one makes in these different presences, the more anemic the engagement, interactions, and overlaps become. Let's explore each type of presence in detail and some strategies for how you can enact these in your online course.

Social Presence

Social presence is the level at which the learner feels that the other person has projected themselves as a real and authentic person (Rourke et al., 1999). The concept of social presence was first developed to help explain the effect a particular medium (mainly telephone, radio, and television) had on how an individual perceived the communication (Short et al., 1976). However, with the advent of online learning, social presence found new favor as researchers examined and instructional designers planned for its implications with online forms of communications (e.g., email, discussion forums, synchronous instruction). Originally, social presence was measured by two variables: (1) intimacy or the sense of connection that one feels toward another and (2) immediacy or the psychological distance between individuals. Interestingly, the instruments initially used to measure these variables used such terms as *unsociable* and *sociable*, *insensitive* and *sensitive*, *cold* and *warm*, and *impersonal* and *personal* to anchor their scales. Each of these paired terms underscores the essence of what was envisioned to project one's self as a real person—sociable, sensitive, warm, and personal—whereas someone who lacked social presence or was unable to project themselves well came across as unsociable, insensitive, cold, and impersonal.

In early research, social presence was often defined through the lens of face-to-face or in-person interactions. As a result, it emphasized nonverbal cues like smiling, eye contact, gestures, and posture that convey immediate engagement. Similarly, verbal cues like using the person's name, praising their contributions and/or work, using humor, or talking about topics unrelated to class were all viewed as ways to achieve social connectedness. In an online learning environment, many of the same verbal cues can still be employed. You can begin an email to a student with their name. You can still use humor in your own participation in discussion forums. You can use some time when students are in a synchronous class as an opportunity to chat about a previous night's sporting event or other local happenings before beginning class in earnest. Nonverbal cues can be a little more difficult, especially in asynchronous interactions, but they are not impossible. This is why tools like chat, texting, and other asynchronous communication flourish: humans find many ways to foster connectedness. Emoticons or text-based expressions of emotions, such as :), ;), :D, or :O can be used in text-based communication like email, discussion forums, or even written feedback. In Stephanie's online classes, she often starts written feedback to students by using their name first and will incorporate emoticons to convey humor, light-heartedness, or sympathy. Most learning management systems and virtual classrooms have emojis or visual expressions of emotions to provide nonverbal communication, along with other visual cues such as images to represent yes and no, speed up and slow down, or the need for a break (see examples in Figure 5.2).

Another common way nonverbal cues are conveyed is through explicitly describing nonverbal reactions. Any online forum is rife with these—shrugs, salutes, or descriptions in parentheses or brackets like {nods head}. In some ways, online learning makes you stop and think about the messages you are sending students and more carefully

Figure 5.2 Emojis available under the "reactions" feature in Zoom, which even include the ability for an individual to change the skin tone of their emojis to match their own identity.

consider what you what to convey and how. For example, as you read a paper, you may think to yourself, "This is a really intriguing point" but not express that to a student. In online learning, pausing to think about what your reactions or thoughts are and how you can convey those productively to students is an opportunity both for pedagogical reflection and for thinking through how to communicate subtle, unspoken messages. Some additional ideas for how to facilitate social presence are provided in Table 5.1.

Table 5.1 Ideas for Creating Social Presence in Your Online Class

Introductions	Share an introduction of yourself (live, recorded video, an "About Me" page with a video and pictures). Ask learners to provide introductions as well. You can also ask them to share personal trivia or photos (make sure you emphasize that they should only share what they are comfortable sharing). Any sort of sharing should be optional.
Interest groups	Ask students to share what they are interested in as it relates to the class. Have them read what others share and then create study groups or work groups based on common interests.

Social time	Create time for social interactions. This could take the form of setting aside time at the beginning of live sessions or hosting a live session one day a week that is just social chat time with no agenda. Or this could be periodic gatherings that are social, such as to celebrate completed work or upcoming holidays or just time to share good news and celebrate each other.
Social space	Create a place in your online course—or, better yet, ask students to cocreate a class page where they can share and connect. This can be a place to share interests or strengths or identify who to reach out to for what type of support. This should be a much more flexible, student-led space.

Activity: Creating Social Presence

What are some ways you can convey a sense of you as a person for your learners?

What are some of your own communication idiosyncrasies that you think convey a sense of you as a teacher? How can you capture those and convey those online? For example, if you like to wear different hats for different occasions, can you change your picture periodically? Or use an avatar?

What about your personality do you like to convey to your learners? How can you capture your personality and convey that online? For example, if you teach government classes and like to share newspaper clippings and convey a sense of "coffee table talk" about current events, could you create a "coffee corner" where you use images of newspapers and coffee to set the scene? If you prefer a professional demeanor with a tie, can you turn your tie into a sort of icon for your presence?

What does it mean to you to be authentic in your class? How can you express emotions in a way that conveys to your students that you are a real person, too, perhaps even modeling for them how to manage emotions? For example, if you are teaching young children in a unit about life cycles and decide to hatch chicks and let the children watch the chicks hatch, you could share your emotions and help them process their emotions if some of the chicks do not hatch or do not survive.

Similarly, what are some ways your students can convey who they are to you and to their fellow classmates? Consider ways you might do this in a classroom, like having young learners create drawings of themselves to communicate their identities, that they can similarly do online. For older learners, they could create "learning community profiles" designed to help them meet new friends and form study groups.

Cognitive Presence

Whereas social presence helps convey the warmth of and connectedness to a real person, cognitive presence relates more to design features of the course and strategies that get learners interacting with the content. *Cognitive presence* is defined as the extent to which a learner is able to understand and make meaning of the content (Garrison et al., 2000). In short, you want to get your learners interacting with content in meaningful ways, not just reading or viewing it. Within the CoI framework, a learner would begin to interact with the content through a triggering event that gets them curious about a topic, which is then followed by further exploration of that topic. As the learner explores the topic, they attempt to integrate the information they find or from the individuals they interact with. Finally, the learner comes to some resolution. If their learning was successful, that resolution is an understanding of the topic and the ability to apply it to their own contexts or in practice. However, if the learning was unsuccessful the resolution can take the form of frustration or a sense of psychological distance from the content.

Our goal as educators, of course, is to try to make that learning successful. We have a host of different strategies we can use to facilitate learner interaction with content. Recall that in Chapter 4 we started with theorizing how learning happens online. The activity in Table 4.1 identifies the different ways educators can structure a class to facilitate learner interaction with the content. The learning outcomes and standards we write for our classes, the materials we select or create, and the assignments, activities, and discussions we develop all exist to facilitate learner interaction with the content. (For more detail on specific strategies for learner-content interaction, see Chapter 6.)

Teaching Presence

Teaching presence is often envisioned as the individual standing in the front of a classroom in a physical, brick-and-mortar environment. As Anderson et al. (2001, p. 2) describe it:

> In that more physical, more observable environment, it is easy to see the function of the teacher as consisting of three major roles: First, as designer of the educational experience, including planning and administering instruction as well as evaluating and certifying competence; second, as facilitator and co-creator of a social environment conducive to active and successful learning; and finally, as a subject matter expert who knows a great deal more than most learners and is thus in a position to "scaffold" learning experiences by providing direct instruction.

In their original article, the authors of the CoI framework indicated that teaching presence was the binding element, without which the community would not exist. In fact, if you consider the descriptions social presence (e.g., addressing students by their names or using humor in their instruction) and cognitive presence (e.g., the presentation of content or the assessment of learning), these descriptions are reflected in the above quote.

Maintain Balance

Keep in mind that it is important to balance structure with dialogue and autonomy in your course design. Too much structure makes a course feel rigid, which can lower social presence and increase learners' sense of distance.

In a traditional sense, teaching presence would include things like the ability to clearly communicate course objectives and instructions, facilitate student progress and learning, and provide meaningful feedback. We continually reference the idea of *structure*, and structure is critical for online learning. Structure conveys to students what they should do when. The more structured and organized a course is, the more it supports learners in understanding what they need to do so they can be successful. That structure is created and communicated through clear objectives and expectations, clear course organization, and ease of access and usability in the course (how easily students can access what they need for a given lesson or week). In short, how you organize and communicate your course to your learners facilitates teaching presence in the course. And this teaching presence is essential scaffolding for learner success. We summarize some tips here; Chapter 9 includes a host of ideas and recommendations on organization and communication to get you ready for launching your online course.

Tips for Creating Teaching Presence Online:
- ☐ Create an easy-to-follow course menu and organization.
- ☐ Organize the flow of information on your course site in a logical manner (see Chapter 9 for ideas).
- ☐ Clearly articulate goals, and share those with students.
- ☐ Provide strategy-focused, constructive feedback throughout the course.
- ☐ Respond to students in a timely manner in discussions, emails, etc.
- ☐ Create rubrics that communicate assignment/assessment expectations and that scaffold students as they work or prepare, not just used as after-the-fact evaluations.
- ☐ Create a course matrix (weekly schedule in a table format).

Note that, in the online learning context, teaching presence can be diffused into specific roles undertaken by different individuals (Barbour, 2019). You may be in a system where different people take on different roles that each facilitate some aspect of teaching presence. For example, your district may have a team (or a contract with a provider) to provide *designers* who design instructional materials and work with teachers to construct online courses and present activities, manages pacing and rigor, interacts with students, and conducts the assessment and grading; and *facilitators* or local mentors who advocate for students(s), proctor assessments, record grades, or other activities (Davis et al., 2007a). Regardless of whether these roles are diffused or carried out by one individual, these tasks all contribute to teaching presence as they create the structure and organization of a course that communicates to students what is expected.

Academic Communities of Engagement

While the CoI framework is one of the most used in online learning environments, it was originally designed and has been most commonly used with adult learners, who are thought to have a greater level of self-regulation and possess a higher self-efficacy toward learning. Many of the early K–12 online learning programs described the typical student as highly motivated, self-directed, self-disciplined, independent learners who could read and write well, and who also had a strong interest in or ability with technology (Haughey & Muirhead, 1999). This could reflect the fact that many online efforts originally started because high-performing adolescents like Olympic athletes wanted to maintain educational options. As of today, however, this does not reflect the typical K–12 student enrolling in online learning, and it probably does not describe the students who are electing for online learning today and thus who you will teach in your online learning program.

Moore did make some accommodations in his theory of transactional distance based on the level of learner autonomy. For example, he argued that the more autonomy a learner possessed, the less the amount of structure and dialogue impacted their sense of isolation or transactional distance. Conversely, he believed that the less autonomy a learner inherently had, the more important it was to control the level of transactional distance in an online learning environment by ensuring that it had a low level of structure and high level of dialogue. However, it is not easy to design for or teach in an online learning context where the learners may be reluctant, may be immature, and may lack self-efficacy in their own ability to learn.

The Academic Communities of Engagement (ACE) framework was specifically designed based on adolescent learners and was then further refined to be more inclusive of both child and adult learners (Borup et al., 2020). Let's explore the ACE framework as a model that you may feel helps you better address today's young online learners. In Figure 5.3, the inner triangle represents a student's independent engagement, which is separate from how others try to support their engagement. Course community support for engagement is represented in the middle triangle, and the student's personal community support is represented in the outer triangle. The order of the support the student receives is interchangeable in the figure and does not reflect a necessary sequence. The goal of the support communities is to help the student increase engagement to the level of engagement necessary for academic success, as represented by the dashed line (Borup et al., 2020, p. 810).

Figure 5.3 The Academic Communities of Engagement framework (Borup et al., 2020).

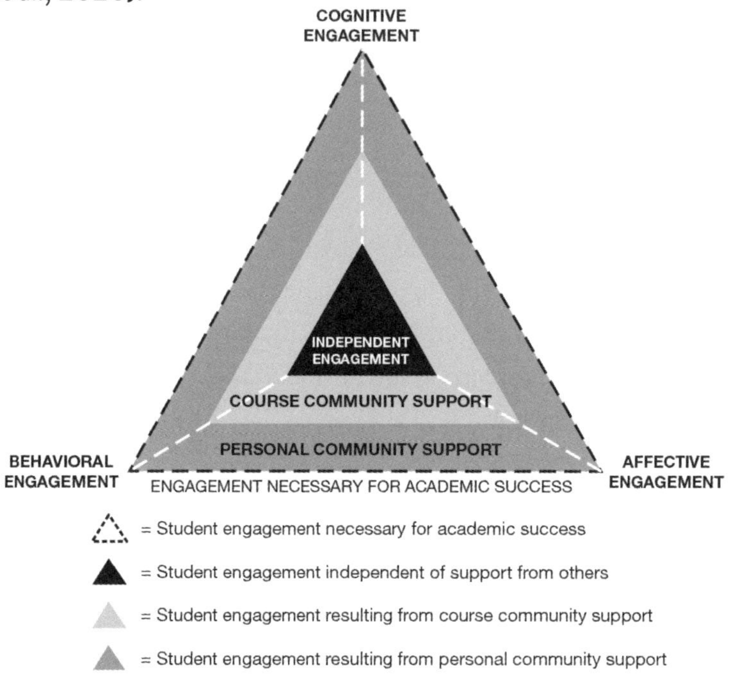

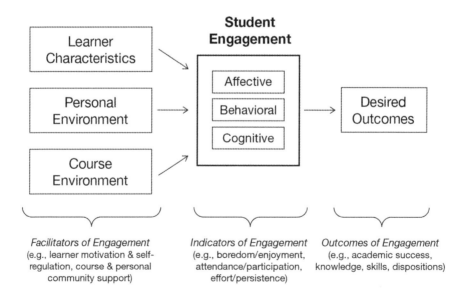

Figure 5.4 Facilitators, indicators, and outcomes in the general model of student engagement (Borup et al., 2020, p. 811); adapted from Halverson and Graham (2019).

At the heart of the ACE framework is engagement, specifically, engagement related to course tasks and activities (as opposed to other forms of student involvement, such as extracurricular activities or community-based activities that may have curricular goals). Borup et al. (2020) break engagement down into facilitators, indicators, and outcomes (Figure 5.4). Starting with the desired outcomes first (backward design), the *outcome* of the engagement would be the student having academic success in the desired knowledge, skills, and/or dispositions that were intended by the instructional experience. The *indicators* of engagement are observable behaviors that would suggest engagement, such as boredom or enjoyment, attendance or non-attendance, participation or nonparticipation, and presence or absence of effort and persistence. According to Borup et al. (2020, p. 813), the three different types of engagement indicators are as follows:

- **Affective engagement,** defined as "the emotional energy associated with involvement in course learning activities"
- **Behavioral engagement,** defined as "the physical behaviors (energy) associated with completing course learning activity requirements"
- **Cognitive engagement,** defined as "the mental energy exerted towards productive involvement with course learning activities"

Examples of affective engagement include beliefs that impact the student's willingness to interact with the content or learning process. For example, if a student believes they are inherently bad at a subject (e.g., "I'm not a good writer") or that a group of students are inherently good or bad at a subject (e.g., the myth that girls are bad at math), that negatively impacts their learning engagement. Conversely, if they believe they are good at the subject or that a group of individuals are good with the subject, that positively impacts their learning engagement. Similarly, if a student perceives that a teacher does not like them, that can lead to decreased engagement; if a student perceives that a teacher does like them, that can lead to increased engagement. Behavioral engagement in online learning could be indicated by the frequency and regularity with which a student logs into the learning management system or attends synchronous classes or tutorial sessions. Cognitive engagement can be indicated by such student behaviors as taking notes on a video-based lecture, emailing their teacher to ask a content-based question, or posting a response to a prompt in the discussion forum.

The *facilitators* of engagement are the different things that impact the student's engagement. Interestingly, the original ACE framework (originally named Adolescent Community of Engagement framework) did not focus on facilitators of engagement (Borup et al., 2014b) but assumed that engagement came from specific actors (i.e., teachers, parents, and peers). The focus on specific actors or individuals placed the burden of responsibility for having those interactions on those specific individuals, and it ignored the complexity of being a student attending a school that is located within a community—and all of the other possible ways that those environments could engage and support the student. As such, in the revised ACE framework, Borup and his colleagues expanded this aspect of engagement to focus on the different facilitators of that engagement.

Vygotsky's concept of the zone of proximal development is a helpful idea here. Vygotsky posited that learning is a social process that relies on communication and interactions. As part of that social process, the student must engage with more knowledgeable others in order to learn. Those "more knowledgeable others" form what Vygotsky (1962) referred to as the *zone of proximal development*, defined as "the distance between the actual developmental level as determined by independent problem solving and the level of potential development as determined through problem solving under adult guidance or in collaboration with more capable peers" (Vygotsky, 1978, p. 86). You may commonly think of the zone of proximal development as a space between a student's comfort zone and discomfort zone, but a better way to think about it is as the supports available to students from within the course community and their own personal community that facilitate their ability to grow and learn. Access to available resources—in the form of course materials, peers, the teacher, others within the school environment, and their supports outside the school environment (such as family, friends, and local resources)—helps create that zone or that space for growth and development. These sources of support include the individual student, the course community, and the student's personal support community (recall Figure 5.3). Let's begin our exploration of these facilitators of engagement with the individual student at the center.

Individual Engagement

At the center of the ACE framework is independent or individual engagement. Students are inherently able to complete some learning tasks and activities independently or by themselves. They may have a specific interest in the topic or subject area, or it may be something that they have excelled at in the past. The topic might be something that the student had learned from a parent or relative, or they could have learned about it on a visit to a museum, historical site, or national or state park. It may have been something that they saw during the educational programming that television stations often broadcast on Saturday mornings, or something they may have read in a book that they borrowed from the library. There are any number of intrinsic and extrinsic factors that make up a student's independent or individual engagement—and these factors will vary from course to course and topic to topic, as well as varying based on the learning environment.

Figure 5.5 A triangle representing a student who can independently achieve high levels of affective engagement but has relatively low levels of behavioral and cognitive engagement (Borup et al., 2020, p. 816).

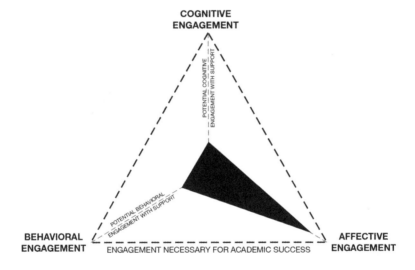

For example, you could have a student who inherently possesses a high degree of affective engagement but a low degree of behavioral engagement and cognitive engagement (see Figure 5.5). In this instance, the student may have a high degree of self-motivation to learn the topic (i.e., affective engagement). However, they may not have the self-regulation to invest the time needed to learn the task (i.e., behavioral engagement). Additionally, the student might not have the prerequisite knowledge to be able to understand the basic concepts of the specific thing that needs to be learned (i.e., cognitive engagement). The ACE framework would suggest that those designing the formal learning experience, as well as the student's own personal support system, need to make up the difference to ensure that the student is able to fully engage on all three dimensions, in order to have academic success. Chapter 4 discussed how self-regulation is very important for online learner success and covered several different ideas for you to help learners develop self-regulation (treating this as a dynamic learner characteristic rather than a static characteristic). Stephanie's book *SEL at a Distance* (Moore, 2021b) includes an entire chapter on self-regulation online. As that book focuses on social and emotional learning (SEL) in the online environment, so it can also be particularly useful for identifying strategies to help learners with their affective and behavioral engagement. You can use ideas that you mapped out in Chapter 4 to help support individual engagement in your class.

In addition to strategies for self-regulation and SEL, you can roll ideas from motivation research into your course design. Keller's (1987) ARCS framework—attention, relevance, confidence, satisfaction—is a common way to remember potential motivational strategies. Figure 5.6 uses this framework to summarize motivational strategies, to give you some ideas for how to engage individual learners. We want to draw particular attention to relevance and confidence, because strategies that help to build these are often overlooked. Such strategies can help address a range of issues or concerns, such as lack of motivation, low engagement, and even cheating behavior.

Figure 5.6 Keller's ARCS theory of motivation.

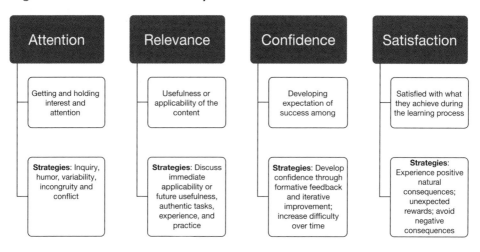

Idea Sparks: Authentic Assessment for Engagement

Milman and Wessmiller (2020) suggest several ways to apply Keller's ARCS to online instruction. The following is a sampling of their many ideas:

Attention: Include visual elements such as videos and visuals; create activities that require frequent interaction; encourage debate where appropriate; use questions to peak curiosity (e.g., start your weekly overview with questions to consider).

Relevance: Base curriculum on real-world issues or scenarios; target the content to learners' needs; have students develop links between the content and their future goals; create opportunities for learners to exercise choice in activities or topics; draw in student experiences and examples; invite guest speakers applying content in the real world.

Confidence: incorporate practice opportunities with feedback and opportunity to improve or revise based on feedback; scaffold the course and assignments (e.g., with rubrics, interim deliverables with low-stakes or no-stakes grading); let students self-assess and identify their areas of strengths and opportunities for growth; provide strategy-focused feedback that helps a learner know what to do to improve.

Satisfaction: Provide positive feedback that underscores what a student does well or where they are creative; reinforce what they are doing well; allow hands-on practice and ability to crezate a product they can share with their families.

Course Community Support

Borup et al. (2020, p. 816) defined the course community as "organized and facilitated by those associated with the course or program who have knowledge of course content, expectations, and procedures." Put another way, the course community includes the "instructors, support staff, and students brought together because of the course/program" (p. 817). From an online learning perspective, these supports would include the specific content, resources, tasks, and activities that are planned into the course. For example, planning for multiple ways to support the student through the course community would be having a topic presented through (a) a video-based lecture, (b) an image- and text-based resource like a textbook or static webpage, and (c) a synchronous session with the teacher. However, these are just the online elements that could be put into place to support the student in the course. Human resources can also be put in place.

Describing K–12 Online Learning

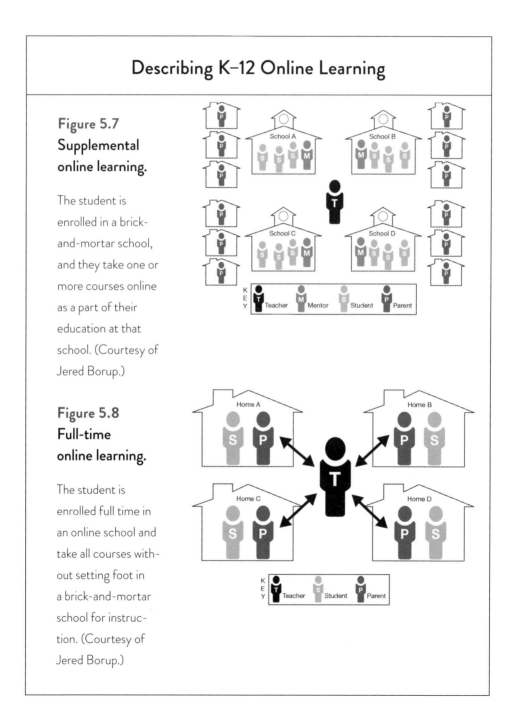

Figure 5.7 Supplemental online learning.

The student is enrolled in a brick-and-mortar school, and they take one or more courses online as a part of their education at that school. (Courtesy of Jered Borup.)

Figure 5.8 Full-time online learning.

The student is enrolled full time in an online school and take all courses without setting foot in a brick-and-mortar school for instruction. (Courtesy of Jered Borup.)

Earlier, we described how the role of the teacher in the online learning environment is diffused into three separate roles—designer, teacher, and facilitator—often undertaken by three separate individuals. Davis et al. (2007a) outlined how it was common for one individual or a team of individuals to design the online course itself, while a different individual who may or may not have been involved with course development was responsible for teaching or actually delivering the course, and a third individual at the local level (e.g., a parent or guardian in a full-time online setting or a school-based teacher in a supplemental online setting) who was responsible for supporting the student as they engaged in their online learning. More recently, Ferdig et al. (2009) described eight different sets of educators who were or could be involved in the online learning environment:

> *Instructional Designers:* The creators of the online course in accordance with content standards using effective strategies for the learners and the content
> *Teachers:* The educators with primary responsibility for student instruction within an online course including interaction with students and assigning course grades
> *Online Facilitators:* The people who supports students in a virtual school program, who may interact with students online or may facilitate at the physical site where students access their online courses
> *Local Key Contacts:* The professionals who assist students in registering and otherwise accessing virtual courses
> *Mentors:* The academic tutors or course assistants for students
> *Technology Coordinators:* The people who facilitate technical support for educators and students
> *Guidance Counselors:* The academic advisers for students
> *Administrators:* The instructional leaders of the virtual school

In addition to the eight individuals outlined by Ferdig and his colleagues, the ACE framework also envisioned the student's own peers as being part of the course community. Individuals within the school structure who provide support both in a face-to-face and in an online setting is a peer tutor. Depending on the nature of the online learning program, not all of these individuals may be applicable to your specific context. But each one should be considered and, if possible, planned for, because the teacher and program are generally unaware of the level of individual support and personal community support that each student will bring to the online learning experience.

How to utilize all of the individuals described above is something that all online programs need to plan for when they are considering how support students through the course community. For example, an online program can provide online technical support between 8 a.m. and 4 p.m. Monday through Friday, as one level of course community support. It would be a very different level of support if the online program used those same 40 hours to provide that technical support from 6 p.m. to 10 p.m. Monday through Friday, 10 a.m. to 6 p.m. Saturday, and 10 a.m. to 10 p.m. Sunday. This alternative schedule assumes that online teachers and other actors within the course community, who may be active during the school day, should be in a position to be able to provide technical support to the student from 8 a.m. to 4 p.m. and considers that students really need access to extra technical support at times when these other course community actors may not be as readily available. Another example is how online learning programs plan for the availability of content- or subject-specific mentors and peer tutors—both in asynchronous and in synchronous online contexts, as well as in person environments.

Table 5.2 Sample School-Based Drop-In Schedule

School	Drop–In Availability
George Washington High School	Monday 9 a.m.–noon / Tuesday 1 p.m.–4 p.m.
Rosa Parks High School	Tuesday 9 a.m.–noon / Wednesday 1 p.m.–4 p.m.
Tecumseh High School	Wednesday 9 a.m.–noon / Thursday 1 p.m.–4 p.m.
Cesar Chavez Middle School	Thursday 9 a.m.–noon / Friday 1 p.m.–4 p.m.
Thomas Jefferson Middle School	Friday 9 a.m.–noon / Monday 1 p.m.–4 p.m.

Depending on the nature of the online learning program, there may be ways to create opportunities for students to drop in to obtain support. For example, a district-based online learning program could rotate among the different schools in the district to allow students greater geographic flexibility. The sample schedule outlined in Table 5.2 provides students two separate days at each of five different schools when the online learning program will have online teachers and content-focused tutors available for face-to-face interactions. Each school has both a morning and an afternoon window to try to better accommodate student schedules. The use of multiple schools gives the student greater flexibility to choose not just a convenient time but also a geographically accessible location.

Online learning programs can deploy this kind of in-person support in a variety of ways. Some programs require students to begin their online learning experiences in a school setting, which allows students to engage in their online courses with all of the local or in-person support that the online learning program has available. Some programs use a model where students take their online courses on site or in person until they have achieved a certain threshold or demonstrated a certain ability to have success in the online learning environment—essentially earning the right to engage in their online courses outside of the school building. Still other online learning programs require that their students spend a minimum number of hours learning at an in-person location. Thus, there are several ways that online learning programs can plan for this kind of course community support.

Michigan Virtual Learning Research Institute

Figure 5.9 Screenshot of the various online learning guides page on the Michigan Virtual Learning Research Institute website.

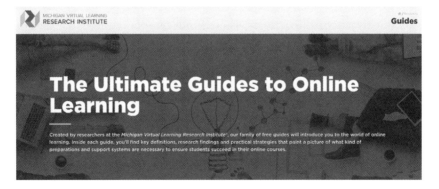

The Michigan Virtual Learning Research Institute has developed research-based guides (see Figure 5.9) to online learning for students, parents, mentors, teachers, school board members, and administrators (see https://michiganvirtual.org/resources/guides/). Online learning programs can adopt or adapt these guides based on their own context.

Finally, online learning programs can look for opportunities to provide support for students beyond the traditional course elements and actors. Some programs provide training or instructional guides for individuals within the daily school environment and those outside of the formal school environment (e.g., the Michigan Virtual Learning Research Institute has one of the most developed sets of research-based guides for a variety of stakeholders, as noted here).

Additionally, most online learning programs provide an orientation for students (and, in some instances, for other actors within the online learning environment). In most cases these orientations are limited to the specific policies and procedures that students need to know or understand to be able to engage in the online learning environment. However, some of the better online learning orientations for students also include instruction and resources on the skills necessary to be able to succeed in the online learning environment. Some online learning programs provide similar orientations for parents and/or guardians, often focusing on how to access academic records of their child, along with expectations of them for overseeing their child's progress. Further, many online learning programs provide a variety of cocurricular and extracurricular activities for students. Having partnerships with local museums, historical sites, parks, art galleries, and music venues provides the ability to offer cocurricular learning opportunities for students. For example, a neighborhood heritage home or community-based art gallery may not have the resources to provide educational brochures and displays, but in partnership with an online program, students could be tasked with researching and creating these materials. Similarly, an online program could organize a sports day in a local park or some other cultural outing as an extracurricular activity. These kinds of opportunities are designed to engage students affectively (e.g., giving them a sense of community), behaviorally (e.g., an activity that students don't have to do but want to undertake), and cognitively (e.g., providing opportunities for students to learn or apply something they previous learned). In many cases, these cocurricular and extracurricular activities often focus more on one or two indicators of engagement.

Personal Community Support
Personal community is described as extending beyond the context of the specific course, program, or school. It is something that the student develops over time, based on the actors and resources available to them, such as "family and friends who have connections to a student outside of a course/program" (Borup et al., 2020, p. 817). Borup and his colleagues also remind us that students are connected not only

with specific family members and friends but also the networks family members and friends can tap into on behalf of students. For example, a student may have an uncle who is a university professor who can review their writing for each assignment. A family member who works at a mechanic shop or a local farm could be a great resource for a class project. The student whose next door neighbor or best friend has an older child might be able to provide some support with math homework.

The personal community can also be much broader than simply family and friends with connections, as Borup and his colleagues envisioned. Countless community organizations can also provide intentional and unintentional support for students. In an intentional manner, local or neighborhood clubs, as well as many church support groups, provide homework and tutorial support for students. You may recall from Chapter 2 the example of the Gem Prep online school, which has "learning societies" that meet in churches or community centers. Access to an older counterpart has the potential to broaden that child's personal community support network. For example, organized sports and other service organizations often group children in two- to three-year age ranges. In this context, a nine-year old child would play alongside other nine- and ten-year-old children on an under-ten little league or soccer team. Further, many youth organizations provide unintentional academic support as a part of their own activities. Across the country each year the scouts sell millions of cookies. Fundraising is not inherently academic in nature, but these scouts interact with the public, accept money and make change, and create signs and other marketing materials, offering many English Language Arts, mathematics, and social studies lessons in these practices. Thus, a student's involvement in these kinds of organizations can provide them with direct academic support, a broader network they can look to for support, and unintentional support through the reinforcement of real-world academic lessons.

The personal community could include physical resources that can support the student, for example, the student's ability to access a local community library outside of the school, as well as the robustness of the resources contained at that library. In addition to learning resources, the local library might also have computers that students can access or provide a public WiFi network that students can use. Additional locations, like fast food restaurants, coffee shops, and major big box stores, also often provide free WiFi. While these are examples of supports available through the student's personal community, the online learning teacher and program can also play a role in facilitating knowledge of and the use of these resources. For example, in its course materials the online program could include information about the location, hours of operation, and holdings/resources of the community-based libraries. The online program could also create a list of known locations of internet-connected computers for community use and/or WiFi locations that allow students to use WiFi. The online learning program could develop partnerships with some of these community-based entities to encourage their students to take advantage of these resources. Each of these items would help students who don't have access to a home computer and need to find reliable internet access. In fact, many online learning teachers and programs often assume that students have reliable computer and internet access outside of school, but this is not always the case. Although a growing number of online programs do not provide technology to students to engage in their online learning, you could work with community partners to identify resources and solutions.

Activity: Create an ACE Plan

☐ **Individual Engagement:** What are some strategies you can employ to facilitate individual learner engagement? What are scaffolds (e.g., self-regulation strategies) you might integrate to support individual students in supporting themselves?

☐ **Course Community Supports:** Who are the various actors in your course community? What are ways they can each support learners? Perhaps a planning meeting with individuals can help you map out different ways each actor in the course community will support learner engagement.

☐ **Personal Community Supports:** What are some activities you can create for the online class that would facilitate intentional interaction between your students and one or more of their community supports? Where are some areas where a community partner might be drawn into your online learning ecosystem?

Applying the ACE Framework

The overall goal of the ACE framework is to provide an online learning teacher and/or program with a structure for planning student engagement at its fullest level to ensure academic success (see Figure 5.10). Unfortunately, the teacher and/or program are unable to know exactly what levels of independent engagement and/or personal community support a student may bring to the online learning environment. Thus, the online learning teacher and program must ensure that the course community is structured such that it can provide the missing level of affective, behavioral, and cognitive engagement necessary for academic success (see Figure 5.11).

Figure 5.10 The ACE model with support elements aligned to the three types of engagement (Borup et al., 2020, p. 817).

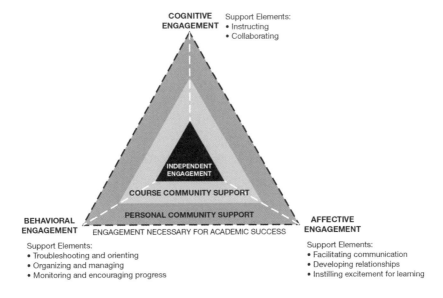

Figure 5.11 Example of an online learning teacher and/or program that planned for and provided only a small amount of support for affective, behavioral, and cognitive engagement.

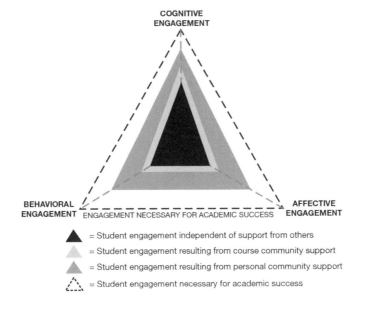

If the online learning teacher or program makes assumptions about the level of independent engagement a student is capable of or the amount of support a student may receive from their personal community, it could result in a lack of course community support—which would result in a lack of academic success for the student. The student represented in Figure 5.5 possessed an above-average amount of cognitive engagement but below-average amounts of affective and behavioral engagement. While they were able to rely on a reasonable amount of support from their personal community, the amount of course community support provided by the online learning teacher and program was inadequate. As such, the student was not able to reach the levels of engagement necessary for academic success, and they failed their online course.

As online learning teachers and programs do not know what levels of affective, behavioral, and cognitive engagement their students will have, or the amount of support that students can count on from their personal community, they need to plan a full range of course community supports to be able to pick up the slack in any area. To use the example of our fictional student from Figure 5.5, as the student's own personal community was only able to provide a small amount of support toward their affective, behavioral, and cognitive engagement, the online teacher and

Figure 5.12 An illustration of the level of course community support required for a student with a high affective engagement, but low behavior and cognitive engagement, and only a small amount of support from their personal community.

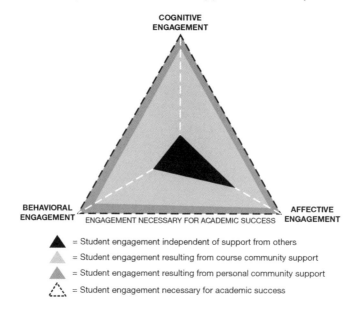

program had to provide a high degree of support through the course community in all dimensions (Figure 5.12). While this support could be provided on a student-by-student basis, it is far less work for the online learning teacher and program to plan for a full range of course community support opportunities as part of their initial development. This planned support is then readily available for use by any student, regardless the shape of their own individual and personal community triangles.

 ## Instruction and Planning Handshake

If you want to take a community-based approach to online learning, then you will need tools and infrastructure that support this approach (see Figure 5.13). Throughout this chapter, we've mentioned several ideas for activities and tools. These instructional decisions should be aligned with system-level planning, such as technology selection and procurement. Often, educators are bound in their instructional practices online by the tools available to them. In systems that are working well, they approach planning through the ecosystems lens, making sure they procure the suite of tools that support their instructional design and visions. In this case, technology evaluation and selection criteria should include features that support community and interaction and will allow for multiple users to create different types of supports, not just standard course templates. Inspect technologies for whether students can create pages to connect with each other, whether the software has a feature that allows them to chat with whoever is online, and other features that support community and engagements.

Figure 5.13
Interaction between instructional decisions and systemic planning.

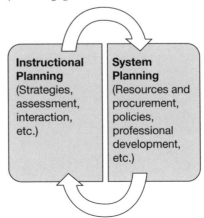

Summary

As learners ourselves, most of us at some point in our educational careers have experienced a sense of isolation and psychological or transactional distance—and not necessarily just in a distance or online learning environment. Most of us have had the experience of sitting in the middle or back of some large lecture hall, feeling somewhat disconnected from both the teacher and the content of that learning experience. At the same time, many of us may have also had the experience of being an online student in a course where we felt connected with our peers and the teacher, like we all knew one another within this tiny learning community. Isolation does not have to be a feature of online learning. That is a result of design decisions—decisions made with the aim to create a flourishing online community. The CoI and ACE frameworks can help you think about how to create a community in your online class and how to wrap community supports around your online courses or programs.

The challenge is that the online learning environment forces us to mediate our interactions with learners in ways that we are generally not used to doing. As educators we are used to explaining things to students in person in real time. Mediating our communications with students through email, discussion forums, or other text-based mediums, and particularly in an asynchronous environment where it may be moments or days between when you engage or interact with a student and when that student actually receives it. The coming chapters examine the different ways and types of engagement within the online learning environment through the lens of the ACE framework, as well as different instructional and assessment strategies that you can leverage to maximize student engagement.

Chapter 6

Fostering Student Engagement and Interaction

The teachers preparing to teach online for the Applewood district were keen to make their classes highly engaging. They did not want students or their families feeling like online learning consisted only of watching videos and reading textbooks. While they knew they wanted to make class more interactive, they didn't have a framework for how to think about engagement. Did the research have any insights into engagement online? How could teachers get students to interact with them, with each other, and with the content? What other types of interaction needed to be considered? What strategies would help students learn the content and also feel motivated to learn? Furthermore, as they planned for high-quality instruction, how could they ensure that what they wanted to do in their classes would be supported by planning decisions made higher up?

Chapter 5 introduced the importance in online learning settings to establish cognitive presence, teaching presence, and social presence to create an effective Community of Inquiry (CoI) for students to learn. In fact, it wasn't simply the establishment of these three types of presence but how they interacted with one another to allow teachers and students to create an effective online learning community. We also examined the Academic Communities of Engagement (ACE) framework, exploring how students need to be fully engaged in an affective, behavioral, and cognitive way, through their own inherent abilities and the support provided by their personal community and the course community, to achieve academic success. The type and nature of that engagement were based on how the student interacted with those supports. Our goal in this chapter is to examine different types of interaction students can engage in as part of the online learning setting, as well as different ways that interaction can be categorized.

What Students Interact With

The basic premise of the ACE framework is that students need to interact with supports provided by their course community and their personal community. There is no way to know what type or level of support an individual student's personal community will be able to provide, so it is imperative that the online school or teacher put in place plans for a robust course community to ensure academic success. That focus on students' interactions with supports provided by the course community forces online teachers and online schools to think about the variety of people and things that students might interact with as they engage in their online learning.

Michael Moore (1989, p. 1) first suggested three different types of interaction in distance learning, casually laying them out in an editorial: "I suggested that, as a minimum, distance educators need to agree on the distinctions between three types of interaction, which I labelled learner–content interaction, learner–instructor interaction, and learner–learner interaction." He likely never intended for his own thoughts for a panel discussion to become such a foundational idea in the field of distance education and online learning. As suggested in Chapter 5, the timing of this idea is important: 1989 represents a period when distance education was transitioning from primarily correspondence education (i.e., the use of course packets sent via traditional postal mail) toward some of the internet-enabled tools that would evolve to become what we commonly associate with online learning today.

A year after Moore proposed his original three types of interaction, the first software-based learning management system, FirstClass, was developed. The early 1990s also saw the development of several forms of computer-mediated communications, the kinds of systems that led Garrison et al. (2000) to propose their CoI framework discussed in Chapter 5. As Moore predicted, learner–content, learner–instructor, and learner–learner interactions were only the beginning to the types of interaction identified in online learning environments. As online learning continued to evolve, Hillman et al. (1994, p. 34) added a fourth type of interaction: "Learner–interface interaction is a process of manipulating tools to accomplish a task." Before the end of the decade, both Blackboard and Desire2Learn (now marketed as BrightSpace) would be created. As the development of learning management systems and other tools to provide online learning matured, Sutton (2001) added a fifth type of interaction, vicarious interaction: the interaction that occurs when the student observes the interactions of others.

Each of these types of interaction focuses directly on the learning environment. However, as we have seen within the ACE framework, numerous individuals and learning resources support the course community yet are outside of the formal learning environment, plus students have their own personal communities that also support their learning. Given this oversight, Burnham and Walden (1997) proposed that the student's interactions with these people and things be described as learner–environment interaction. The following sections look at each of these six types of interaction: student–content, student–teacher, student–student, student–interface, vicarious, and student–environment.

Student–Content Interaction

The first and most obvious thing that students interact with is the content. This reality is true of both face-to-face and in-person learning and distance learning, regardless of the nature of the distance learning provided. Historically, when students were sent packets in the mail by correspondence education programs, their primary interaction was with the content. Even today, in most online learning environments students interact with asynchronous course content. In fact, Moore (1989, p. 2) actually identified student-content interaction as the "defining characteristic of education," regardless of setting. Thinking back to Chapter 5, students' planned interaction with the subject matter is essentially the cognitive presence described by the CoI framework.

Students interact with content in an online learning environment through reading texts, listening to audio, watching videos, working with a simulation, taking a practice quiz, and the like. In the early days of online learning, there was a lot of reading of text. The internet, and even personal computers at the time, did not support all of the options we have today for content. The different options available now for online learning content allow for a great deal of flexibility in design choices, and using varied types of content can help keep students engaged. Do not, however, fall into the myth of learning styles as a rationale for using different types of content. There is no support for basing instructional decisions on learning styles

Table 6.1 Presentation, Generative, and Assessment Strategies to Support Cognitive Presence (adapted in part from Morrison et al., 2013)

Tools needed: ability to record explanations that include visuals with audio narration; examples that include pictures, visuals, and/or videos; quiz tools; sorting activities; productivity tools like Google Docs, Google's Padlet, or Microsoft Office online.

Learning objective	Presentation strategies	Generative strategies	Examples	Assessment strategies
Facts and Concepts *Objective: Remember / understand*[b]	• Present the fact; provide the concept name; provide a definition and explanation, give examples	• Rehearsal or practice (e.g., saying, spelling, writing); mnemonics—recall; ask learners to elaborate or explain; ask learners to generate or find new examples	• Create a product (table, presentation, etc.) in which they distinguish between examples and non-examples; ask learners to identify key characteristics; ask learners to categorize and compare; create a concept map	• Knowledge checks (quizzes and tests)—recognition, retention, and near transfer items; drag-and-drop activities for sorting and comparing or categorizing; activities to generate lists or tables with categories or have learners re-sort examples you provide
Principles, Rules, and Procedures *Objective: Apply / analyze / evaluate / create*[a]	• Explain procedures, provide a range of examples across contexts; in some cases, a simulation may be useful (e.g., application of principles in STEM)	• Opportunities for the students to practice the procedure and submit their product or effort • Simulations which students can test and/or manipulate • Generate examples and/or instances in which the methods	• Demonstrate the procedure or application (e.g., create a video and submit it or perform it live) • Explain the steps (could also ask students to explain steps while they demonstrate performance in a video—i.e., a talk-aloud)	• Explain back to you their understanding of the procedure • Create a concept map or visual model • Write a brief explaining what principles where applied where and how • Create a video doing a narrated tour or explanation of work • For labs or exercises/stretches (e.g., for PE or science), record

		or procedures being used are applicable (and not)	• Analyze a recorded demonstration applying principles from readings (record or submit a written analysis)	themselves doing an exercise or completing an activity like building a prototype or testing and gathering data and submit a video or connect on live video to demonstrate and get immediate feedback • Produce an authentic product (design, work of art, lab report, business plan) and submit for feedback
Interpersonal or Attitude *Objective: Affective*	• Seeing examples, reading case studies, watching a simulation	• Examples (worked examples, demonstrations, talk-aloud on how you solved a problem, etc.) • Role-playing • Case studies or scenarios • Simulation • Diverse teams	• Consider what sort of diversity is central to your objective—disciplinary, cultural, skills/capabilities, racial, geographic, etc.	• Reflection journal; participation in a role-playing exercise; participation in a simulated exercise (e.g., decision-making with different stakeholder groups where students have to take on different perspectives; after-action review of a simulation or exercise; open questions during an oral or written exam; structure a quiz that is designed around self-assessment instead of knowledge assessment

a Objectives using Bloom's taxonomy (Anderson et al., 2001).

(Khazan, 2018; May, 2018). (Chapter 8 covers research-anchored approaches to designing content that facilitates learning and information processing.)

Morrison et al. (2013) describe presentation strategies (strategies for presenting new content to learners) and generative strategies (strategies for engaging learners more deeply with the content). Assessment strategies are also an important part of the cognitive presence tool kit—they drive a lot of how learners engage with the content. Table 6.1 provides some ideas for how to facilitate different types of cognitive presence and learner–content engagement, depending on the content and objectives. (Chapter 7 also discusses types of interaction in more detail, including student–content interaction.)

Table 6.2 can help you identify strategies for learner–content interaction based on different types of objectives, and can be used and reused multiple times. We then provide ideas on how this should "handshake" with institutional planning and vice versa.

Table 6.2 Planning Aid: Strategies for Learner–Content Interaction Based on Objective and Content

Strategies for learner–content interactions
What is the learning objective?
What type of objective is it?
☐ Knowledge/comprehension
☐ Application
☐ Analysis
☐ Synthesis
☐ Evaluation
Presentation strategy:
Generative strategies (practice/activities):
Assessment strategy:
What tool(s) do I think I need to implement these strategies?

Instruction and Planning Handshake

Types of learner–content interactions should significantly inform system-level planning, especially technology evaluation and selection. You may also need to develop policies, support adoption with professional development, or even offer professional development that supports teachers in thinking through possible ways to facilitate learner–content interaction. If, for example, STEM faculty identify simulations and virtual labs as strategies and resources they need to support active learning in their courses, then that need should be included in procurement and resource acquisition. Consider the following necessary handshakes between instructional strategies for online and technology infrastructure.

Presentation Needs and Tools (circle or add):

Ability to record explanations that include visuals with audio narration

Examples that include pictures, visuals, and/or videos

Other: _____

Other: _____

Practice and Assessment Needs and Tools (circle or add):

Knowledge checks (quizzes and tests)

Drag-and-drop/sorting activities

Wiki/Google Docs

Simulations/virtual labs

Other: _____

Other: _____

Student–Teacher Interaction

Regardless of one's relationship or level of expertise with education, when the average individual thinks about learning, the interactions that happen between the student and their teacher often come to mind. Moore (1989, p. 2) defined *student–teacher interaction* as "interaction between the learner and the expert who prepared the subject material, or some other expert acting as instructor." He suggested that many teachers felt that this form of interaction was essential, while many students would describe it as highly desirable. At the time he outlined this kind of interaction, Moore primarily had such things in mind as the development and sequencing of the asynchronous course content, trying to stimulate students' interest in that content and motivate them to complete it, and providing formative feedback on course activities and summative comments on graded assignments.

Even accounting for these more modern tools, student–teacher interaction may still bring to mind students asking questions or teachers grading assignments and providing feedback to students, but there are many other types of student–teacher interaction in online teaching and learning. Table 6.3 is a job aid to support you in identifying different possible types of learner-instructor interactions that are possible today. Start by identifying what learner–instructor interactions you want to make sure are featured in your course. You can also begin to make notes on when you want each type of interaction to occur.

Table 6.3 Planning Job Aid: Ideas for Student–Instructor Interaction

Select the desired types of student–instructor interaction. Make notes in the white space about when/how frequently you will make these happen.

- ☐ Virtual office hours
- ☐ Live synchronous sessions—optional
- ☐ Live synchronous sessions—required
- ☐ Asynchronous forum/discussion board discussions
- ☐ One-on-one Q&A and support
- ☐ One-to-many message/information distribution
- ☐ Formative feedback on student work as they develop it
- ☐ Summative feedback on student work after they complete and submit it
- ☐ _____
  _____
- ☐ _____
  _____

Student–Student Interaction

Moore (1989, p. 4) defined *student–student interaction* as the interaction "between one learner and other learners, alone or in group settings, with or without the real-time presence of an instructor." In his introduction to this kind of interaction, Moore acknowledged that this would challenge both educators' thinking and their practice in the future, an indication that distance learning provided at the time had not featured a great deal of student interaction. Three decades or so later, there is a great deal of focus within online learning to create opportunities for student–student interaction, to help students develop collaborative skills, maintain student motivation, challenge their understanding, and facilitate the coconstruction of knowledge.

Affordances and Challenges

Synchronous Interaction

- Students can interact in real time, as their thoughts come to them.

- Students can be spontaneous in their interactions.

- Students often interact more socially (as opposed to only content or procedural interactions).

- Students must have reliable and stable internet connections to participate.

- Students are often limited in their interaction by the physical device they are using (e.g., the app versions of many live classrooms do not have the same functionality or are not as user-friendly as the web version).

Asynchronous Interaction

- Students can work on their own time but can also procrastinate until the deadline.

- Students have more time to think and reflect on their interaction.

- Students also have more time to edit and revise their interaction.

- Students can feel a greater sense of isolation and disconnection from their online learning experience (i.e., create a greater level of transactional distance).

While not specific to student–student interaction, we often think of interaction in two ways: synchronously and asynchronously. Synchronous interaction is interaction that happens live or in real time. In the traditional in-person environment, it would be the interaction that happens in the classroom. It assumes all students are in the same location at the same time. Within the online environment, the most common example of synchronous interaction is the live class delivered in Zoom, Microsoft Teams, Google Meet, or some other virtual classroom online tool (a good example of student–teacher interaction). In contrast, with asynchronous interaction students can become involved on their own time and schedule. The most common example of asynchronous interaction is the flipped classroom model where students review videos and other instructional content at home to allow them to engage in more project-based learning activities in class the following day (a good example of student–content interaction). As indicated by these examples, it is easy to find both synchronous and asynchronous ways to have students interact with the content and with the teacher, and there are many purposeful ways that online schools create opportunities and encourage students to interact with other students in asynchronous and synchronous ways.

Online teachers can create numerous activities for students to interact with their peers in an asynchronous manner. One of the most common methods in online learning environments is for students to participate in an online discussion forum. While the instructor provides the initial prompt, it is important to create parameters that encourage students to meaningfully interact with one another. Too often teachers will rely on a numerical requirement to try to encourage that interaction (e.g., required comments on at least two other students' responses). An alternative way to encourage students to interact with their peers is to focus the assessment criteria on student behaviors, and we provide generic discussion guidelines as an example. You can also use these discussion guidelines to create a rubric to encourage student to interact with their peers. This kind of activity is most commonly associated with text-based discussion forums but could also be applied to student blogging or tools that are designed to encourage more audio- and/or video-based interaction (such as Flipgrid, Padlet, and VoiceThreads).

Another method often used to encourage students to interact asynchronously with their peers is to use online collaborative tools. For example, whenever students are required to read their textbook or something online, or review a website,

---

Discussion Guidelines Focused on Behavior

Keep in mind that this is a graded discussion, so the more interaction between you and your fellow students, the more we will all learn about each of the cases overall. While there is no formal rubric for the discussion activity, to perform well in these tasks you need to have a high degree of interactivity. This means that to do well you do need to be reading what others have to say, commenting on their ideas, and responding to comments made about your own posts. Use the behaviors described below to help guide both your own entries and the level of interactivity you should strive for in these discussions.

- Post a well-focused response to the prompt provided.

- Post frequently and regularly.

- Frequently offer in-depth comments that further the discussion.

- Comment widely on posts by many classmates.

- Respond regularly in a specific, engaged manner to others' responses and their comments on your response.

- Write concisely.

- Frequently show clear sentence-to-sentence cohesion.

- Use correct grammar and punctuation.

---

podcast, or video, this is an opportunity to organize the students into groups to create sets of content notes in a collaborative fashion. Students can use a wiki or some form of productivity tool (such as Google Docs or Microsoft 365) to build a set of notes together.

Many of these opportunities for students to interact with their peers asynchronously are also examples of ways that students can interact with the content (e.g., read a chapter in the textbook or watch an instructional video) or with their teacher (e.g., respond to the teacher's prompt in a discussion). The challenge for online teachers, and online schools in general, is to be purposeful about creating opportunities for students to interact with their peers in an effort to motivate one another and coconstruct their own knowledge.

When we think of synchronous or live instruction in the online learning setting, we often think of the virtual classroom and tools like Zoom, Microsoft Teams, Google Meet, or Webex. In fact, such tools were commonly used during the pandemic to provide some level of continuity of learning for students (to the extent that the phrase *Zoom school* became common in the media and among educational stakeholders). Again, while this could be a form of a student–teacher interaction, if planned in a purposeful manner it can also be an opportunity for student–student interaction. For example, most of these virtual classrooms allow students to engage in text-based chat with one another while the teacher is presenting the lesson. Students could use this chat feature as a way to ask questions, and the teacher could encourage other students to respond to questions—as opposed to

Table 6.4 Planning Job Aid: Student–Student Interaction Strategies

Select the desired types of student–student interaction (and add additional ideas):

☐ Small-group activities where students read in small groups or complete an activity together (e.g., a SeeSaw activity, a presentation in Google Slides)

☐ Social time at the start of the class for students to chat

☐ Social space in the class site for students to share about themselves and connect with others

☐ Discussion on asynchronous forum/discussion boards

☐ Construction of a single artifact/product by more than one individual

☐ Ability to share draft and final documents/products with each other

☐ Group work on joint project—synchronous

☐ Group work on joint project—asynchronous

☐ Peer review on individual work—synchronous

☐ Peer review on individual work—asynchronous

☐ Self-organized student meeting groups—asynchronous

☐ Self-organized student meeting groups—synchronous

☐ Real-time messaging to peers for Q&A

☐ _____

☐ _____

always relying on the teacher. Students could also be encouraged to simply interact with one another about the lesson in the chat. Beyond the specific live lessons, teachers could create open synchronous rooms for students to log into and use on their own to meet with their peers. Teachers should always be concerned with how these open rooms are used and the potential for use by nonclass actors or for cyber bullying and other negative actions; when creating these rooms, the teacher can limit the ability to access it to only users who are registered with the online school. The teacher can also limit the information about the room number and passcode or the link to access the room by sharing it only inside the learning management system. Finally, it is always a good idea to have these rooms set to automatically record, not because the teacher wants to intrude on the interactions students are having with one another but as a way to review those interactions if any negative behaviors need to be looked at.

Table 6.4 is another planning job aid to help you identify possible ways you can support student–student interaction.

Student–Interface Interaction

In much the same way that the setup of a physical classroom can impact how students interact with their learning, it is also important to consider how students interact with the technological environment. As described above, the 1980s and 1990s saw the development of numerous types of systems that allows individuals to interact with one another over the internet. While numerous sole-purpose technologies developed or became widespread (e.g., email, online discussion forums, and other forms of computer-mediated communication), during these decades systems were developed to bring together these individual tools into a single platform (e.g., bulletin board systems and multiuser dungeons). "While the introduction of a medium into the communication [learning] process may not fundamentally alter it, it does have consequences depending on the medium" (Garrison, 1989, p. 17). A lot of these examples were developed for professional or social purposes, but many were also adopted for educational purposes. However, not until the development of FirstClass in 1990 were all of the educational elements of each of these types of systems brought together in a single environment specifically designed as a learning management system. It was in this historical context that Hillman et al. (1994, p. 34) described student interface interaction as "a process of manipulating tools to accomplish a task," or types of interactions the learner has with the technology itself. The most basic measure of how students interact with the technology is whether they are successful in their use of it: Could they get the technology to do what they wanted it to do, or was the technology a barrier to student learning? In this respect, it is of the utmost importance that the online school choose tools that are user-friendly and that provide the necessary technical support.

Another way that students interact with the technology is with the delivery of content within the learning management system. There are two ways to think about online content delivery: how the student navigates the content, and structure of the course content. For navigating the content, most learning management systems allow the teacher to customize both the specific menu items available for students and the order in which those menu items appear (see Figure 6.1).

Figure 6.1 An example of the navigation menu items within the Canvas learning management system.

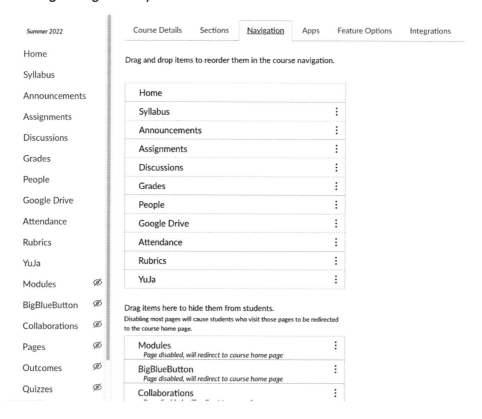

Students need to be able to find their way around their learning management system. For example, how students submit their assignments should be consistent within a course, as well as across different courses offered by the online school. If there is a specific pattern to the nature of instruction, that pattern should also be consistent. For example, if each unit begins with a course announcement or an email from the instructor, followed by a specific presentation of the asynchronous course content, followed by some form of student interaction, followed by a summative evaluation of student learning—these things should be consistent both within the course and across courses. It is important that the online school create a consistent navigation structure and predictable learning experience for students.

Figure 6.2 An example of structure and consistency in presentation of content in a learning management system (from Barbour, 2007).

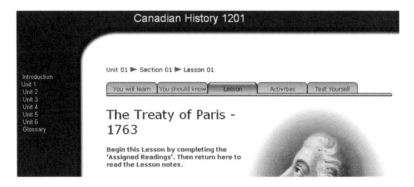

The second way to think about how the student interacts with the learning management system is the structure of the course content. As you can see in Figure 6.2, this course is broken down into six units. Each unit is further broken down into a variety of thematic sections. Each section is then broken down into individual lessons that are designed to represent approximately one hour of instruction for the student to complete. In addition to this course structure, the example in Figure 6.2 shows how the individual lesson is also broken down into five individual components:

1. You will learn: briefly lists, in student-friendly language, the instructional outcomes for the lesson
2. You should know: lists and, when necessary, elaborates on outcomes the

student is expected to have mastered prior to the lesson (i.e., in previous lessons or courses)

3. Lesson: presents the actual content the student is expected to complete, which may be broken into multiple pages (e.g., text, image, multimedia, and/or video instruction)

4. Activities: contains further instructional events the student may need to carry out in order to master the lesson outcomes (e.g., practice questions, additional resources)

5. Test yourself: offers a formative opportunity for students to gauge the degree to which they have achieved the lesson outcomes

This is not to suggest that teachers should break up their lessons in this specific manner or that instructional designers should plan out their asynchronous course content using individual pages corresponding to these five categories—this is simply an illustration of a consistent model that presents the content to students in a way that allows them to proceed in a predictable and bite-size manner. Many online schools create a template that their asynchronous course content must be developed in, and there are many examples to consider.

The main goal that online teachers and online schools should have with respect to student–interface interaction is to ensure that the technology is not an impediment to student learning.

Vicarious Interaction

It is somewhat puzzling that vicarious interaction was chronologically the last type of interaction identified. Readers of this volume will all have had the experience of sitting in a class and watching a fellow student ask a question of the teacher—often a question that you might not have thought of yourself—and the response given by the teacher helps clarify your own understanding of the topic or allows you to learn something new. While you were not a direct participant in the interaction, you were still a part of that exchange. Sutton (2001, p. 227) formally defined *vicarious interaction* as "when a student actively observes and processes both sides of a direct interaction between two other students or between another student and the instructor." This form of interaction is characterized as students observing the interactions of their peers and/or the teacher in an online setting without actively participating. Within the online, noneducational community this vicarious experience was often called *lurking*. Student lurkers are still interacting with their subject matter, peers, and teacher—even if it is only passively.

According to Sutton (2001), vicarious interaction is part of the social learning necessary for students to be able to engage with the supports provided by both their course community and their personal community. You may recall from the ACE framework that students are inherently able to complete some learning tasks and activities independently or by themselves. But for students to have academic success, they need to interact with more knowledgeable others to stay in their zone of proximal development (Vygotsky, 1962). While we often associate the interaction with more knowledgeable others as students directly interacting with online content, a textbook, their peers, or a teacher, it could also be the student vicariously witnessing the interaction between their teacher and another student in a synchronous class or between two peers in an asynchronous discussion forum. It could be a situation where the teacher has received a question from a student in their inbox and, instead of responding directly to the student, the teacher posts an announcement, creates a discussion post, or emails the full class with the response because they determined that the full class would benefit from the response.

Student–Environment Interaction

Each of the types of interaction described thus far have been a part of the formal course community, which Borup et al. (2020, p. 816) defined as "organized and facilitated by those associated with the course or program who have knowledge of course content, expectations, and procedures." However, the ACE framework indicates there are also personal community supports that extend beyond the context of any particular course, program, or school—online or in person. This is what Burnham and Walden (1997, p. 52) had in mind when they proposed *student-environment interaction*, which they described as "reciprocal action or mutual influence between the learner and the learner's surrounds that either assists or hinders learning." In this situation, the type of interaction is characterized as student interaction with environmental or situational factors external to the learning environment.

Table 6.5 Teaching Roles Outside of the Direct Instructional Environment in Online Learning–(from Davis et al., 2007a & Ferdig et al., 2009)

Facilitator: Local mentor, advocates for students(s), proctors, records, grades, etc.
Online Facilitator: Supports students in an online school program; may interact with students online or facilitate at the physical site where students access their online course
Local Key Contact: Professional who assists students in registering and otherwise accessing online courses
Mentor: Academic tutor or course assistant for students
Technology Coordinator: Facilitates technical support for educators and students
Guidance Counselor: Academic adviser for students
Administrator: Instructional leader of the local or online school

Put another way, there are numerous personnel at the local school level who may not "have knowledge of course content, expectations, and procedures." Table 6.5 uses the teaching roles outlined by Davis et al. (2007a) and Ferdig et al. (2009) to list potential individuals. While many of these teaching roles are indeed outside of formal supports provided to the course community by the online school, online teachers and online schools can better prepare these individuals for interactions with online students. As mentioned in Chapter 5, organizations like the Michigan Virtual Learning Research Institute provide research-based guides for students, mentors, teachers, school board members, and administrators (see https://michiganvirtual.org/resources/guides/).

Another option available to online schools is the use of agreements with individual students and parents/guardians who enroll in their courses or individual schools/districts who offer their online programming. In these instances, the students and parents/guardians or schools/districts must agree to either undertake specific tasks or provide certain resources and supports. For example, in the Canadian province of Ontario has historically used an agreement between the Ministry of Education and school districts that districts had to sign to gain access to the Ministry's e-learning program (which provided a student information system, the learning management system, and asynchronous course content). The agreement (which can be viewed at https://k12sotn.ca/wp-content/uploads/2022/11/

ONeLearningMasterUserAgreement.pdf) outlines specific responsibilities for the student's local school district, the student's local school, the student's local school principal, the online school principal, the online teacher, and the online student. An individual with the legal authority to make the commitment to maintain all of the roles and responsibilities of these different stakeholders on behalf of the school district was required to sign the agreement to gain access to the e-learning program.

In addition to these teaching roles outside of the formal course community, under the ACE framework, support is also provided by students' personal community. As a reminder, Borup et al. (2020, p. 817) described personal community support as "family and friends who have connections to a student outside of a course/program," as well as the community organizations and physical resources (e.g., public computer access sites and WiFi hotspots). Basically, the very environmental and situational factors external to the learning environment that Burnham and Walden (1997) had in mind when they envisioned the student–environment interaction. Many online schools also provide guides for parents/guardians of their online students, such as the Florida Virtual School (see https://www.flvs.net/docs/default-source/full-time/flvs-full-time-student-parent-handbook.pdf) and the North Carolina Virtual Public School (see https://ncvps.org/guide-for-parents-and -mentors/). Further, some online schools provide students with a list of locations where they can access computers, WiFi, and other learning resources in their local communities. The lesson from these examples is that, while the online school may not be able to control the type or level of support an individual student's personal community will be able to provide, online teachers and online schools can take actions to assist this group with their support role.

Ways Students Can Interact

The main theme from this exploration of the types of interaction that students might engage in is that it is important to ensure that the online teacher and the online school have planned and enacted purposeful opportunities for students to interact with each of these components (see Figure 6.3): direct interactions not only with the content but also with the environment, with teachers, with other students, and with the interface, plus passively observed vicarious interactions.

Figure 6.3 Sources of interactions for students in an online environment.

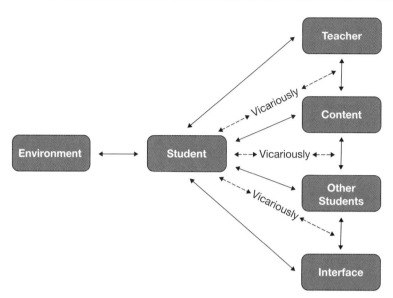

Once we have thought about and planned for interactions between students and all of these different peoples and things, it is important to focus on what forms those interactions will take. Burnham and Walden (1997) suggested that grouping interactions by type is insufficient and that interactions should also be categorized by their subject: What should they interact *about*? Heinemann (2005) suggested that online teachers think about their interactions in terms of the purpose of those interactions, which he believed fell into three categories: *intellectual interactions* are instructional or content-focused interactions; *organizational interactions* refer to the procedural or administrative interactions that students have within an online course; and *social interactions* are generally non-course-related interactions, which often generate a sense of social presence. The following sections look at each of these categories in greater detail.

Intellectual/Instructional Interactions

Intellectual interactions are exchanges related to the course content. This particular category, and all of Heinemann's (2005) categories, was based largely on an examination of the work of online learning pioneer Zane Berge (1995) and his description of the different tasks of the online teacher. One of these tasks he described as follows:

Pedagogical (intellectual; task)
Certainly, some of the most important roles of online discussion moderator/
tutor revolve around their duties as an educational facilitator. The moderator
uses questions and probes for student responses that focus discussions on
critical concepts, principles and skills. (p. 23)

Essentially, intellectual interactions include most of what we consider to be "teaching," such as presenting and clarifying the course content, responding to student
questions, and providing feedback to students on coursework and assignments.

Intellectual interactions are most consistent with activities that fall under the
teaching presence in the CoI framework. This includes such things as designing
the asynchronous course content that online students will interact with. It might
also include delivering the online instruction, in the case of a synchronous environment, or scaffolding student learning experiences in either a synchronous or
an asynchronous environment. Intellectual interactions would also involve evaluating students. However, some ways to encourage intellectual interactions do not
involve students interacting with content or teachers. For example, many teachers
have a discussion forum specifically designed for students to pose content-focused
questions. There may be only one teacher, but there are many more students, so
there is a strong likelihood that one of these many students will know the answer
and see it before the teacher has the opportunity to see it and respond. Additionally, if one student has this particular question about the content, there is a chance
that other students will have the same or similar questions, which means that all
of these students would benefit from a public response. Thus, while it would be
easy to assume that, because the teacher is the subject matter expert, intellectual
interactions would focus on the teacher or the course content, but they also present
opportunities for student–student interaction.

While the use of Heinemann's categories of interaction by scholars as a way
to guide research has been slow, the initial research that has been undertaken has
shown that in online learning environments the vast majority of interactions fall
into the intellectual/instructional category. In fact, Hawkins et al. (2011) reported
that between 60% and 95% of interactions by online teachers were instructional
and focused on content. Given this result, it is all the more important to purpose-
fully plan for ways that students are able to interact with their peers about the
course content.

Organizational/Procedural Interactions

Organizational interactions are exchanges related to course policies, procedures, and student progress. Interestingly, this was the only category that Heinemann (2005) proposed that combined two of the tasks outlined by Berge (1995, p. 23):

Managerial (organizational; procedural; administrative)
This role involves setting the agenda for the conference: the objectives of the discussion, the timetable, procedural rules and decision-making norms. Managing the interactions with strong leadership and direction is considered a *sine qua non* of successful conferencing.

Technical
The facilitator must make participants comfortable with the system and the software that the conference is using. The ultimate technical goal for the instructor is to make the technology transparent. When this is done, the learner may concentrate on the academic task at hand.

As Davis et al. (2007b) suggested, online teachers need to undertake a different managerial role than performed by traditional classroom teachers. Online teachers need to ensure that the interface and content are organized and structured, with obvious deadlines to help keep students on track. Online teachers need to access the course data generated by the learning management systems to understand trends in student participation, to help identify which students are on pace and which students are exhibiting behaviors that suggest that they may need assistance.

One of the easiest ways to address or minimize organizational interactions is to facilitate student-interface interactions. If students are able to navigate their online learning in consistent and predictable ways, this lessens the burden on procedural and administrative teaching role (which would allow teachers to focus on more intellectual and, in particular, social interactions). Another strategy that online teachers can use to try to minimize the amount of organizational interaction is to collect all of the managerial and technical queries that they receive throughout the course and then use that information to create and post a thematically organized Frequently Asked Questions document for students to find answers to the most common questions past students have had. This document can be revised and updated each semester or even throughout the semester. Yet another strategy to minimize the amount of student–teacher interaction focused on organizational issues is for online teachers to create an open discussion forum specifically for that purpose, similar to the strategy used for intellectual interactions to encourage student–student interaction.

While the concept of trying to minimize the amount of organizational interaction, to create more time for intellectual and social interaction, is important, we would be remiss if we didn't discuss recent research into data analytics and the potential that it has to make organizational interactions more purposeful and meaningful. For example, Hung et al. (2012a) found that students tended to perform lower in entry-level courses regardless of the level of student engagement and suggested that online schools focus more effort on finding the right balance of structure in these entry-level courses. In a similar study, Hung et al. (2012b, p. 89) found that "discussion participation (replies and posts) was the most important behavior for predicting students' overall performance." At its most basic level, Dickson (2005) found that students who clicked on more items in the learning management system performed better than students who clicked on fewer items. This suggests that students who interact more with the various aspects of the course (e.g., visit more of the content, read more of the discussions, watch more of the videos) perform better. Online teachers should know how to access student course activity or participation data and engage in organization interactions with the student when they notice a lack of this basic level of engagement in the course (or, if the learning management system is sophisticated enough to allow it, create automatically alerts around certain student behavior or lack thereof).

Social/Supportive Interactions

Social interactions are exchanges that offer support, encouragement, and perceptions of immediacy and connectedness. This category aligned with the following task:

Social

Creating a friendly, social environment in which learning is promoted is also essential for successful moderating. This suggests "promoting human relationships, developing group cohesiveness, maintaining the group as a unit, and in other ways helping members to work together in a mutual cause," are all critical to success of any conferencing activities. (Berge, 1995, p. 23)

Numerous studies have pointed to the importance of supportive interactions for online student motivation and progress (Borup, 2016; Borup et al., 2013, 2014a, 2019; DiPietro, 2010; DiPietro et al., 2008; Mulcahy et al., 2008; Nippard & Murphy, 2007; Roblyer, 2006; Weiner, 2003). The common theme in these studies is the importance of social interactions with students to nurture, encourage, motivate, and retain them in their online learning journey.

Much of the social interaction in an online learning setting is designed to allow for both the online teacher and the online students to be able to project social presence. As suggested in Chapter 5, online teachers can use their students' names when sending them email, when responding to a post in a discussion forum, or when students join the synchronous class. The online teacher can also use humor and other things to display their personality, in each of these kinds of interactions with the students. Many online teachers create open discussion forums that students can use to engage in non-course-related topics; some even open up the synchronous classroom for virtual "happy hours" when students can simply hang out and get to know one another. In this instance the synchronous classroom is quite useful, as it provides both a main room and breakout rooms that smaller groups of students can use to congregate around topics of mutual interest. Many online schools organize cocurricular and extracurricular activities—sometimes online using the same tools that the students use for learning, and other times in person to allow students the opportunity to get to know one another and their online teachers without the interaction being mediated by a computer screen or mobile device.

As has been foreshadowed by the previous categories, some of the online teachers in the Hawkins et al. (2011) study reported that they had no social interactions with their students at all, whereas others suggested that they only had minimal social interactions with their online students, in the form of personal comments students left in assignments or the occasional word of encouragement that teachers left in the feedback they provided to those assignments. One of the main barriers given by the online teachers was the lack of mechanisms in place to encourage social interactions. Essentially, the online schools or the online teachers themselves had failed to plan for opportunities for students to interact with their peers, with their teacher, or within the tools being used to deliver the online instruction. Other barriers raised by online teachers included a lack of time due to class size, a concern about revealing too much about themselves online, and a perception that intellectual interactions were more important and should take priority. The lack of social interaction did mean that both the online teachers and their students felt a lack of social presence or connection to the course.

Summary

With all of these types and categories of interaction, you may be asking yourself, how do I plan for them all? Are they all of equal importance? Terry Anderson (2003, p. 4) proposed his equivalency theorem regarding Moore's original three types of interaction:

> Deep and meaningful formal learning is supported as long as one of the three forms of interaction (student–teacher; student–student; student–content) is at a high level. The other two may be offered at minimal levels, or even eliminated, without degrading the educational experience.
>
> High levels of more than one of these three modes will likely provide a more satisfying educational experience, though these experiences may not be as cost or time effective as less interactive learning sequences.

While Anderson focuses on Moore's original three types of interaction, the principle applies to all six types of interactions that students can have in the online learning setting. For example, if there are times when you know you that you will be grading large projects and will have less time for direct student-teacher interaction, then you may want to make sure your students have ample student-content and student-student interactions. You can budget more time for direct student-teacher interaction at times when your responsibilities in the other roles allow it. The key is to ensure that students can interact or engage in multiple ways and that they have ample opportunity to interact in intellectual, in organizational, and especially in social ways.

Wolcott (1995, p. 42) asked five basic questions of online teachers that are still applicable today:

1. Am I considering methods because they are familiar and comfortable?
2. Are the methods under consideration those which utilize the medium to its best advantage, or are they attempts to reproduce face-to-face instruction?

3. What strategies would optimally achieve expectations in light of the variables of students, content, and context?
4. What adjustments are required to accommodate instructional activities and visuals to distance [online] delivery?
5. Are the methods and techniques likely to encourage participation and interaction?

These questions can help you consider what your students are interacting with in their online learning setting and how they are interacting with them. Are you planning for a high level of student–teacher interaction because it is familiar and comfortable, or because it is consistent with how you teach in a face-to-face setting? Given your goals for a particular lesson or topic, have you provided students with a means for interaction that is suitable to achieve those goals? Are there other ways the students could interact within the online learning setting that would allow them to achieve those same goals but also provide the students with choice and agency in their learning (see Chapter 4)? Do the methods and techniques that you have planned to encourage interaction allow you to project your teaching presence and allow both you and your online students the ability to exhibit your social presence (see Chapter 5)?

Chapter 7

Using Effective Instructional Strategies for the Online Environment

It was clear to the teachers in the Applewood district that merely dumping content online was not the equivalent to education or learning. They wanted more for their learners, and even for themselves as they engaged with students. What strategies could teachers use in their online teaching that would engage the learners with the content? What would help them choose between learning at the same time synchronously versus work and interactions that could be asynchronous? How could they think through what different options offer, and how might they leverage the best from a range of tools to support a variety of strategies, including some direct instruction, class discussions, and collaborative learning? What might be some other strategies that research shows are effective in online learning? What about STEM content, where students may conduct labs or do more hands-on experiments, or art classes where students are creating tangible artifacts?

Chapters 4–6 have outlined several more theoretical concepts and frameworks. Chapter 4 introduced the concept of transactional distance, or the sense of psychological distance (also often described as isolation) that students can feel if their distance learning does not have the right balance of structure, dialogue, and autonomy. As we learned, the balance of course structure (i.e., the degree to which it is organized, has a reliable rhythm, and has clearly communicated expectations) and dialogue you foster with your students is largely dependent on the student's level of autonomy, or their ability to provide input into the class or direct some aspect of their learning. And as educators we know that student autonomy is largely impacted by student age.

Chapter 5 explored the Community of Inquiry (CoI) framework and how it is important that the online learning we plan have overlapping opportunities for students to experience our teaching presence (i.e., the sense that we have planned our their learning experience in a purposeful manner), their own cognitive presence (i.e., the opportunity for them to make meaning of the content), and both our and their own social presence (i.e., opportunities for us to project ourselves as real people). We also explored the Academic Communities of Engagement (ACE) framework, which stresses the importance of understanding that, while the student will bring certain inherent interests and abilities to their online learning—as well as support from their own personal community—the main aspect an online teacher or online school has control over is the support provided by the course community. Because of this reality, the onus is on us to ensure that we examine all of the individuals and resources that make up that course community, and how each can be leveraged to support our online students. We also learned from the ACE framework that students need to be engaged affectively, behaviorally, and cognitively in order to have academic success.

One of the ways we can engage our students affectively, behaviorally, and cognitively rests in strategies we can use to support their interactions with online learning. As outlined in Chapter 6, students will interact with a variety of other actors and things in their online learning. In a more traditional sense, students will interact with the course content, their teacher, their fellow students, and the environment outside of the formal learning context. In a distance learning context, how students interact with the technology or interface that provides the learning is also important. As we stressed, it is important for online educators to consider how students will be interacting and plan to ensure that they are interacting with multiple actors. A solid instructional plan for online learning does not solely focus on the content or course procedures but also includes a good mix of social interactions that are intentionally planned and incorporated into your online courses.

In this chapter, we turn to specific instructional strategies you can use in your online teaching. We hope that, as you make decisions about how to design and deliver your online learning, as well as assessing student learning, you will consider which strategies to use and how to implement them with a larger framework in mind, along with the visions for online learning those frameworks reflect.

You may recall from Chapter 6 Morrison et al.'s (2013) breakdown of presentation strategies and generative strategies. This chapter explores a specific set of strategies commonly used in online instruction that can facilitate presentation and generative strategies: direct instruction, discussion, collaboration, and worked examples (by no means is this a complete set of strategies you could use). We also have incorporated some examples of strategies and tools for content areas that teachers often feel less clear on how to teach online, such as art and STEM classes. These strategies also work well together as a strategy set, so we conclude the chapter with ideas for how they can be used together.

Instructional Strategies

During the pandemic a lot of the teaching or instructional emphasis was placed on delivering lectures and other forms of direct instruction live through a virtual classroom environment like Zoom. In fact, as can be seen in this journal entry by Kadambari Baxi from April 2020, the use of Zoom was so prevalent that many students and parents referred to the remote learning their teachers provided as "Zoom school":

> Live/work in our apartment remains surreally calm, but outside in the real world, Governor Cuomo, reading the numbers, warns us daily that the crisis is dire. Meanwhile, a door down the hall remains shut. We are not allowed to interrupt our son's Zoom-school. (Baxi et al., 2020, para. 13)

The reality is that the use of Zoom as an instructional tool to simply replicate the traditional classroom environment was one of the weaker instructional strategies for online learning we have seen in recent years, as it does not take advantage of many of the strengths and affordances of online learning.

In this section, we introduce the idea of "affordances" and explore the different instructional strategies that online learning can afford. Well before the pandemic, Skylar (2009, pp. 71–72) argued that teachers often "emulate traditional instructional methods in the online learning environment through the use of synchronous . . . lectures." The traditional classroom environment is often how we think about engaging in online teaching activities, so let's examine some instructional strategies that we regularly use in the classroom and how those might be implemented in an online setting. Regardless of the specific instructional strategy selected, you must decide whether to employ that strategy in a synchronous or an asynchronous fashion. Therefore, as we describe each of the individual strategies, we will attempt to provide some of the advantages and disadvantages of each modality.

Strategies for Direct Instruction

Direct instruction is often one of the easiest instructional strategies to implement both in the traditional face-to-face classroom and in online learning. In the face-to-face classroom teachers can simply talk to the students while presenting material that they wish to cover. Teachers can also use slides that include notes or visuals to help guide the direct instruction they are providing. Depending on the topic and subject area, teachers may make use of a whiteboard to work through different problems or write out notes that accompany the lecture. In a less direct fashion, teachers can provide students with handouts or point students to a particular section of the textbook that accompanies the material. All of these things can also be done in various fashions in an online learning setting.

Building Your Online Learning Vocabulary

Pacing versus Modality

One major confusion often arises around the term *asynchronous*. People will sometimes confuse *asynchronous* with *self-paced*, but these are not synonymous terms. One has to do with pacing, and the other with modality.

Pacing Options	Modality Options
Self-paced	Synchronous
Class-paced	Asynchronous
Blend of both	

Synchronous means everyone is participating at the same time but not at the same place. *Asynchronous* means everyone is participating at different times from different places. Many online classes use both synchronous (live) and asynchronous (on your own schedule) activities and options.

Self-paced means learners work through the content at their own pace, independent of where any other learners are in the content. Some online learning is designed this way, but a lot of online learning in schools and universities is class-paced. This means students work through the content at a similar pace. This allows for a much higher degree of interaction among learners.

Instruction within a week can be a mix of class-paced and self-paced, but the structure from week to week is class-paced. You can also have a class that is entirely asynchronous but is class-paced.

As an online teacher, one of the first decisions to make with respect to direct instruction is whether the specific content is better presented in a synchronous or an asynchronous format. The synchronous perspective is one that we often associate with the description of Zoom school referenced above—a situation where the online teacher is attempting to replicate in an online environment many of the methods of direct instruction that one would find in the face-to-face classroom. However, it is important to note that, depending upon the nature of the content, the use of a synchronous virtual classroom may be the most appropriate way to provide direct instruction. For example, the topic being covered might be one that students often have difficulty with. The synchronous virtual classroom allows students to stop their teacher and ask them to go over a specific idea or concept again, or to ask clarifying questions of the teacher to ensure that they understand the content.

Interestingly, the online learning environment affords both the teacher and the student specific opportunities to interact that the face-to-face setting does not. In a traditional classroom, students who have questions about the content being presented have two choices. First, they can raise their hand and, when called upon, ask their question of the teacher in front of their peers. For a variety of reasons, many students are reluctant to demonstrate in such a public manner that they don't understand what the teacher just went over. Or, they can wait until after class and ask the teacher their question in a more private setting. However, if the student needs clarification to understand the rest of the class content, such as needing to understand Step 2 in order to be able to grasp Steps 3–5, this option means these students are likely unable to understand the remainder of the lesson.

Figure 7.1 A sample poll in Zoom from the instructor's perspective.

At present, most virtual classrooms allow online teachers to poll their students, presenting the opportunity to check for understanding or determine the pace of the lesson, as shown in Figure 7.1—after the online teacher has clicked on the "End poll" option, they can share the results of the poll with the class—it provides an aggregate response, maintaining individual student confidentiality—or they can just use the results to adjust their own instruction.

Figure 7.2 Emojis available under the "reactions" feature in Zoom that allows students to indicate a positive or negative response to the teacher, as well as the need to speed up, slow down, or take a break.

Online teachers can also have their students use the reactions feature included in most virtual classrooms to give students their own agency in providing feedback (see

Figure 7.2). Online teachers can scan the thumbs-up icon or the green check and red X icons to periodically check for understanding. Early in the course, the teacher can develop norms or guidelines for online course "netiquette" that includes using the rewind icon (the gray button with the two less than signs) and the fast-forward icon (the blue button with the two greater than signs) to request the teacher slow down or speed up. Determining how these reactions will be used at the beginning of the course is actually a good opportunity to create some student autonomy by asking them to help generate these expectations. For example, a class might develop a norm regarding whether students should use the raise-hand function in Zoom or simply type a message in the chat box when they have a question.

One of the limitations of the reactions feature in most virtual classrooms is that it is public, so all students would see if one student asks the teacher to slow down. However, most virtual classroom environments allow the online teacher to turn on the chat function and allow students to send messages to the class or in private to another user or the teacher (see Figure 7.3). These virtual classroom tools also allow the teacher to disable the public chat, in which case all chat messages would be seen only by the teacher. The teacher can also disable chat altogether, which might be useful if the chat would only serve as a distraction during a particular lesson. The affordances of the tool should be considered in light of the specific goals of the lesson.

Figure 7.3 The chat feature in Zoom. The view on the left is the default, where everyone (i.e., the teacher and all of the students) would see any message posted in the chat. The view on the right is an option for the student to change that default and choose to send their chat message privately to the teacher.

While the affordances of most virtual classrooms provide online teachers with feedback from the students that they would often find difficult to obtain (especially privately) in the traditional classroom, if the specific topic of the lesson is straightforward and students are often able to understand on their own, the use of a video (e.g., a narrated presentation or a recording of a worked example) may be the best option to provide direct instruction. Additionally, the use of a video to provide direct instruction gives the students agency over how they view that video. They can choose when they watch it, allowing them to select a time of day when they feel most ready to focus and learn the content. They can also pause a video, which affords them the opportunity to think more deeply about the material that has just been presented or to work through an example problem you may want them to work out on their own. Recorded videos also afford learners the ability to rewind the video and replay the last bit or rewatch the video entirely. Learners also often use features such as slowing down or increasing the speed of the video. Given all of these affordances, online teachers should always record synchronous classes used to present content and post those recordings where the students are able to access them for these purposes. In our online courses, we usually post a link to the recording in that same week so students can always find the recorded session in context with the rest of that week's materials.

One of the affordances of using video or text and images to provide direct instruction in an asynchronous fashion is the analytics that most learning management systems maintain. Most systems track both how many times a student interacts with a particular piece of content and how much time the student spends accessing each item. Thus, as an online teacher you can see if the student actually clicked on the web page or the video where are you provided the content (Figure 7.4). Additionally, many systems, or the third-party vendors that integrate into those learning management systems, will actually track how much of a video an individual student has watched (Figure 7.5). While this data is useful to the online teacher on an individual student basis, the aggregate data for the entire class can also be quite useful as it can inform a teacher whether multiple students in the class watched the same portions of the video multiple times. That can indicate instructional needs such as students having difficulty with the content that was discussed in that particular portion of the video.

Figure 7.4 Individual usage data from a single student captured by the learning management system.

Access Report

Content	Times Viewed	Times Participated	Last Viewed
⬇ remote-teaching-1.png	2		Aug 4, 2020 9:41AM
⬇ plus.png	4		Aug 4, 2020 9:41AM
⬇ header.png	4		Aug 4, 2020 9:41AM
🏠 Course Home	2		Aug 4, 2020 9:41AM
⬇ remote-teaching.png	2		Jul 10, 2020 11:10AM

Figure 7.5 The aggregate analytics from a third-party video hosting system integrated into the learning management system.

These examples are good illustrations of the affordances of synchronous and asynchronous modalities when it comes to direct instruction. The question you as an online teacher want to answer is what makes the most sense for the content of the lesson and the students engaged in the course. Is the content such that it would be beneficial for students to be able to provide real-time feedback on their understanding or to be able to ask questions as they occur? Or would it be better to record that direct instruction and have the students watch that video on their own time, which would also give you the opportunity to use your allocated synchronous time for other activities that may allow students to be more active participants in their online learning? Maybe in the past you have covered this content by providing a worked example using text and images on a page in the learning management system, but this time you feel the students need a more interactive presentation of the content? Perhaps you've demonstrated worked examples in a live virtual classroom in the past, but the students you have this time around are more independent and would just as easily learn the content through a recording? Alternatively, maybe to this point in your online teaching you have primarily used recorded videos (i.e., student-content interaction), and you are deciding to cover the next topic in a synchronous session to encourage more student-teacher and student-student interaction? Which modality encourages students to exhibit the greatest cognitive presence, or which modality allows you as the online teacher to demonstrate a greater sense of social presence? These are just some of the questions that you need to consider as you plan out your instructional strategies within the broader frameworks that we have discussed thus far.

Strategies for Class Discussion

Consider the following scenario: You are a classroom teacher with 30 students and you want to engage your students in a class discussion. The previous day or as homework, you asked the students to review some content so they would be prepared to participate in the upcoming class discussion. As the teacher, you have thought about and revised your opening comments and specific prompts you want to use to invite students into the discussion and encourage them to participate. Your 60-minute class begins, although you've missed the first three to five minutes as students have been filing into the room, chatting with one another, or simply just interacting with you in a social manner before the formal lesson begins. You take another two or three minutes to provide your background context and deliver the prompt to your students. With a class of 30 students, if you factor in the five to eight minutes that have already passed before the students even begin their participation, if each student were to simply respond to the prompt occupying the same amount of time that it would take for you to read aloud—only what has been written in this paragraph thus far—it would occupy the next 40 minutes of class time (or about 80% of the class). This is not even considering any interaction that students might have with points raised by their peers—this is only the time that it would take for each of your 30 students to deliver their initial response to the prompt that you have given.

We begin our consideration of the use of discussions in online learning with this illustration because, as noted in Chapter 6, a common instructional strategy for online teachers is to add a prompt in the discussion forum and then to ask each student to post a response to that prompt, and often also include a requirement that they interact with or respond to a specific number of their peers' responses. We aren't suggesting that this is a poor instructional strategy, but if we are thinking about the affordances as well as the limitations of the technologies that we have in the online learning setting, this particular strategy may not be the best choice.

Taking into consideration some of these issues, the first question you want to ask yourself as an online teacher is, what are the benefits of conducting this discussion in a synchronous fashion compared to an asynchronous fashion? For example, if the discussion were a part of a live session using the virtual classroom software, it would mean that the student responses would be less polished, as they would be thinking on their feet like in a traditional brick-and-mortar classroom discussion. The lack of time to reflect and revise one's remarks might lead to more overlap in the content of student responses—particularly for those who aren't among the first to respond. However, the choice to hold the online discussion using a synchronous tool affords the instructional ability to require students to respond immediately and be quick on their feet. It also affords students the ability to actually hear the tone and intonation of each speaker as they contribute to the discussion. The students can see one another's faces and the gestures they make while speaking. The use of synchronous time for the online discussion, and the lack of time to prepare and carefully revise their comments, also means that what students have to say is often a more accurate reflection of what they know and think about the topic in that moment. If you want immediacy for an instructional reason—for example, students should be able to debate, or you want them to simulate a discussion or meeting where they have to arrive at a solution or agreement like they might in an authentic context—then synchronous discussion makes sense. However, if you want students to take their time to think through their response and consult resources on how they construct a response—such as a post that integrates ideas or readings from class or where they should consult worked examples—then asynchronous would be a better fit.

Defining Discussion Norms With Students

In the guide *Leading Synchronous Online Discussions*, Fedesco (2020) suggests that online teachers create a set of norms with their students on how they will conduct their online discussions in the virtual classroom. These are some of the areas that she recommends teachers explore with their students:

- Should students have their video and audio on during class?

- What protocols should be put in place for students who may not easily be able to leave their video and/or audio on, because of poor internet connection, distracting learning environments, health issues such as migraines, and so on? For example:

  - How should students communicate with the instructor when they are unable to be seen or heard?

  - Can students display a fun photo instead of a black box when their video is muted?

- You can suggest that everyone dress as if they are going to a face-to-face class so that students feel more comfortable showing up on video.

- Should students raise their actual hand or virtual hand when they want to speak?

- Should students signal that they would like to speak in the chat?

- Should you encourage all students to contribute to the conversation in the chat if they aren't comfortable sharing via audio/video?

- You can encourage students to nod along, smile, mime nonverbal feedback, or use Zoom signals like hand clapping or thumbs up, emphasizing that nonverbal cues are helpful in facilitating conversation, but typical backchannel responses like "uh-huh" or "oh wow" can be more disruptive in Zoom.

If the benefits of conducting the online discussion in a synchronous manner align with the overall goals of the lesson or with the course objectives, then the next step would be to plan how best to implement the synchronous online discussion (e.g., developing a set of norms, as suggested by Fedesco, 2020). The importance of these kinds of norms cannot be overstated. For example, if one of the reasons that you decided to conduct the online discussion in a synchronous format was because of the physical and other nonverbal cues that seeing and hearing the speaker provides, how the students use the chat feature and the reactions in the virtual classroom could hinder that affordance.

It is important to note that we aren't dismissing the idea of conducting your online discussion in an asynchronous format. While the traditional threaded online discussion forums generally lack much ability to convey nonverbal social cues and can often be more time-consuming for students to participate in, they do offer many affordances that real-time discussion lacks. Asynchronous discussions allow students the ability to reflect on their responses and to revise their contributions to the discussion prior to posting. Asynchronous discussions also allow students the time to consult with additional resources. Given that asynchronous discussions are often conducted over an extended period of time, it lets students engage with the contributions of many more of their peers then they would have the opportunity to do in a real-time discussion. Further, the ability of an asynchronous discussion forum to simply generate more interactions than a synchronous discussion provides students with more opportunities to interact vicariously with the coconstruction of knowledge by their peers.

Online teachers need to consider both the goals that they have for an activity and the benefits and disadvantages associated with how they implement that strategy. One of the considerations that you should have as an online teacher in determining that goal is whether you were trying to encourage student–teacher or student–student interaction. For example, if your goal for using online discussion is to get students interacting with one another and building on one another's ideas (i.e., leaning more toward student–student interaction), then it is important that both the instructions and how the discussion is graded (assuming it is a graded activity) focus on that particular goal. In Chapter 6 we included "Discussion Guidelines Focused on Behavior," which listed first, "Post a well-focused response to the prompt provided." If the student's specific answer to the prompt doesn't matter that much, and your goal is really just to get the students interacting with one another as they coconstruct knowledge around a specific topic, this kind of statement in the instructions or in the grading rubric would deter that goal. Even how active you, as the online teacher, are in the online discussion will either enhance or limit your ability to achieve your instructional goal. Often exerting more teaching presence in asynchronous discussion decreases student–student interaction. (We often wait for our students to post and then interject some comments toward the end of a discussion period.)

As we consider this strategy, it is also important that we aren't limited by our perceptions of the tools and technology available. Above we suggested that one of the advantages of the synchronous discussion in the virtual classroom was the ability to hear the tone and intonation in people's comments, as well as the ability to see physical and nonverbal cues. Similarly, we also suggested that the inability to access these things was one of the limitations or drawbacks of using asynchronous discussions. However, if we focus our attention on student–interface interaction, we quickly realize that many of today's online learning tools allow us to engage in video-based or audio discussions in an asynchronous format. Tools like Voice-Thread or Flipgrid are specifically designed to allow students to post video responses to an instructor's prompt. In fact, most modern learning management systems also include this functionality (although in many cases it is less user-friendly than tools specifically designed for this purpose). Use of video instead of text for the asynchronous discussions allows students and their online teacher to demonstrate a much higher degree of social presence. If conveying tone or gestures is important but you still want them to be reflective and take their time, you can also use a video discussion where you ask students to share and post videos responses using a tool like Flipgrid.

Finally, our consideration of discussion as a strategy thus far has focused solely on the instructional interaction that online discussions provide. However, online discussions could also be used for students to introduce themselves to their teacher and peers. Students could be invited to share interests or personal trivia they feel comfortable sharing as a part of the instructions or prompt. Another opportunity to combine instructional, procedural, and social interaction would be for online teachers to schedule a regular synchronous discussion session and make it a blend of both task-focused and social time. To create an aspect of flexibility for the students and allow them to exercise their learner autonomy, you could make these synchronous sessions optional or record them to allow the students to access them based on their own schedule. Instead of meeting in one large group, online teachers could meet with students in smaller groups based on schedule availability. An additional way to provide students with the opportunity to interact instructionally, procedurally, and socially is to create a space for students to self-organize and talk with one another. This space can be a combination of things like discussion forums where they can post questions and answers, a link to a synchronous or live virtual classroom where they can meet in at any time, or using some form of presence tool often embedded in learning management systems where students can see who is in the course at the same time as they are and chat with them. Each of these opportunities to dialogue in both structure and unstructured ways will help decrease the sense of isolation or transactional distance that students can feel in their online learning.

As you may be able to tell, we believe that classroom discussions are a fundamental strategy for online learning. Discussions are how students are able to express their ability to understand and make use of the content. Discussions are where you, as the online teacher, are able to see that understanding in real time in a synchronous discussions or students' ability to apply and build on that understanding in an asynchronous discussion. By using both synchronous and asynchronous discussions, you will also model effective communication skills and give students the opportunity to practice different types of communication.

Strategies for Class Collaboration

Collaboration is the generic term we have chosen to group together a variety of student-focused instructional strategies, similar to how we group teacher-focused or teacher-led strategies under *direct instruction*. From an online learning standpoint, some traditional examples of these kinds of strategies include the use of WebQuest, online activities where students are introduced to a topic and then given a task. Either individually or in small groups, the students are supposed to use the resources in WebQuest, as well as their own problem-solving and critical thinking skills, to complete the task by generating an artifact. (See https://webquest.org/ for more information, sample WebQuests that you can use with your students, and Quest-Garden, a tool that allows you to create your own WebQuests for your students.)

In an effort to leverage more interactive tools, online teachers could have their students undertake activities or create artifacts using any variety of collaborative tools. For example, students could be exposed to a common experience during their synchronous or asynchronous instruction, and then be asked to work individually or in small groups to document what they learn from their experience or to apply the content from that experience in a collaborative tool like Google Docs or a wiki. To move away from using text as the sole mode of learning, online teachers could have their students create artifacts to document their learning using concept mapping tools, image-generation programs, animation tools, or video-creation programs. Further, tools such as Camtasia, iMovie, and other screen recording programs—even using virtual classrooms to record and capture a desktop screen being shared—could be used by students themselves to record and document learning.

Another common online collaborative strategy is to have students work in groups. Because the online environment presents certain physical barriers to student collaborations that aren't present in a face-to-face setting, it is important to scaffold these types of learning activities throughout the course. Often teachers will start by placing students in smaller groups at the beginning of the course, and as they learn strategies to work together in the online environment, the teacher can begin to have students working in larger groups. One of the strategies for working together in the online environment is to set clear guidelines in terms of how students will communicate with one another, the specific tools they should use, and the different roles group members should be willing to assume. Similar to a classroom environment, the online teacher needs to find ways to encourage full participation in these groups, to ensure that some students are not able to leverage the hard work of their peers for their own gain. In this respect, one of the affordances of online group work is that the selection of tools and guidelines the students use and how they communicate should provide an electronic footprint of each student's activity within the group.

Thinking more broadly, students do not need to be actively online to engage in student-focused learning. There are many things around the home and within the student's own neighborhood that an online teacher can use to help guide the student through a learning experience. One of the most common examples of this is the use of kitchen science. For example, you could have students pour water into a bowl and then shake pepper into the water; then the student places a finger into the water and sees the pepper stick to the finger; next the student puts soap on the finger and repeats the same process, the pepper floats away from the finger. You could even have the student repeat the experiment substituting different household liquids in place of the water (such as milk, juice, or cooking oil) to see if the same reaction occurs. Moving outside of the kitchen, you could have students use a measuring tape to calculate the area of their home. Similarly, you could have students create a scale drawing of their home to practice their mapping and other geography skills. We understand that these kinds of home- and community-based examples are often not associated with online learning. However, one of the things that the pandemic has taught us is that teachers need to be able to generate instructional strategies that may not rely on tools that require connectivity or significant bandwidth. Having said that, most of these activities could also be incorporated into an online environment by asking students to record or somehow document in an electronic fashion what they were doing within their household or neighborhood as they undertook these activities.

Strategies for Worked Examples

In their book *e-Learning and the Science of Instruction*, Clark and Mayer (2016) present multiple principles, many relating to the design of multimedia content and materials (Chapter 8 covers these in more depth). One principle, worked examples, is particularly noteworthy as an instructional strategy, as well as a content presentation strategy. *Worked examples* are a form of modeling for learners and thus can be used as part of a strategy of cognitive apprenticeship originally developed for both reading and mathematics education (Collins et al., 1987; Brown et al., 1989; Jekielek et al., 2002). Cognitive apprenticeship involves six steps: modeling, coaching, scaffolding, articulation, reflection, and exploration (see Figure 7.6).

Figure 7.6 The cognitive apprenticeship strategy.

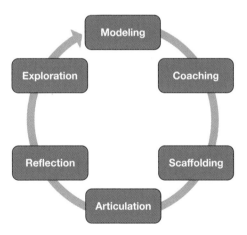

You may already be familiar at least with parts of the cognitive apprenticeship approach. The commonly used strategy of "I do, we do, you do" is a simplified version of cognitive apprenticeship. Worked examples are an excellent strategy where you can record yourself or provide a live demonstration of you as an expert working out an example (modeling). For instance, if you teach math or other STEM topics like science or engineering, you can record yourself working out an equation as a worked example and then follow this by providing learners with problems they should work out on their own. One strategy that an engineering instructor uses for an online accelerated academy for juniors and seniors is to record videos of himself using tablet technology where he writes out the equation and explains as he goes. He then provides these videos to students for them to work on in their own time. They then meet for synchronous sessions where the first half is devoted to students working through the problems they were provided, as he coaches them and provides them real-time feedback, and the second half to new problems of the same type that are harder, where they work on them together. This use of multiple examples, structured from a worked example to independent work to increased difficulty, scaffolds students toward their ability to work on these problems on their own and also helps them develop confidence (which, as noted in Chapter 6, can help with motivation and engagement).

This strategy can be applied in different content areas. Perhaps you want to present your students with case studies, and you begin by presenting a case and modeling how you would work through it yourself. Perhaps you want students to apply grammar lessons, so you present a paper that has examples of errors in the grammar rules you're covering, so you model for your students how you identify those errors and fix them. Perhaps you are teaching a science class and you want to model a procedure for your students. Recall in Chapter 6 the structure of presentation strategies and generative strategies from Morrison et al. (2013). Using modeling as a presentation strategy is particularly effective for any content where you are presenting principles, rules, procedures, interpersonal skills, or attitudinal content (see Table 6.1). Thus, you can use this strategy whether you are presenting on science content, language arts, history, government, social and emotional learning (SEL), or any other content area.

Special Considerations: STEM and Art Strategies

Many strategies are useful across a broad range of online learning environments, including STEM and art. We receive many questions from educators about these areas in particular, so here we present ideas that are particularly useful for these traditionally hands-on areas—ideas that teachers in other content areas will also find useful as well.

STEM Courses: Labs and Simulations

STEM courses often rely on activities like labs where students get hands-on practice applying their learning and practicing procedures. While some of these can be difficult or even dangerous for students to do at home in an uncontrolled environment, most labs can be integrated into online learning using one or more different strategies. Figure 7.7 summarizes the different types of strategies for remote labs in an online format that we have seen in action or in case studies that describe what schools are doing, with a lot of creative solutions for online learning. Below we list several different resources with example labs, materials, and other tools that teachers can use or adapt for their courses. While several of these are in higher education, they were developed with an eye toward sharing with middle school and high school educators.

Figure 7.7 Different strategies for remote labs.

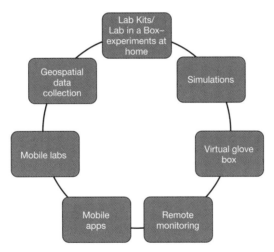

- https://www.cpp.edu/facultycenter/teaching-continuity/labs-studios-and
  -activity-courses/—features labs, studios, activity courses
- Multimedia Learning Objects repository, Center for the Advancement of
  Faculty Excellence: https://elearning.cpp.edu/learning-objects/—various
  visualizations, animations, simulations, and other learning objects
- Virtual Labs for Science Education, BCcampus, *Virtual Lab and
  Science Resource Directory* (A. Cheveldave, Ed.): https://opentextbc
  .ca/virtualscienceresources/

- Enhancing Digital Teaching and Learning in Irish Universities, *EDTL Approach: Considerations for Lab-Based Subjects*: https://edtl.blog/the -edtl-approach/edtl-approach-considerations-for-lab-based-subjects/ —infographic on process for developing remote labs; site also features case studies, resources, and exemplars (videos)
- "KPU Physics and Astronomy Online Labs Promo": https://www.youtube .com/watch?v=uG4Ho5gRpBQ&feature=youtu.be—brief video showing examples of physics and astronomy labs where students received a kit and completed experiments at home and recorded and shared those experiments back with the instructor
- Heriot Watt University Learning and Teaching Academy, "Practice-Based Activities: Labs, Studios, and Fieldwork": https://lta.hw.ac.uk/wp-content/ uploads/03_RBL_Practice-based-activities.pdf—a guide on online and blended labs, studios, and fieldwork; includes a planning guide, ideas, and links to resources, media articles, and academic articles
    - Covers labs in STEM subjects (home labs, lab recordings, lab simulations, remote labs, citizen science)
    - Includes ideas on studios and workshops in design subjects (social media like Pinterest, virtual studios)
    - Also discusses fieldwork—local field trips, broadcasts from the field, virtual field trips (capture real world data/pictures/cartography), and virtual museum tours
- Lecturemotely, "Lab Science Resources": https://www.lecturemotely.com/ copy-of-lab-courses—webinars specifically on lab courses

The following are additional resources with existing virtual labs and simulations, as well as tools for creating your own labs or simulations:

- Virtual Labs, by MERLOT, SkillsCommons, and Partners: https:// virtuallabs.merlot.org/
- MERLOT Materials: https://www.merlot.org/merlot/materials.htm? page=1&keywords=&sort.property=overallRating&category=
- PhET, University of Colorado, "Interactive Simulations for Science and Math": https://phet.colorado.edu/

- LabXchange science education site: https://www.labxchange.org/—created by Harvard
- Labster virtual labs: https://www.labster.com/—also offers the ability to create your own simulations

Art and Studio-Based Classes

Figure 7.8 **Strategies for art and studio-based classes.**

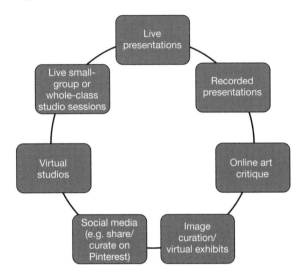

Some of the examples above include ideas that can be used for design content areas or studio-based classes. Here are some additional ideas teachers are using that are more specific to art and studio-based classes in an online format (see Figure 7.8). The following resources are different tools and sites being used to support online art and related classes:

- VoiceThread
- Social media tools
- Discussion board in your learning management system
- Live video chat (e.g., Zoom, Collaborate, WebEx)
- Video recording tool in the learning management system—either for assignment submission or for discussion submission

- Virtual exhibit tools
  - *Exhibbit*: https://exhibbit.com/home/
  - *ArtSteps*: https://www.artsteps.com/
  - *VAS* virtual art space: https://www.3dvas.com/
- Digital portfolios (e.g., ePortfolios in Canvas, D2L or other LMSs; or students can use tools like Google Slides, Seesaw, Flipgrid, and other general-use tools)

Bringing It Together:
Using Multiple Strategies in Online Teaching

In the example above from the engineering teacher, he made use of both asynchronous and synchronous modalities together, and specifically used each based on their own affordances. It also shows a host of strategies coming together: direct instruction, discussion, collaboration/group work, and worked examples. Let's explore some ways you can bring these ideas together and how you can carefully structure and sequence both asynchronous and synchronous strategies, as well as sequence instruction within a block of synchronous time.

Figure 7.9 Making good use of synchronous time with multiple strategies.

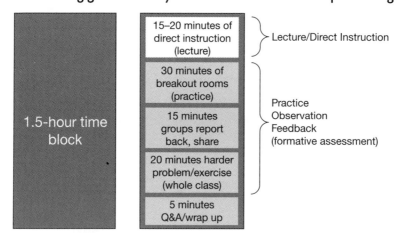

Let's start with a basic block of time for instructional planning—say, 1.5 hours of instructional time before a break. You can chunk this time into time for direct instruction and the time for practice, discussion, and feedback (formative assessment). Figure 7.9 provides an example of how synchronous time might be planned using several of the strategies we have discussed. Notice how there is time for direct instruction but the instructional time is not all "sit and get." Significant time is allocated for practice and discussions in small groups, discussion as a whole group, and then more practice with a more difficult problem. You can also use an approach that blends asynchronous and synchronous together, and you can even move the time for direct instruction around in our sequences. Figure 7.10 depicts a plan for asynchronous first that involves modeling with direct instruction and a worked example or two, followed by different options for a follow-on synchronous section. The middle box is the same instructional plan as in Figure 7.9. In the third box, the content is resequenced based on how it flows from the asynchronous plan. The first and third boxes together are representations of the example from the engineering teacher described above.

Figure 7.10 Sequencing asynchronous and synchronous strategies.

Asynchronous: Recorded lecture presenting information and working through an example or two; students must watch before class. Give students an activity, problem or example they have to work on and come to class ready to share and discuss.	

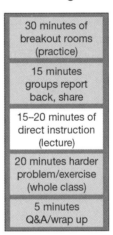

Planning for Instructional Strategies

First, decide whether you will use asynchronous, synchronous, or both modalities. In the boxes in Worksheet 7.1, detail what strategies you will employ in either modality.

Asynchronous (e.g., recorded video, discussion forum)	**Synchronous** (e.g., live video, live small-group, or whole-class work)

Worksheet 7.1

Once you have decided what you will deliver in an asynchronous format, it's time to carefully plan your synchronous time. Worksheet 7.2 provides empty boxes for you to fill in for when you will do direct instruction and for how long, and any other activities, such as small groups, whole-class activities or discussions, time for wrap-up and Q&A, and so on. If you find this format is limiting, you can create your own structured schedule using Word or any other planning tool you find useful.

	Detail your lesson block. Write in the blocks when you will do direct instruction, small-group activities, whole-class activities, discussions, a quiz for understanding, etc.

Worksheet 7.2

Summary

As you consider the different ways to implement these common instructional and assessment strategies, it would be easy—even familiar—to select a series of options that are limiting in their focus. For example, it would be easy to select a synchronous option for how we deliver our lectures, how we do discussions, and how we do formative assessment. Similarly, it would be easy for us to choose a teacher-led option for how we present content, a teacher-led option for how we have students interact with each other, and a teacher-led option for how we assess students. The main reason we have invested so much time in the previous chapters looking at different theoretical concepts is to encourage you to consider varying how you deliver this lesson or undertake that assessment. For example, as you are planning out your online learning, if you decide that a particular topic is better suited as a synchronous lesson in a virtual classroom environment, it may be useful to consider an asynchronous way that includes less teacher involvement as you engage the students in a discussion or how you assess the students.

Similarly, instead of using a teacher-led way to deliver content (such as a lecture during a synchronous class or through an asynchronous video), consider having the students interact directly with the content by creating text- and image-based instruction for a particular topic. This might be particularly useful in an instance where you have a topic that is likely to encourage a robust discussion among students during a live synchronous class, which you can follow up on in an asynchronous discussion forum in the learning management system. This allows students to interact with the teacher and with their peers in multiple interfaces that they are familiar with in their online learning environment.

Chapter 8

Presenting Digital Content to Facilitate Learning

After thoughtful planning and preparation around effective strategies for online teaching, teachers at Applewood started to turn their attention to pulling their instructional materials together. This led them to ask questions about the creation and use of digital content. They wanted to create their own content, like videos or PowerPoint talks or activities, and they also wanted to use content they were finding online. Was there any guidance from research on what features or qualities they should design into their online materials or use to evaluate existing digital materials? Was it good enough to use anything online, or where there some things that made some videos or other digital content more effective for learning? How could they present their material online in a way that helped learners understand and apply their learning? Additionally, how could they ensure they have access to the tools they need to create their multimedia content as well as access to existing online resources? That would have to be coordinated with school and district support staff and leaders.

To this point, most of our emphasis has been on strategies for interaction and community building, in large part because these strategies help address most of the concerns with online learning. When online learning is treated as a content dump—as if all you need to do is post content or deliver it to learners, and they'll learn on their own by watching and reading—both satisfaction and learning start to drop. While it is important to make sure that online learning is not merely a content dump, this of course does not mean that content is not important, just that content is not equal to education. Even well-designed content requires strategies that engage learners with the content, with one another, and with the instructor in meaningful ways to support learning, as earlier chapters have explored.

Additional Resources

This chapter is not comprehensive but covers some main ideas from several resources. If you are interested in learning more, here are the key resources we are drawing from:

Clark, R., & Mayer, R. (2016). *e-Learning and the science of instruction: Proven guidelines for consumers and designers of multimedia learning* (4th ed.). Wiley.

Lohr, L. (2007). *Creating graphics for learning and performance: Lessons in visual literacy* (2nd ed.). Pearson College.

Mayer, R. (2020). *Multimedia learning* (3rd ed.). Cambridge University Press.

Williams, R. (2014). *The non-designer's design book (4th ed.).* Peachpit Press.

How content is organized and presented can either inhibit or support learning. Presentation strategies are an important component in the online class. This chapter covers two overall strategies for content presentation: instructional strategies for presenting content, and strategies for designing digital material that facilitates learning instead of interfering with comprehension and retention. For content presentation strategies, we focus on how the content is introduced to learners depending on the nature of the content. For digital material design strategies, we cover some basic multimedia design principles that facilitate learners' ability to remember, retain, apply, organize, and integrate content cognitively. In Appendix C, we have included some additional resources on accessibility of digital materials and online learning and resources on other additional considerations, such as privacy and safety in online learning. These principles can inform both development of your own materials and evaluation and selection of existing materials. As with other strategies we share in this book, these principles can also be applied in your classroom practices as well.

Content Presentation Strategies

Chapter 7 focused on strategies that facilitate application and get learners to deeply engage with the content so they can apply and transfer their learning. This chapter focuses on content presentation. You may recall from Chapter 6 (see Table 6.1) Morrison et al.'s (2013) distinction between presentation strategies and generative strategies for helping learners recall or apply content, depending on the nature of the content they are learning. These are strategies you can employ for content in any modality. Table 8.1 summarizes some strategies for content presentation, depending on the type of content you are covering, drawing from Morrison et al. (2013).

Table 8.1 Instructional Strategies for Presenting Content

Content	Strategies
Facts	• Rehearsal-practice (e.g., practice repeating, writing, spelling, etc.). • Provide a mnemonic to aid memory/recall. • Elaboration—ask learners to explain a fact or elaborate on a topic.
Concepts	• Provide the concept name and a definition. • Give an example. • Give a range of additional examples to refine understanding, and ask students to explain differences and similarities in the examples. • Can also use the same strategies as for facts. Support *integration* of new knowledge with prior knowledge: • Ask learners to find or generate additional examples. • Have learners compare and contrast examples and non-examples to support *organization* of knowledge (schema development). • Ask learners to identify characteristics. • Create categories that allow learners to compare. • Create a concept map.
Principles or Rules	• Provide an example. • Provide a demonstration of the principle or rule as applied/in action. • Can use the same strategies as for facts. • Can use the strategies for *integration* and *organization* as for concepts.

Procedure	• Demonstration/provide examples (e.g., recorded video, pictures, live video). • Ask for examples. • Ask learners to list the steps or describe the process.
Interpersonal	• Model or demonstrate (role playing in a live session, recorded video example, etc.). • Ask students to identify key features or point these out (narrate the role playing or the recording). • Discuss examples or cases.
Attitude	• Model or demonstrate (role playing in a live session, recorded video example, etc.). • Reflection activities. • Discuss examples or cases.

Materials Design Principles for Cognitive Organization and Integration

Although instructional strategies are important for helping learners organize and integrate new learning, some principles for the design of digital instructional materials can also support learners in organizing and integrating new knowledge. These principles can be applied to videos you create for your class, PowerPoint slides you design and then lecture on, and handouts you provide for class, as well. These are also really good principles for evaluating existing digital content and resources you may come across. For example, many online videos or resources from publishers may have good content but can often lack design features that facilitate memory and comprehension, or may even have design features that interfere with learners' ability to remember and understand. In her book, Lohr (2007) explores three ideas in particular that anyone can use for to design instructional materials that better facilitate cognitive organization and integration of new information: hierarchy, gestalt, and figure/ground.

Hierarchy
Hierarchy helps communicate "relative importance between elements" (Lohr, 2007, p. 203). A good example of hierarchy is a topical outline or the outline of a chapter.

Using headers as organizers immediately helps readers develop an understanding of how the content should be organized—this facilitates schema development in a learner's mind. Different levels of headers communicate top level or main ideas, subordinate ideas or organization, and coordinate levels. By using different sizes and even different colors, boldface, or italics, you can create distinctions among these levels. Typically, though, any ideas within a single main idea should be treated similarly, because shifting colors, bolding subordinate but not main ideas, and other conflicts with your hierarchy create confusion—those subtle design changes communicate subtle information to a reader or learner. Color changes signify a shift to a new idea, and bold attracts attention as a main idea. Using sizing, coloring, and bolding strategically can help highlight main ideas, indicate relationships between similar or separate ideas, and suggest how to organize the information mentally. If you are presenting a procedure or a process, using numbering and arrows or lines for flow can also facilitate cognitive organization of the information that facilitates better memory. Figure 8.1 provides two examples of hierarchy for design, with some additional design principles applied, including "chunking," repetition, and proximity (Lohr, 2007; Williams, 2014). For color handouts or other materials, use color to highlight the main idea and subordinate ideas. Notice how Figure 8.1 also uses sizing and spacing to separate the explanative header from the example.

Figure 8.1 Examples of hierarchy created using sizing, bolding, italics, chunking, and space.

Example of using size, bolding, italics, and spacing to indicate organization:

Digital Content That Facilitates Learning

Content Presentation Strategies
Presenting Facts and Concepts
Presenting Principles and Rules
Presenting Procedures
Presenting Interpersonal and Attitudes

Principles for Cognitive Organization and Integration
Hierarchy
Gestalt
Figure-ground

Principles for Recognition, Retention, and Transfer
Multimedia Principle—words and audio
Redundancy Principle
Spatial Contiguity Principle
Temporal Contiguity Principle

Example of using size, numbering, italics, and spacing to indicate organization:

The Scientific Process

(1) *Define a Question to Investigate*
Ask why something is the way it is. Formulate a question.

(2) *Make Predictions*
Develop a hypothesis: what do you think will happen and why?

(3) *Gather Data*
How will you gather data? Observations, perform an experiment, run a model, or some mix? Document your procedures so others can validate your findings.

(4) *Analyze the Data*
Once you have your data, run analyses that help you see the patterns in the data or otherwise answer your questions. Visualizations or tables are also often helpful in reporting analysis.

(5) *Draw Conclusions*
Did your prediction(s) come true? If so, explain what this means. If not, provide possible explanations for why.

Gestalt

Gestalt as a design principle comes from gestalt psychology which focuses on perception. For the design of learning materials, we are concerned with the perceptions that learners develop based on how those materials are designed. They may perceive ideas as related or the same, or as distinct or disconnected, depending on how the different ideas and parts are presented.

Consider Figure 8.1. The numbers in circles help create the perception that those items are related to one another but different from the left side of the figure. On the left side, extra spacing between the three sections communicates that these three are separate, and similar spacing between the subheaders and their tertiary items indicates they are grouped together. These subtle design decisions communicate organization and help create learner perceptions of what is related, what is unrelated, and how different parts relate.

Gestalt can be a really important design tool in learning content because it can help communicate to learners where they are in the material. It can also help learners understand how the parts relate to the whole, allowing them to understand both the details of the part and its connection to the larger whole or idea. Consider, for example, if you are sitting through a talk or a recorded lecture where the speaker uses several slides, but it is hard for you to tell whether they are in the middle of a talk or nearing the end. Often, slides also use the same layout over and over, meaning the learner is unable to distinguish meaningful differences or see how the part connects to the whole.

Figure 8.2 provides two different examples of slides. In the first example, the speaker simply presents information on slides with the same layout without applying gestalt or hierarchy principles. In the second example, the speaker incorporates a visual indicator along the bottom that helps the listener understand both where they are in relation to the other parts and where they are overall in the presentation (and also applies hierarchy).

Figure 8.2 Examples of gestalt and nongestalt design. The slide set on the left has no indication of where the learner is in the content or how each slide relates to the whole (note that hierarchy is absent). The slide set on the right uses gestalt to orient learners: a menu at the bottom indicates where learners are in the content, and a header at the top relates to the rest of the content (with hierarchy applied).

These design elements are relatively simple features to add to most digital materials. It may take a little more time to add the features and adjust sizing, coloring, and so forth, depending on the tool you are using, but the difference in a learner's ability to organize and develop a robust schema of the content based on these design principles is significant. In the example on the right in Figure 8.2, any slides in the same section can retain the same menu variation to indicate where learners are in the content. Additionally, if this is developed in something like PowerPoint, the boxes along the bottom can even be linked to the first slide for that section so learners could interact with the slides to click back to a section and revisit it, if you wanted to provide them more ability to revisit topics easily. Menus in particular, or "breadcrumbs" (see Figure 8.3), provide learners cues that help them understand how the content is organized and where they are in the content, which also helps them better understand how it is related. *Breadcrumbs* refers to features that allow a user to retrace their steps back through the levels in a website or digital material. Sometimes, visual organizers also help learners understand how the content is related— you may recall from Chapter 5 the Community of Inquiry (CoI) model (Figure 5.1) and the student engagement model (Figure 5.5). Those figures could also be used as visual indicators to help chunk and organize digital content; for example, the section you are discussing can be highlighted in color, with the other sections grayed out, or you can create an icon that is used in a lower corner of slides to indicate what section you are discussing.

Figure 8.3 Example of a breadcrumb that can appear toward the top or bottom of a page or screen in a website or digital material.

Situated Cognition → Cognitive Apprenticeship Model → Modeling

Figure/ground

For the purposes of designing instructional materials, Lohr (2007, p. 175) defines *figure/ground* as "the perception principle that describes the mind's tendency to seek figure and ground distinctions; as a visual designer the figure is typically the information you want to stand out, and the ground is the information you want to recede or support the figure." One challenge presented to learners by digital materials is that they can't figure out what to pay attention to—everything has been foregrounded and nothing has been backgrounded. This can happen when there is too much information on the page or screen, there is a conflicting background that makes it hard to read or decipher the main content, or the colors between the background and foreground do not contrast enough. Figure/ground is a particularly helpful tool for breaking down complex visuals or representations. For example, consider the Academic Communities of Engagement (ACE) model presented in Chapter 5—Figure 5.4 has a lot of information in one visual. To break this down, in each section discussion a different part of the model, we provided separate instances of the same visual with a different part highlighted (see Figures 5.6, 5.12, and 5.13). This strategy helps readers know that the information being covered relates specifically to that section of the model.

Figure 8.4 provides an example of how a visual can be used to communicate a complex idea and the relationship between different parts, and then how figure/ground can be used in subsequent versions to focus attention on a particular part and still include the rest of the information grayed out as background to help learners retain a sense of how the part relates to the whole. Even in gray scale, we can use darker shading to bring focus on a part to the foreground and lighter gray to send other information to the background. This can be accomplished similarly in color with lighter versions of the same color.

Figure 8.4 Example of using figure/ground and gestalt together to communicate focus and relationship to the whole.

Figures 8.5 and 8.6 provide examples of how figure/ground, gestalt, and hierarchy can all be used together, as applied to a handout that can be shared as a document or PDF (Figure 8.5) and to PowerPoint slides (Figure 8.6). These same concepts can similarly be applied to other digital creations, such as videos, Prezi presentations, Google Slides, or other content presentation tools.

Figure 8.5 All three design principles—figure/ground, gestalt, and hierarchy—applied to a handout.

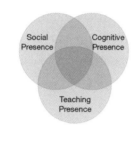

The Community of Inquiry (CoI) Model

This is a great model for designing a community of learning in your online classes. There are three different types of presence in the CoI model: Social Presence, Cognitive Presence, and Teaching Presence.

Social Presence

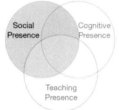

Social presence relates to opportunities for students to interact with each other. Social supports and access to informal conversations are important for learners. You can facilitate this with discussions, social spaces for students, a cybercafe, and other opportunities for students to interact with each other.

Cognitive Presence

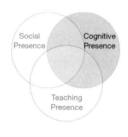

Cognitive presence refers to supports in your online class that clearly support student learning. Strategies for cognitive presence are those that support students engaging with content. This includes intentional design decisions and guidance for students where they apply content, demonstrate their understanding, and do something based on what they are reading, watching, or observing.

Teaching Presence

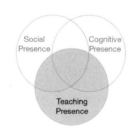

Teaching presence relates to learners' sense that you as an educator are present and helping to guide their learning. That sense is created through clear objectives and expectations as well as through interactions between you and learners. This includes engaging with them on discussion boards and providing them with feedback on their work.

Figure 8.6 All three design principles—figure/ground, gestalt, and hierarchy—applied to content presentation tools like slides or videos.

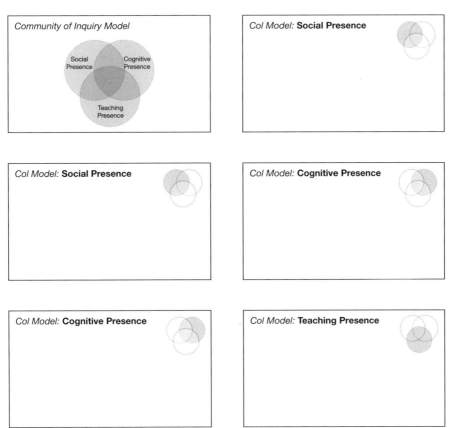

Lohr (2007) offers many other principles and tips, but these three—hierarchy, gestalt, and figure/ground—are a good place to start both for evaluating existing materials to see if they support memory and understanding and for designing or revising your own learning materials that you have developed for your students. *The Non-designer's Design Book* (Williams, 2014) covers additional principles you can explore, such as contrast, alignment, repetition, and proximity. These design principles in particular support hierarchy, gestalt, and figure/ground, so they're good companion ideas if you want to expand your tool set for visual design principles that facilitate learning.

Multimedia Learning Principles

While the word *multimedia* in this section title may seem to connote the use of technology, Mayer (2008, 2020) offered a different definition of multimedia that is based on what information humans process. He suggested that *multi* means "multiple means of information," such as visual information, auditory information, tactile information, and so on. This is very different from learning styles, a theory of learning that is not supported by research. Theories of learning styles suggest that some learners are visual learners, some are auditory learners, and so forth. In contrast, Mayer's research demonstrated that as humans we take in all kinds of information through our senses: we take in visual information through our eyes, auditory information through our ears, tactile information through our sense of touch, and so on. These are very different types of information, and although a learner's brain processes all of these types of information, it processes these different types quite differently. This has implications for how we design learning materials. Mayer focused specifically on visual and auditory information because these are by far the most common types of information transmitted in education.

When Mayer tested his theory of how humans process information, he repeatedly found significant learning gains for learning materials that were designed according to two key parts of his theory. The underlying theory, *information processing theory*, is based on theories of how memory works—how we move new information from short-term memory into long-term memory. He also drew on *cognitive load theory*, which explores how much humans can attend to at one time and how much information we can process (spoiler alert: it isn't much—the old 7 ± 2 rule turns out to be 4 ± 1; see Cowan, 2010). Based on studies supporting these theories of memory and information processing, Mayer posited that learners can process only so much information at a time. He suggested that many instructional materials present too much information to learners at once, thus overloading their capacity to process the information. He also suggested that how information is often presented in instructional materials—especially when text explaining a visual is not connected to the visual it explains—creates additional cognitive work for learners as they try to map content in one place to content in another place and figure out how they relate. In short, most instructional materials create a sort of cognitive traffic jam in the brain, making it hard for the brain to sort and organize or even to know what to pay attention to.

As he tested and validated his hypotheses, Mayer developed several principles that have been replicated by others in research as well—a very good indicator that these are reliable principles for the design of multimedia materials. Over time, Mayer has developed 12 separate principles. We do not cover them all here but instead focus on five: the multimedia principle, the modality principle, the redundancy principle, and the spatial and temporal contiguity principles. We also throw in a dash of a the coherence principle. This is a widely used set of principles for designing learning materials, so to read further you can readily find online resources that include excellent additional visual and video explanations of these principles (e.g., Water Bear Learning's website: https://waterbearlearning.com/). Mayer's (2020) book also details the research supporting these principles; and Clark & Mayer (2016) elaborate on these principles and others in much more detail. For now, let's explore a starter set of solid multimedia design principles to have in your digital content design toolbox.

The Multimedia Principle

The first principle that Mayer developed is the *multimedia principle*, which is simply that humans learn best from words and pictures together than from just words alone. Applied to content presentation, this means that a PowerPoint slide that is just a bulleted list of words is much less effective and harder to remember than a visual with some on-screen words. In Figure 8.7, the slide on the left is too text heavy; instead, applying the multimedia principle, we might generate something like the slide on the right.

Figure 8.7 Applying the multimedia principle to content presentation.

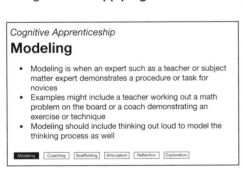

One thing you may quickly notice in the differences between the two presentations is that the text from the first slide has been moved into the Notes section of the second slide and turned into narration. If you have difficulty applying this principle, a good place to start would be to develop your slide as you might with the bullet points, and then cut and paste those bullet points into the Notes section and add in a visual that demonstrates or models what you are discussing (*not* clip art but specific or actual images that are instructional rather than visual filler). The redesigned slide on the right still has some text on, but it is minimal. The section below on spatial and temporal contiguity principles discusses how to use animations to sequence content so that what you are saying or explaining is timed to align with what appears visually for learners.

The Modality Principle

This leads us to the Modality Principle. The *modality principle* states that humans learn better from visuals plus spoken words than from visuals plus print words. Print words are particularly difficult for humans to process (setting aside reading difficulties) because they are encountered first as visual information and then our brains reprocess them using a *phonological loop*, encoding visual words as sounds. Thus, to interpret visuals (letters, characters) into the sounds they represent, the brain has to do extra work. In most educational instances, we can lower that cognitive load and effort for our learners by moving words into the auditory channel and keeping pictures in the visual channel. In Figure 8.7, this is precisely what we have done in the redesign, applying both the multimedia principle and the modality principle at the same time.

The modality principle does not mean that all words should be spoken. It's often important to present to learners such words as key terms, new names, and new concepts or terms. This helps them learn to spell them and supports their understanding. However, we often present too many words—or extraneous information. Mayer called this the *coherence principle*: Humans learn best when extraneous or distracting information is removed. A good balance to strike is to include only terms, labels, or new names as visual words and otherwise offload elaborations and explanations to auditory words. In an online setting, auditory words can include both what you say during a live online session and what you say during a recording as you narrate a video or explain something to students. Figure 8.8 is a good example of common instructional situations where you may want to have some on-screen text for main ideas or terms but offload the detailed explanation to auditory words (narration).

Figure 8.8 Example of the modality principle, with some key words presented visually.

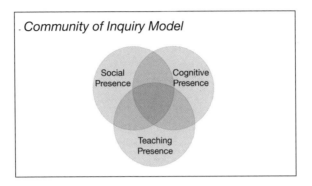

Narration:
Social presence relates to opportunities for students to interact with each other. Social supports and access to informal conversations are important for learners. You can facilitate this with discussions, social spaces for students, a cybercafe, and other opportunities for students to interact with each other.
Cognitive presence refers to supports in your online class that clearly support student learning. Strategies for cognitive presence are those that support students engaging with content. This includes intentional design decisions and guidance for students where they apply content, demonstrate their understanding, and do something based on what they are reading, watching, or observing.
Teaching presence relates to learners' sense that you as an educator are present and helping to guide their learning. That sense is created through clear objectives and expectations as well as through interactions between you and learners. This includes engaging with them on discussion boards and providing them with feedback on their work.

The Redundancy Principle

Mayer's *redundancy principle* states humans learn better with narration and visuals than with narration, visuals, and text. In other words, adding a bunch of words creates a real cognitive traffic jam: there is too much for the learner to pay attention to, and they are trying to figure out how the words they are hearing relate to what they're seeing visually. Learners end up spending their cognitive resources trying to figure out what parts of what they're looking at relate to the words they're hearing. As a result, they don't process the information in either channel well and can't remember or connect what they heard or saw with what they saw or heard. Figure 8.9 is an example of a serious redundancy problem that was solved by Figure 8.8. If you are feeling overwhelmed just looking at Figure 8.9, that is exactly the feeling of a learner who is trying to process content presentation where there is redundancy between the visual and auditory channels.

Figure 8.9 Redundant information causes difficulty and cognitive overload for learners.

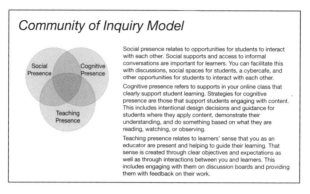

Narration:
Social presence relates to opportunities for students to interact with each other. Social supports and access to informal conversations are important for learners. You can facilitate this with discussions, social spaces for students, a cybercafe, and other opportunities for students to interact with each other.
Cognitive presence refers to supports in your online class that clearly support student learning. Strategies for cognitive presence are those that support students engaging with content. This includes intentional design decisions and guidance for students where they apply content, demonstrate their understanding, and do something based on what they are reading, watching, or observing.
Teaching presence relates to learners' sense that you as an educator are present and helping to guide their learning. That sense is created through clear objectives and expectations as well as through interactions between you and learners. This includes engaging with them on discussion boards and providing them with feedback on their work.

The Spatial and Temporal Contiguity Principles

Thus, far, we have learned that it is best to not put a lot of text in the visual channel—reserve that channel for visuals and offload words to the auditory channel as much as possible. However, we can still overwhelm learners if we present them with too much information visually at one time. This is why, in addition to these other principles, the spatial and temporal contiguity principles are so important.

The *spatial contiguity principle* is quite similar to Williams's (2014) principle of proximity covered in her book mentioned at the beginning of the chapter. The spatial contiguity principle states that text and visuals that relate to each other should be close to each other. If there is too much distance between different parts or between a visual and its label, then learners will not perceive them as being related to each other. You want to place relevant words by the visuals they relate to. In slides this is not often a challenge, but in online and printed or PDF materials it can become a real challenge because the text describing a visual may be on another page. As best as possible, try to keep text and visuals next to each other when they are related. You can use additional white space to separate ideas, as reflected in several examples throughout this chapter.

The temporal contiguity principle is perhaps the more interesting and novel principle that can add a layer of sophistication to your digital materials. This principle states that humans learn best when corresponding words and visuals are presented together at the same time rather than apart. Mayer typically uses this principle to explain animations or simulations, stating that the narration should play along with the animation or simulation. Stephanie has adapted this along with the idea of chunking to focus on how instructors can break down complex ideas and visuals using animation features in something like PowerPoint, exemplified in Figure 8.10. When you have a complex visual with a lot of different parts, presenting it all at once to learners may be overwhelming, because they don't know where to focus first. You can chunk it down into parts and fade in one part at a time as you explain just that part. Figure 8.10 compares a slide with a complex visual presented all at once to a series of animations in a slide (or a series of slides) that chunks the visual down to create temporal contiguity.

Figure 8.10 A slide without versus with temporal contiguity (using animations).

Without Temporal Contiguity

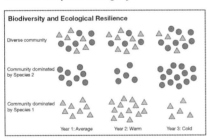

In a community dominated by one species, you may see any average population in one year, and then even more of that species in a warmer year, but then in a cold year that species struggles so there are fewer of them.
For a community dominated by another species, again you might see an average population in one year, but then in a warmer year perhaps that species struggles. In a colder year, it may over-populate.
But in a diverse community, we see some resilience in it in different conditions over time. Even if one species has more in some years or less in other years, the population overall remains stable over time.

With Temporal Contiguity

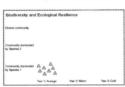

In a community dominated by one species, you may see any average population in one year

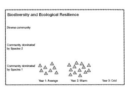

and then even more of a that species in a warmer year,

but then in a cold year that species struggles so there are fewer of them.

For a community dominated by another species, again you might see an average population in one year,

---

Pro Tip: STEM Content

In content areas like STEM disciplines where you may be explaining ideas or working out equations or diagrams that you annotate, you may want to consider getting a tablet tool that allows you to write on a white board and talk at the same time, or record yourself talking as you write. This is akin to writing on the chalkboard in a classroom, which works well in part because it forces temporal contiguity: if you are drawing out an equation, diagram, or other visual, you can draw only so much at a time, and ideally you are explaining as you draw. This chunks the information together and ensures corresponding words and visuals are presented at the same time. For an online learning setting, recording what you write or draw while you narrate off-camera centers the visual information in the visual channel and offloads most of the words to the auditory channel. This is also a great way to provide your students worked examples, another of Mayer's principles (see Chapter 7).

Summary

Content development and selection are necessary parts of any instructional planning. However, simply providing content to learners does not mean they will be able to learn from it. The way that content is presented to learners can enhance or detract from their ability to make sense of the material and remember it long term, or to develop accurate mental models of the content. This chapter has covered strategies and design principles for content presentation, emphasizing design principles that apply to digital materials in particular.

Three design principles—hierarchy, gestalt, and figure/ground—are a good starting place for designing, revising, or selecting more effective instructional materials (Lohr, 2007). Hierarchy helps a learner understand the structure and organization between main ideas and sub-ideas. Strategies that can help create hierarchy include using headers and different sizing or emphasis (e.g., boldface or italics) to clearly chunk information and indicate organization. Gestalt relates to perceptions, and for learning materials this includes what they perceive about how different ideas are related or distinct. Relatedness and disconnection can be conveyed through elements being close together or far apart, for example. Visuals can also help learners better understand the whole and how parts relate to the whole. Figure/ground helps a learner know what information to attend to and what information to ignore. Foregrounding key information and backgrounding (or removing) extraneous information helps a learner know what to focus on. Using all three of these together can help you develop or select learning materials that better support learners' cognitive processes.

Multimedia learning principles that have been extensively tested provide further guidance for designing and selecting effective learning materials. Mayer (2008, 2020) redefined multimedia to focus not on the technology being used but on the type of information being processed. Specifically, he focused on how learners process visual information and auditory information both separately and together. Based on multiple studies, he identified several principles; we focused on a subset of these as a starting point for designing more effective multimedia content: the multimedia principle, the modality principle, the redundancy principle, and the spatial and temporal contiguity principles. These principles suggest that it is better to present visual information in the visual channel and offload as much text as possible to the auditory channel (spoken or recorded narration). These principles also suggest that we can lower learners' cognitive load and increase their ability to remember information if we do not present competing information in both channels and if we segment information using spatial and temporal spacing so that learners know exactly what words go with what visuals.

Chapter 9

Developing Formative and Summative Assessments

The teachers at Applewood had a *lot* of questions about assessing learning online. Some questions related to things they had heard or read about proctored exams and surveillance. Other questions were specific to whether and how different types of learning outcomes could even be assessed online. And was it even possible to shift assessment online from assessment *of* learning to assessment *for* learning? How could assessment practices reflect more of a learning community and actively support student learning rather than feeling like teachers distrusted their students? What sort of learning culture was being created by their assessment decisions? And even more practically, just what could even be assessed online, and what tools could be used to support more than tests and quizzes?

Assessment strategies are perhaps some of the most important decisions you make. Online assessment strategies are often critiqued as part of the online learning experience, and those critiques reflect decisions that can be made differently. Overreliance on practices like proctoring, for example, creates a certain class culture that conveys a sense of distrust. Moore and Tillberg-Webb (2023) also discussed some ethical and legal issues related to proctoring and assessment methods that rely on tools that scan students' rooms. We have discussed a number of ideas throughout this book related to assessment, including issues with tools like these. Here, we want to reframe the discussion on assessing learning online into assessment as a strategy that supports student learning, not assessment as a behavior management strategy.

We can approach assessment in different ways that are common across all modalities. The most common perspective focuses on the assessment *of* learning, a process for determining how effective the instructional strategies were in allowing the student to master the content (*summative assessment*). However, another perspective is to use *formative assessment* as a strategy to support learning—assessment *for* learning (Chappuis & Stiggins, 2016; Stiggins & Conklin, 1992). This chapter covers both approaches to assessment—in reality we often use both assessment strategies together. Stephanie has written more in *SEL at a Distance* (Moore, 2021b) on how assessment creates class culture, strategies for addressing concerns about cheating, and self-assessment online and provides more details on formative assessment and how to better balance formative and summative assessment. We draw on the same frameworks and concepts here to provide aligned support.

Developing Your Assessment Strategy

Means et al. (2014) identified five different roles that assessment strategies and tools serve online:

1. Determine if a student is ready for new content.
2. Tell the system how to support the student (e.g., adaptive learning technology or instruction).
3. Provide the student or teacher with information about the student's learning state.
4. Determine and input a grade.
5. Identify students at risk of failure.

These are not mutually exclusive options. You could use assessment for all, a subset, or just one of these roles. As you plan for assessment—both instructionally and at the system level—it is important to understand the role of online assessments and how they will be used, so you can make intentional decisions around both the strategies and the technologies that enable those strategies. This also can help you better evaluate technologies during vendor sales pitches. Consider the following questions to help you start selecting assessment strategies and tools:

Checklist: Deciding the Role(s) Assessment May Play

☐ Do you want assessments to be automatically graded?

☐ Do you want to be able to provide students written, verbal, or video feedback?

☐ Will students have an opportunity to act on any feedback they receive?

☐ Do you want them to share their work with peers and provide feedback to one another or collaborate on a project or product that will be assessed?

☐ Will students have the ability to view their assessment results?

☐ Will students receive supports based on their assessment results?

The answers to these questions can vary widely, and those different questions suggest very different assessment approaches. For example, if students will *not* receive supports, have the ability to review results, or have an opportunity to act on feedback, then that is assessment *of* learning. Assessment *for* learning means you intend to use assessment methods and data to support the students in their learning process, not simply to provide a result at the end of it.

Before you proceed, take some time to think through these various roles and your answers to the questions in the checklist. The five roles listed earlier can be thought of as design options. Circle the assessment strategies you wish to employ, make notes on who will use assessment data for that purpose, and then identify what tools you will need to support that assessment strategy. To help you with this decision process, Table 9.1 lists the roles for online assessment, with space for you to fill in your answers, and Table 9.2 lists the questions above for selecting assessment strategies and tools, with space for answers.

Table 9.1 Roles for Assessments in Online Learning

Role of assessment	Who will use the data	Possible tools
1. Determine if a student is ready for new content.		
2. Tell the system how to support the student (e.g., adaptive learning technology or instruction).		

3. Provide the student or teacher with information about the student's learning state.		
4. Determine and input a grade.		
5. Identify students at risk of failure.		

Table 9.2 Questions to Guide Assessment Strategy and Tool Selection

Do you want assessments to be automatically graded?	
Do you want to be able to provide students written, verbal, or video feedback?	
Will students have an opportunity to act on any feedback they receive?	
Do you want them to share their work with peers and provide feedback to one another or collaborate on a project or product that will be assessed?	
Will students have the ability to view their assessment results?	
Will students receive supports based on their assessment results?	

Chances are, you will want a suite of strategies and tools that support various types of assessment. For example, if you want assessments to be graded automatically, then you will need a system with assessment tools such as quiz features that enable automatic grading. If you want to provide students feedback, then you'll want to evaluate tools based on your ability provide automated feedback or authentic written, audio, or verbal feedback. If the system should adapt to support learners based on how they perform on assessments, then you will probably want to look at adaptive learning systems—note, though, that this suggests you'll be implementing a self-paced learning design. If it should adapt to students within a class-paced environment, then you want to carefully evaluate tools for whether they assume self-paced or class-paced learning.

Generally, there is a significant push right now as well to consider how students have agency in their own learning processes. Online learning and educational technologies have ushered in significant increases in the collection and use of data to assess and evaluate students. While the technology is zooming ahead, policies and practices have not necessarily kept pace. As we discussed earlier in this book, these tools have significant issues related to bias, discrimination, accessibility, and data rights and privacy. Any assessment plan should include careful consideration of these issues. If you have completed the activities in earlier chapters, then you need to incorporate those decisions and ideas into your assessment planning process here. The impacts of technologies result from our design and implementation decisions, so if you want your assessment strategies to have more equitable and just impacts, that should be an explicit part of your evaluation and selection process.

A Framework for Assessment: Types of Learning Mapped to Tools and Methods

Once you have laid a foundation of major design decisions for assessment, then we can move on into specific assessment strategies. We have adapted the following assessment framework from Stiggins and Conklin (1992) and Chappuis and Stiggins (2016) to online learning, and we have overlaid Bloom's taxonomy for those who use it to organize their instructional and assessment planning.

Your assessment strategies should depend on the type of learning you are assessing. We use five categories as suggested by Stiggins and Conklin (1992) and Chappuis and Stiggins (2016): knowledge, reasoning, skills, products, and dispositions.

- **Knowledge:** Assesses mastery of discrete elements of knowledge, such as important history facts, spelling words, foreign language vocabulary, and parts of plans
- **Reasoning:** Assesses blocks of knowledge rather than pieces of detached information, such as causes of environmental disasters, the carbon cycle in the atmosphere, how one mathematical equation can be derived from another, or the concept of checks and balances in the government; helps identify whether a student has strong reasoning or problem-solving abilities

- **Skills:** Determines whether a student can skillfully complete a task or perform in a desired manner, such as mixing chemicals correctly, engaging in skilled debate, holding a conversation in a foreign language, or making a decision in a legal case based on constitutional law
- **Products:** Determines whether a student can create a quality product based on what they have learned. These might include a business presentation, a lab report, a health and fitness plan, a balanced checkbook register, a creative work of art, or even a news article or broadcast
- **Disposition:** Gathers information about students' dispositions and their ability to reason about their attitudes and beliefs, and allows you to probe more deeply; can take the form of interviews, student journals that you read and respond to, open questions during instruction, and oral exams

Figure 9.1 Assessment for different types of learning, adapted to the online context.

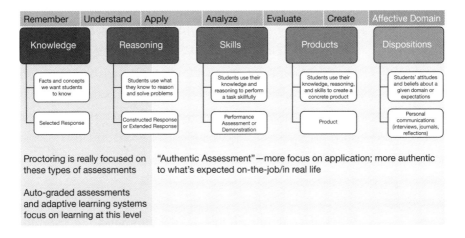

In Figure 9.1, you can see the definitions of each followed by examples of the type of assessment method. For online, we have also indicated how proctoring and autograded assessments really only apply to assessment of knowledge and possibly reasoning. That means there's a vast space of learning assessment that these tools cannot cover, even if you do decide to use them. Most of the rest of the types of learning require *authentic assessment* strategies: assessments that focus more on applying learning and better reflect on-the-job and real-life expectations. Figure 9.2 provides specific examples of how each of these types of learning can be assessed online.

Figure 9.2 Examples of online assessment for different types of learning.

Knowledge	Reasoning	Skills	Products	Dispositions
Facts and concepts we want students to know	Students use what they know to reason and solve problems	Students use their knowledge and reasoning to perform a task skillfully	Students use their knowledge, reasoning, and skills to create a concrete product	Students' attitudes and beliefs about a given domain or expectations
Selected Response	Constructed Response or Extended Response	Performance Assessment or Demonstration	Product	Personal communications (interviews, journals, reflections)
Examples for online: • Quiz or test tools (objective items) • Audio voice threads (e.g., language instruction) • Recitations (record something that has to be memorized)	**Examples for online:** • Quiz or test tools (open-ended items) • Sorting activities • Record solving a problem and submit that recording • Paper on a topic • Presentation on a topic (record and submit as assignment or share in a discussion forum) • Case studies requiring students to apply course content and derive a solution	**Examples for online:** • Students record themselves performing a skill (e.g., a lab, an exercise routine, a talk-aloud on their design process for a product) (assess using a rubric) • Students perform a skill during a live video session (e.g., labs) (assess using a rubric) • Simulation or role playing	**Examples for online:** • Students complete a project—individually or as a group—and submit (assess using a rubric) • Students construct a writing sample—individually or together—on a wiki or GoogleDoc (e.g., mimic a writer's style or revise an essay with issues that you load for them)	**Examples for online:** • Students maintain a reflection journal throughout class with prompts that focus on beliefs and attitudes • Personal communications—open questions during instruction, oral exams, one-on-one feedback loops

Rather than starting with the tools, starting first with considering what type of learning you wish to assess can help you align the tools you select with what you actually want to assess. The options in Figure 9.2 should start to give you a good idea of the different tools or features you may want to have available in your online learning ecosystem. In what follows we discuss a few specific examples of different strategies for assessment of learning as they align with online instructional strategies we've discussed in previous chapters. We cover ideas for both formative assessment (*for* learning) and summative assessment (*of* learning).

Discussions

In terms of the logistics of an online discussion, the affordances of the different tools and features that can be employed for synchronous and asynchronous discussions, as well as the advantages and disadvantages of each of the mediums, still apply. The main difference between how a discussion is used as an instructional tool, compared to how it is used as an assessment tool, is how the online teacher decides to assign grades to the student's participation.

You may recall from Chapter 6 the "Discussion Guidelines Focused on Behavior," which listed eight online behaviors as criteria for interactivity:

1. Post a well-focused response to the prompt provided.
2. Post frequently and regularly.

3. Frequently offer in-depth comments that further the discussion.
4. Comment widely on posts by many classmates.
5. Respond regularly in a specific, engaged manner to others' responses and their comments on your response.
6. Write concisely.
7. Frequently show clear sentence-to-sentence cohesion.
8. Use correct grammar and punctuation.

It would be easy enough for a teacher to turn these guidelines into an assessment rubric with the addition of some descriptive qualifiers (see Table 9.3).

Table 9.3 Example Rubric for Discussion Assessment

Score	Responding to teacher's prompts	Interacting with peers
4	Posting frequent and regular well-focused entries in response to the teacher's prompts	Widely commenting on posts by many classmates
3	Posting regularly in a way that engages the topic thoughtfully	Commenting on posts by classmates
2	Posting on only a few of the teacher's prompts	Occasionally commenting on posts by classmates
1	Rarely posting on the teacher's prompts	Rarely commenting on posts by classmates
0	Never posting on the teacher's prompts	Almost never commenting on posts by classmates

However, depending on what our goals are for assessment or the specific learning outcome we want to assess, some of these criteria may not be necessary. The criteria "Post well-focused response to the prompt provided" and "Post frequently and regularly" aim to measure the student's understanding of the content and participation patterns in the discussion. This observation is true for many of these statements. For example, the criterion "Frequently offer in-depth comments that further the discussion" aims to measure the student's master of and ability to use the content, whereas "Comment widely on posts by many classmates" aims to measure their commenting patterns. In the example rubric shown in Table 9.1, the criteria in the teacher prompt column begin with a focus on both content mastery (e.g., "well-focused entries" and "engages the topic thoughtfully") and student behavior (e.g., posting frequently, regularly) but then for Levels 2–0 focus solely on student behavior and fail to include any reference to content mastery.

Further, criteria like "Write concisely," "Frequently make clear sentence-to-sentence cohesion," and "Use correct grammar and punctuation" aim to measure the student's writing ability. If the class where this guide was used was an English language arts class, than measuring students' use of writing conventions would likely be consistent with the learning objectives. But if the discussion was a part of a science or social studies class, you would be using three out of eight criteria that may not be course outcomes. This illustrates why it is important to consider both your specific goals for an assessment and the alignment between the specific learning objective and what the assessment measures.

Quizzes

Hodges and Barbour (2021) referred to this category as tests, quizzes, and exams. For this type of assessment they envisioned "closed-book assessments, that are proctored (i.e., invigilated), and usually must be completed within a certain time-frame" (p. 89). However, this is quite a limited view of quizzes in online learning. In some subject areas the use of quizzes, particularly multiple-choice quizzes, is quite common (even the dominant form of assessment). As Fawns and Ross (2020, para. 1) indicated, while "there may be technological means that allow [schools] to proceed with 'business as usual' in the form of closed-book, invigilated, time-limited examinations . . . the moral and pedagogical justification for doing so needs much more scrutiny." While it is true that monitoring features are built into most online quiz tools and third-party proctoring services, the use of these functions raises legitimate concerns about student privacy and academic integrity. There are also concerns about the amount of work required of teachers to create online quizzes that take advantage of these features to address some of these academic integrity issues. In fact, many recommend that online quizzes be limited to low-stake assessments or student self-assessments (Sotola & Crede, 2021)—research has started to show that frequent use of this form of formative assessment can actually improve overall student academic performance.

Having said that, it is important for us to explore some of the options available, should teachers choose to use online quizzes for formative or summative purposes. One feature available in almost every learning management system and online testing tool, the ability to provide individual feedback to student responses, is one that online teachers rarely use. As illustrated in Figure 9.3, these tools allow the teacher to provide students with feedback specific to their correct and incorrect responses.

Figure 9.3 Most learning management systems allow teachers to write descriptive text associated with each correct and incorrect response.

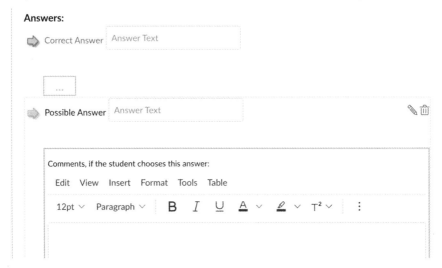

For example, consider a mathematical problem that a student needs to solve, where B was the correct response. Incorrect response for A might be chosen if the student forgot to change a negative sign to a positive sign, whereas incorrect response C might result from using an incorrect order of calculation. If this was a problem that the student had completed as homework and turned in, or if it was a problem on a paper-based test, the teacher would likely show where the student went wrong by hand, using a pen. However, in most online quizzes, when students select an incorrect response, they are told the correct response, but not usually why they may have chosen their incorrect response. Yet, one of the affordances of using quizzes in an online format is the ability to automate this type of feedback.

The online environment also provides a variety of features that would be difficult to accomplish in the traditional brick-and-mortar setting, for example, the ability to personalize the quiz that each student receives (see Figure 9.4). Again, one of the affordances of most online quiz tools is the fact that, with the simple click of a couple of options, the teacher have each student receive the questions on the quiz in a unique order (i.e., shuffle questions), and even the possible responses to specific questions (i.e., shuffle answers). Similarly, if you have created more questions than you wish to use on a particular quiz, the online quiz tool can randomly select a specific number of questions for each student. This means that, with a few simple clicks, you can create a quiz where a specific question might be Question 6 for one student, Question 23 for another student, and not even appear on the quiz of a third student; and for the two students that received the same question, the correct response could appear as Option B on one quiz and Option D on another. Accomplishing this in a face-to-face setting would require manually creating a different test for each student.

Figure 9.4 Quiz options available to teachers in a learning management system.

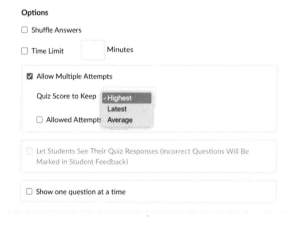

Online teachers who use quizzes in a summative fashion can still allow students to take a quiz multiple times, and have the option to limit the number of attempts (e.g., take the quiz twice, up to five times, or any number the teacher sets). Online teachers can also set the quiz so that a student's grade for that particular quiz is the highest score received from all attempts, the most recent attempt made, or an average of all attempts. Because there are often legitimate concerns about both academic integrity and student privacy when it comes to the use of online quizzes as a form of summative assessment, many teachers choose to use them in a formative way. You may recall from Chapter 6 that Figure 6.3, an example of using structure and consistency in presenting content, the final item in the course structure was "Test yourself," a multiple-choice quiz students could use for self-assessment (i.e., testing themselves). Further, as suggested above, quizzes are also useful for determining how much of the content or prerequisite material students know prior to a lesson. Thus, a teacher could use an online quiz or poll at the beginning of a synchronous class to determine which portions of the instruction to spend more or less time on. Similarly, an online teacher could use a quiz delivered asynchronously through the learning management system at the beginning of a unit for the same purposes. Doing this in an asynchronous fashion would actually allow the instructor the opportunity to personalize feedback to each student in terms of which portions of the content they should focus on. As a way to save time, to create these formative quizzes many online teachers use test banks or question banks often provided by course textbook publishers—some teachers have concerns about students' ability to gain access to these commercial test banks, so the use of this resource as a formative assessment removes that concern.

Written Assignments

Even though the inherent nature of online learning means that students can both consume and create content in a variety of mediums (e.g., audio or video), as Weller (2018, p. 40) noted, "text remains the dominant communication form in education." For example, the vast majority of online discussions are limited to the written word—for that matter, so are most quizzes. In much the same way you would in a classroom environment, students can continue to complete written assignments using traditional word-processing software or an online collaborative tool. For example, students can complete a short essay in an asynchronous fashion around a topic assigned by the teacher. Alternatively, the teacher could devote a portion of a synchronous lesson to have students write a response to a prompt or write a short reflection about what they've taken away from that particular class (also a useful formative strategy to assess student learning).

In her book *Making the Move to K–12 Online Teaching: Research-Based Strategies and Practices*, Kerry Rice (2012) describes a variety of writing assessments that can be used in a formative or summative fashion. Students can engage in reflective writing through a journal or diary. To provide a broader and more public audience for the students, they could blog instead of using a discussion forum, which is often limited to registered users of the learning management system. A teacher could have students use collaborative tools like Google Docs or an online wiki to coconstruct knowledge as a part of a group project. Teachers could even have students write annotations using different social bookmarking tools as a part of or one step in a larger project. As Hodges and Barbour (2021, p. 88) stated, "Written assignments should be familiar to almost anyone, as they have been utilized in education for as long as any of us can recall."

Presentations

If text remains the dominant communication in education—both face-to-face instruction and online learning—what opportunities does online learning have to provide alternatives? Asked another way, if the students are already learning in a technology-mediated environment, how can those tools be leveraged to allow students to create non-text-based artifacts that can be assessed? In a traditional classroom we would often think of the use of student-made posters on a sheet of Bristol board as an example of a student product that was not primarily text based that could be evaluated. At its simplest level, this could be accomplished by having students create a poster in a traditional sense and then scan it or have them take a digital image of it and upload it to a photo-sharing service inside or outside of the learning management system. A more high-tech alternative would be to have the students use an online tool like Canvas to create their poster.

Another common presentation strategy that classroom teachers regularly use is to have students both create the physical artifact of a "presentation" and perform the interactive action of delivering a presentation. The physical artifacts are often created using PowerPoint, Keynote, or some other productivity software, or an online presentation tool like Prezi. This could be a live presentation delivered in a synchronous session in the virtual classroom, or it could be a recorded presentation submitted as an asynchronous video. However, a number of other tools are also available that could extend the more traditional concept of a presentation. Numerous animation tools allow students to deliver their presentation in an asynchronous fashion without actually having to be an active participant in that presentation. Alternatively, the online teacher could use a synchronous session for students to showcase these student-created artifacts.

As most students have access to a video camera as a part of their mobile device or through the standard webcam in most laptop and desktop computers, students can record themselves giving a more traditional presentation, acting out a performative piece, or even undertaking a science lab. According to Hanke (2012), these student-created artifacts are representative of "generative learning." All of these examples could be shared with just the teacher or peers through the learning management system, or through a video-sharing site like YouTube or Vimeo to a much broader audience. Regardless of the format of the presentation or tool used, the goal for this form of generative learning is to have the students summarize, explain, synthesize, evaluate, or apply the content they were responsible for learning through the act of preparing and presenting whatever artifact have created (Fiorella & Mayer, 2016).

Finally, thus far this discussion has focused on different strategies for assessing student learning. However, this is also a good time to remind online teachers that the vast majority of feedback students receive for their assessments, both formative and summative, is in the form of text-based comments. Feedback can be a powerful strategy to encourage student learning. Like any other pedagogical strategy, the more engaging and personal online teachers can make their feedback, the more likely it will have a positive impact on both student motivation and student learning. Using a screen-capture or other recording tool, instructors can review student work in a verbal fashion so that the student can see what instructors are talking while they listen to feedback on different parts of their assignment. As a concrete example, instead of simply using tracked changes in a word-processing document to provide corrections and comments, online teachers could record themselves discussing what they are reading in the document and provide specific comments section by section, paragraph by paragraph, and even sentence by sentence. The use of a more personal form of feedback, like the audio feedback through a screen recorder or video-based feedback, should increase the online teacher's teaching presence and decrease students' sense of isolation and transactional distance.

Bringing It Together: Developing an Assessment Plan

You have probably already jotted down assessment ideas. This section will help you flesh out your assessment plan using types of assessment based on what exactly you want to assess. We provide quick descriptions and examples for each, and under each type (as appropriate) note what you will do, when, and what students will submit. The planning aid in Table 9.4 should help you select the right tools that align with what you want to assess. (If you would like to change the objective questions to map to Bloom's taxonomy, we provided an overlay of Bloom's objectives in Table 6.1, which you can map onto this taxonomy.)

Table 9.4 Planning Job Aid: Selecting Assessment Strategies

Assessment:		
Objective	**Definition**	**Examples for online**
Knowledge	*Facts and concepts we want students to know*	Quiz or test tools (objective items) Audio voice threads (e.g., language instruction) Recitations (record something that has to be memorized)
What are my knowledge objectives?		
What assessment method will I use?		
What tool(s) will I use?		
Reasoning	*Students use what they know to reason and solve problems*	Open-ended quizzes or tests Sorting activities Record solving a problem and submitting that recording Paper on a topic Presentation on a topic (record and submit an assignment or share in a discussion forum) Case studies requiring students to apply course knowledge
What are my reasoning objectives?		
What assessment method will I use?		
What tool(s) will I use?		
Skills	*Students use their knowledge and reasoning to perform a task skillfully*	Students record themselves performing a skill (e.g., a lab, an exercise routine, a talk-aloud on their design process for a product) (assess using a rubric) Students perform a skill during a live video session (e.g., labs) (assess using a rubric) Simulation or role-playing

What are my skills objectives?	
What assessment method will I use?	
What tool(s) will I use?	
Products — *Students use their knowledge, reasoning, and skills to create a concrete product*	Students complete a project (individually or as a group) and submit (assess using a rubric) Students construct a writing sample (individually or as a group) on a wiki or in Google Docs (e.g., mimic a writer's style or revise an example essay with problems that you provide for them)
What are my product objectives?	
What assessment method will I use?	
What tool(s) will I use?	
Dispositions — *Students' present attitudes and beliefs about a given domain or expectations*	Reflection journal maintained throughout class with prompts that focus on beliefs and attitudes Personal communications—open questions during instruction, oral exams, one-on-one feedback loops
What are my disposition objectives?	
What assessment method will I use?	
What tool(s) will I use?	

Summary

Your assessment strategies can set the tone for your class and drive the learning community and culture in ways you may not anticipate. By carefully considering how you can incorporate assessment *for* learning along with assessment *of* learning (i.e., both formative and summative), you can signal to learners that *how* they are learning and growing is as important as *what* they are learning. This is particularly the case in online learning, where commonly used tools are not necessarily the best tools and represent a narrow range of assessment options.

The framework for assessment from Stiggins and Conklin (1992) and Chappuis and Stiggins (2016) helps highlight different types of learning we assess: knowledge, reasoning, skills, products, and dispositions. By better understanding these types of learning, we can select assessment strategies and tools that are suitable for each. This chapter translated these assessment strategies into the online space to identify a host of different assessment methods and tools that better support student learning and your assessments of and for their learning.

Chapter 10

Facilitating Communication and Organization for Your Online Classes

> There was a lot of front-end planning to online learning! Teachers at Applewood were itching to simply "get to it" and start building their online courses and delivering their classes. How could they organize their classes so that students felt very clear about expectations and where to access everything they needed? How were they going to communicate with students both before class started and all throughout class? What were tips for class delivery to help everything go smoothly and support students in successfully participating in their classes? Did the research have any insights on effective organization and communication?

Much of what the preceding chapters have covered falls into phases of planning, design, and development. For good reason, effective online learning relies on a substantial front-end process, so that the learning experience for both educators and students is as smooth as possible from Day 1. While learners and educators adjust to changes during a face-to-face course, these changes can be harder to communicate and facilitate in an online course. As much as possible needs to be in place before the first day of an online class. This helps ensure clear expectations are communicated to learners and lowers the load and stress for instructors, who can focus on teaching and delivery instead of trying to build the airplane while flying it. Like the real estate agent saying, what matters is "location, location, location," in online learning the mantra should be "organization, organization, organization"—and a corollary to that is "communication, communication, communication."

Not only should online courses be well organized and structured, but that organization and structure also need to be clearly communicated to students, even in advance of the first day of class. Any changes to a course syllabus or plan after classes start can cause a lot more frustration and confusion in an online format than in a room-based class. Additionally, as discussed in Chapters 5 and 6, instructor presence throughout the class is key to ensuring that the class runs smoothly and that students perceive the online learning experience to be meaningful and worthwhile. This chapter covers ideas for facilitating organization and communication in online classes, both for setting up the online class and as it is implemented.

Creating the Learning Climate

A useful way to think about organization and communication is that they help you create a desirable climate for learning in the online environment. Parker and Herrington (2015) offer several user-friendly principles for how educators can set the climate in online learning, derived from research on what works online. Their principles, covered more extensively in *SEL at a Distance* (Moore, 2021b), include tips on creating a user-friendly, organized learning environment and building rapport to engender a sense of belonging in the online class. Some general tips for creating the learning climate online are summarized in Table 10.1—you may recognize several from previous chapters. The sections that follow provide more detail on organization and communication, with tips and checklists throughout.

Organization, Organization, Organization

Organization and communication are important companions in ensuring a positive, effective online learning experience. Surveys of students routinely report that ease of use and organization are important indicators of the quality of an online course and learning experience (Fischer et al., 2022). In a study of the effects of online course features like organization, Fischer et al. (2022) found that each increase in course organization (based on the rating used in their study) was associated with a 0.15 letter grade increase. That effect was even larger for traditionally underserved students: a 0.24 increase for low-income students, a 0.20 increase for female students, and a 0.48 increase for underrepresented minority students. They suggest that increased

Table 10.1 Organization and Communication Tips for Creating a Supportive Online Learning Environment (based on Parker and Herrington, 2015)

Organization	Communication
Create a user-friendly course environment • Develop an easy-to-follow course menu for navigation. • Use an uncluttered design style (you can apply principles from Chapter 8 to your course interface design as well). • Organize the flow of information and materials in a logical manner.	*Build positive rapport (social presence)* • Use open and friendly communication styles to decrease distance and isolation. • Actively participate *with* your students in discussions, etc., and offer opportunities for interaction. • Let your personality come through (talk about hobbies, travel, use emojis, etc.).
Promote a clear purpose • Articulate goals and share those with students. • Provide advice and feedback throughout the course. • Provide strategy-focused, constructive feedback, not just corrective feedback.	*Engender belonging* • Use students' names. • Create spaces for students to interact with one another. • Engage students in defining different spaces for different interactions.

course organization and transparency for the learner of course organization relates to greater student performance online because greater organization facilitates better self-regulation, a key to success in online learning (see Chapter 4).

Fischer et al. (2022) noted that course organization is evident through such features as a navigable infrastructure that includes organization of weekly assignments and instructions for getting started, and these features support student autonomy as well. Strong course organization supports a student's ability not just to find resources but to self-regulate learning based on course expectations and organization. Clearly communicating expectations and structure, such as assignment due dates, preparation time, and policies like late submissions, aids students in managing their learning process. Organization relates to how you have structured your online course and how well that structure is conveyed in key course documents, such as a course syllabus, and in how your course site is organized. Organization also means that everything is in place—assignments are created, discussions are created, links to live sessions are created, due dates are established, and everything is laid out in a way that makes it easy for students to access what they need for a given week.

Create a Course Matrix

One of the best ways to organize a course and communicate that organization is with a course matrix that maps out the week, with readings for the week, assignments or assessments due that week, and any recorded or live sessions. Some instructors also add the topic for that week or structure their table to show how a topic spans several weeks; some may also add the course or unit objectives in one column to show alignment. This matrix becomes the structure for the online course site as well and can be used to guide the development and display of information in your course site. Table 10.2 is an example from one of Stephanie's 8-week online courses. A lot of front-end planning goes into finalizing the content for this matrix, but as you work through different design considerations, such as covered in other chapters, it's good to start a table and continue building and editing it until you can finalize your class structure.

Table 10.2 Example Course Matrix From Stephanie's Class on Multimedia Learning Principles

Week	Reading/resources	Discussions and assignments
Week 0 (open 1 week before Day 1)	Orientation: *Instructional Design Primer*	
Week 1 (8/22–8/28)	• Mayer, Chaps. 1–3 • Piskurich, pp. 4–6, Chap. 4 • Baddeley	• Discussions: Applying the readings; Rapid ID • Project: Action Plan due
Week 2 (8/29–9/4)	• Mayer, Chaps. 6, 11, 12 • Lohr, hierarchy principle (reading provided in Canvas) • Chandler and Sweller; types of cognitive load • Piskurich, Chap. 7 (scan this chapter and wrap your evaluation plan into your design document)	• Discussions: Applying the readings; Rapid ID • Project: Design Document due
Week 3 (9/5–9/11)	• Mayer, Chaps. 7 & 8 • Lohr, gestalt principle (reading provided in Canvas) • Williams, Chap. 7	• Discussions: Applying the readings; Rapid ID • Project: Work on Draft Storyboard

Week 4 (9/12–9/18)	• Piskurich, Chap. 5 • Using multimedia in classroom presentations: best principles	• Discussions: Applying the readings; Rapid ID • Project: Draft Storyboard due
Week 5 (9/19–9/25)	• Mayer, Chaps. 9 & 10 • Lohr, figure/ground principle (reading provided in Canvas) • Williams, Chaps. 1–3	• Discussions: Design Throwdown I; Rapid ID • Storyboard tour: Post and discuss your Final Storyboard • Project: Final Storyboard due
Week 6 (9/26–10/2)	• Piskurich, Chap. 6	• Discussions: Applying the readings; Rapid ID • Project: Work on Draft Prototype
Week 7 (10/3–10/9)	• Williams, Chaps. 4–6 • Mayer, Chap. 13	• Discussion: Design Throwdown II • Project: Draft Prototype due
Week 8 (10/10–10/16)	• Williams, Chaps. 9 & 10 (if you're curious, enjoy Chap. 11 just for fun) • Instructional Uses of Typography website	• Discussions: Shared resource—instructional material design principles • Prototype Tour: Post and discuss your prototype • Project: Final Prototype due; Design Debrief due

Create Your Course Materials

Once you have established a structure for your course and summarized it in a matrix or table, that matrix can be integrated into a course syllabus. The syllabus should summarize key information for the class, such as contact information, how to access the class, a description of the course along with class objectives, required readings that will be provided or should be purchased in advance, and the class matrix. Syllabi should also include any class policies, overviews of assignments with grading/weighting information, and due dates. Some educators also include links to resources students may wish to access, such as accessibility services, tutoring resources, career services, or other system supports.

Once you have a clear course structure and syllabus that states policies, due dates, and so on, then building your course in your school's or district's learning management system (LMS) will be more straightforward. You may have already started curating readings and resources. All LMSs have a Files or Resources section where you can load content—this is typically not the student-facing organization for a course but your back-end repository where you can keep materials such as readings, videos, handouts, and so forth. One way to organize this section so you can easily locate things is to keep your main course files, such as the syllabus, in the main folder and then create subfolders for Readings, Handouts, and Rubrics, Videos, and any other types of materials you may wish to use. You will find it is easier to build the student-facing organization for your course in any LMS if you have as many materials as you can loaded into your Files or Resources folders ahead of time. If you plan to use discussions (or any other type of prompts for each week), you may also want to create a document in which you have each weekly discussion question typed up, so you can easily copy and paste them into different parts of the LMS. Also be sure to create assignment handouts and any associated rubrics or grading criteria in advance, so that all of these are ready to be loaded and then linked to as you build your course site.

Rubrics themselves are also another excellent tool for making expectations clear and communicating them to students in advance. Thus, they deserve some added attention during the preparation, development, and delivery process. Rubrics have several benefits that can be particularly supportive of online teaching and learning. While rubrics provide structure for grading and evaluation, a well-developed rubric supports students as they work on their assignments and activities. As you develop a rubric, use language that is strategy focused (guides them on what to do) and clearly communicates what you are looking for (what should be present) rather than language that focuses on errors.

Rubrics can also be a great opportunity for engagement and autonomy in a class. Some teachers engage students in articulating expectations for an assignment as they start their work on it and then polish the rubric with student input, for them to use as a guide as they work. This may be more effective later in a class than at the beginning, but engaging students in articulating expectations is a great strategy for shifting from assessment *of* student to learning to assessment *for* student learning (Chappuis & Stiggins, 2016; Stiggins & Conklin, 1992). Thinking of rubrics as instructional scaffolding—as something for students to use at the beginning, middle, and end of an assignment—can help you create clearer organization and communication in your online class.

Start Building Assignments, Assessments, and Discussions

After you have created your course structure and loaded all the materials you have, the next step is to create assignments and discussions in the LMS. Again, adding, building, and creating anything you can in advance will make the process of assembling everything into the student-facing organization faster and smoother. For assignments (or assessments and quizzes, depending on what you use in your class), students require very clear instructions. Make sure you provide clarity on what to submit and how, and link to any associated handouts for an assignment, such as a rubric. In most LMSs you can either attach or create a rubric that is used for grading. A good rule of thumb is to provide the rubric both ways, if you have that option, so that students can access it while they are working on their assignments, to use as scaffolding toward expectations.

For discussions, create prompts that ask students to do something with the content they have read or learned, not just repeat something from a book. For example, ask them to generate an example of a specific concept they are reading about, or ask them to apply principles or processes to an example you provide or link to. In Stephanie's class on multimedia learning, for example, her discussion prompts ask students to apply the principles they read about that week to materials available online, such as a specific collection on YouTube or another popular repository. Her discussions on rapid design prompt students to generate specific ideas for how they can apply specific rapid design ideas (e.g., rapid analysis or stakeholder input) to their projects for class. In some cases, you may also want to include instructions to clarify for students how they should reply to others. For example, if you use a discussion board for peer review, include an explanation of how the peer review process should work (will you assign who reviews whose work, what is the deadline for feedback, etc.).

Create the Student-Facing Course Organization

Once you have created your materials, loaded those materials, and created assignments and discussions in the LMS, then you are ready to create weekly modules or overview pages. This is the student-facing organization. Figure 10.1 gives an example of modules in Stephanie's multimedia learning course. In Figure 10.2, you can see a different example from one of Stephanie's other courses on ethical issues in educational technology. In Figure 10.1, the headers are simple with dates that help students know which to access when, whereas Figure 10.2 includes more descriptive detail of what will be covered that week. Either way is fine, and you can vary from course to course as you feel best fits your particular needs. Both of these are from courses that are in the Canvas LMS. The key ideas here are that the content is clearly organized and that dates are used in both instances to signal when students should access the content.

Figure 10.1 Example of module organization in Stephanie's multimedia learning class.

Figure 10.2 Example of module organization in Stephanie's ethics and ed tech class.

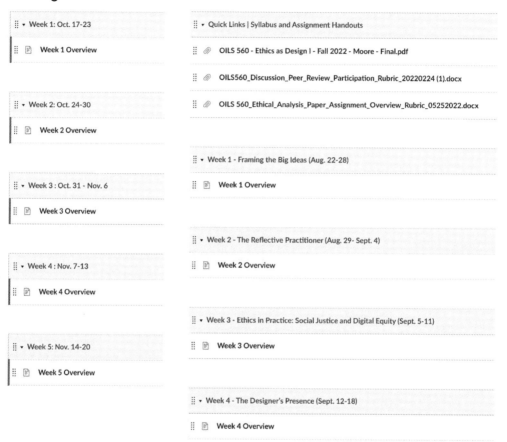

Another thing you may notice in these examples is that, for each module except the welcome module, there is only one item: an overview page. Many instructors may place multiple items under a module. Some LMSs force the approach or adding everything into a module as separate items. Others, such as Canvas, make use of pages where you can organize everything into one stop for students, and they can access everything they need for a week or module or unit from that page.

Generally, a "flatter" design (fewer steps needed to access resources and information) facilitates a more user-friendly experience for learners. If students have to click around multiple places to find things or access materials they need in different locations, they can often become confused and frustrated and miss something vital. This also adds to their cognitive load in the online learning environment, as they're having to work to piece resources together in addition to understanding the content in those resources. When possible, using a flatter organization for a course facilitates ease of access and decreases confusion and frustration. Again, using Stephanie's course as an example, her course has a home page (see Figure 10.3) and then has modules for each week (Figures 10.1 and 10.2). Each module has one overview page where everything for that week is provided (see Figure 10.4). For the home page, a graphic organization or visualization of the course can be useful for helping students understand the course organization or the main ideas of the course. An overview for the entire course helps set the tone and provide an introduction (Figure 10.3). This is a good place to link a welcome video as well. You can also incorporate quick links to modules, key documents for the course, or both.

Figure 10.3 Example of a home page in Stephanie's multimedia learning class.

Welcome to OILS 517
Applied Aesthetics

Overview

Ever wonder how a designer made a handout or a PowerPoint or an instructional web page look so appealing and easy to use? Have you or your learners had the feeling of being totally overwhelmed by a complex graphic where you don't know where to look first? Are you curious about how research on learning can inform the design of effective materials?

In this course, we will explore how to present visual and auditory information to learners in a way that is consistent with research on how people process information and how it sticks in memory. No background in graphic design or visual arts is necessary. In many instances, applying effective materials design principles focuses more on how you organize information than on slick graphics. Upon completion of the class, you should be able to evaluate existing materials and select those that are more effective, modify existing materials, and create more effective materials for your instructional needs.

We will have weekly activities (see Modules) during which you will evaluate some popular materials available online in light of the principles and research we are reading. We will also follow a "rapid design" process that includes a prototyping process during which you will provide and receive peer feedback as well all work together to workshop our materials in a virtual studio. Your readings for the course will include multimedia and visual design principles, underlying research and theory for those principles, and readings on the rapid design process. Thus, in the end not only will you learn techniques for designing instructional materials, but you will also learn why certain techniques are more effective and you will learn a process for quickly generating and iterating on instructional products.

Quick Links to Weekly Modules

- Welcome Module (Orientation to Canvas, supports and resources)
- Week 0 - Introductions and ID Primer (start here with introductions; if you aren't familiar with ID: please work through the ID primer before class starts in Week 1)
- Week 1: October 17-23
- Week 2: October 24-30
- Week 3 : October 31-November 6
- Week 4 : November 7-13
- Week 5: November 14-20
- Week 6: November 21-27

Figure 10.4 Example of an overview page in Stephanie's multimedia learning class.

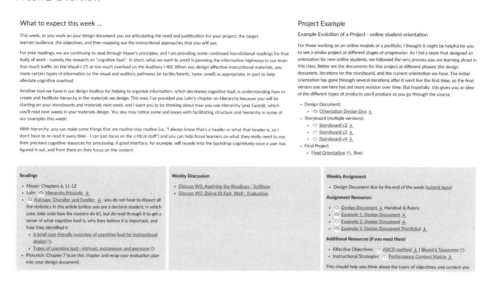

Notice how the weekly overview page shown in Figure 10.4 provides a written overview for the week and then the boxes at the bottom map to the course matrix for consistency. Links to everything students need for the week are embedded there: readings, supplementary videos, discussions, and related assignments and their materials. In this case, Stephanie also adds a "yellow sticky note" sort of area where she posts any reminders, upcoming events, or things to think about (e.g., "thinking ahead").

The example shown in Figure 10.4 is achieved by using two tables on a page in the Canvas LMS. The first table is a 1 x 2 matrix with a larger space for the main content and a "sidebar" space with a yellow background for notes, tips, and other addenda for the week. The second is a 1 x 3 matrix, evenly spaced with readings, discussions/activities, and assignments due that week. Each of these links to the relevant resources, discussions, assignment submission areas, and other supporting materials like handouts and examples for the week.

If you have all your materials in place already, creating these weekly or module pages for organization will be relatively straightforward. It may take you time to consider what you want to say in the course overview, but providing an overview text (and perhaps even a video) really helps students feel organized and clear about what to do and about expectations. You can also revise your course over-view over time as you experience learner feedback, confusion, or questions. The example provided in Figure 10.3 is one that has evolved over time through several course iterations.

Online Course Development Checklist: Creating Organization

The following list summarizes organization items mentioned in this section, to help you get your course organized before Day 1.

- ☐ Create a table that quickly summarizes each week: what students will read, any assignments due, any recorded lectures and any live sessions (with links as necessary to these things).
- ☐ Curate or create your materials for your online course:
  - ○ Readings
  - ○ Links to external resources (e.g., videos, websites, etc.)
  - ○ Assignment handouts
  - ○ Assignment or assessment rubrics
  - ○ Discussion prompts (if applicable)
  - ○ Weekly overviews
- ☐ Create a course site in your school's LMS.
- ☐ Load materials into the Files or Resources folder (name will vary depending on LMS).
- ☐ Create any assignments, assessments, or discussions that will be due (or have support staff help you with this).
  - ○ For online, students require very clear instructions and prompt feedback, so make sure you provide clarity on what to submit and how and any associated handouts for an assignment. In an LMS, you can set due dates, attach files, and write a description for assignments to provide students guidance.
- ☐ In the course site on the LMS, create weekly modules that map to the table you created.
- ☐ Within each of these weekly modules, create an overview page that includes what you want to say to students for/about that week. Be sure to include links to readings and assignments. Arrange this overview page so that it is easy for students to find what they need for the week. You can

create sections or use tables to organize the page other ways such as the examples provided in this chapter. Putting this information on one page so students have one place to go each week quickly takes them to what they need and provides optimal organization.

Communication, Communication, Communication

Course organization facilitates a great deal of the important communication in class. As you attend to the tips and practices above, you will also address a great deal of the communication necessary to support online learners. This section focuses on additional communication strategies and points in the course to attend to. We address three key types of communication in an online course: startup and structure, community building, and feedback throughout the course. These strategies are central to implementing and delivering an online course. Having a plan and solid strategies for communications helps ensure a positive, effective online learning experience.

Communications for Startup and Structure

As noted, many of your documents for your class that are key to organization are also key to communication. For instance, a well-structured syllabus and other materials such as handouts and rubrics communicate a lot of information to students that help them understand the course organization and how to structure their time. But students and their parents also need communications in advance to help them prepare, get a sense of what the experience will be, and be ready for Day 1 of an online class. Consider how, for in-person learning, open houses and "meet the teacher" sessions help students and parents get oriented to the school environment and to their classrooms. This helps students know where to go on the first day when they get off the bus and makes the environment familiar to them so they feel more oriented and less stressed on that first day of school. Similarly, for online learning we want to provide online learners and their support system the information and familiarity that will help them feel more oriented and less stressed on their first day of school. This means that we should plan for interactions and orientations to take place before the first day of online classes. Additionally, planned and structured activities with clear objectives for helping learners familiarize themselves with the online environment are significant opportunities for communication and structure.

One thing that can help you prepare for important communications and communicate messages when needed for students is to develop a communication plan to help students know where to go and what to expect in the online learning environment. Map out communication details like where students should send questions and how, how quickly they can expect you to respond to emails, how quickly you will respond to discussion posts or return graded assignments, and how can they reach you for urgent questions or needs (and what is urgent or not urgent). Additionally, create a plan for yourself for class: decide what regular communications you will send out to your class (e.g., weekly emails at the start of a week or end of a week), what time blocks will you allocate to grading, checking discussions, reading email, or other communicative tasks, and so forth. This is a good time to also consider if you will make optional interactions available, such as additional informal class sessions or online office hours for students. While you do not need to communicate your personal plan for your class to your students, many of these items are things you can share with your students to help shape their expectations and provide clear information and structure to support their engagement. The Communication Checklist below includes several of these ideas to help you develop a communication plan.

Communication Checklist: Having a Plan

☐ Create a class communication plan so students know where to go and what to expect:
  ○ Where to send questions
  ○ How quickly will you respond to emails and to discussion posts
  ○ How to reach you with any urgent needs or questions
  ○ What sort of regular communications you will send out to the class (e.g., weekly reviews and/or updates)
  ○ Any other plans you have for how you will be available to students and how you will send out regular information and updates

☐ Make sure your class roster is added to your class site—typically, support staff can help with this:
  ○ Download your class roster with emails to have on hand for quick reference if necessary (usually, you can save your class roster in a spreadsheet format with this information—it takes less than one minute to do)

    ☐ Communicate your plan to your students:
        ○ Do a quick walk-through of your plan and the course site for
          students—this can be done either in person, if you still have some
          in-person sessions, or as a recorded video you share with your class

Communications for Community Building

Creating a learning community online is one of the best strategies for facilitating communication and organization, as students become sources of communication and structure or support, along with you, in your class community. You will set the tone for your class most especially through the first communications you send out before and during Week 1, so let's focus on different ways you can help set the learning climate and tone for your class early on.

Before Day 1

Send information to parents and learners at least two weeks in advance of class, welcoming them to the class and communicating any important information about the class. For example, this is a good time to send the syllabus in advance, and perhaps even include a welcome video. A video can give them a sense of you from the start and help you convey warmth, energy, or whatever other messages and social presence you want to establish. Often, you may find that resending this message again one week before class begins is helpful. Your language, tone, gestures (if you record a video), and other explicit messages (information about the class, policies you want to highlight, etc.) will all help set the tone. You may also want to offer an orientation period or online open house before the first day of classes. This can be open time for students to come to the course site and join you on live video. During this time, you can show students around the class, answer questions, and even structure no-stakes activities for them to get familiar with the tools or course environment.

Week 1

If it is important to you to build a sense of community in your online class, then the time to start doing so is Day 1 and Week 1. The following are some ideas for activities you can use during Week 1 to help you and your students get to know one another. You could implement all of these or some of these, depending upon your time and schedule:

Week 1 Checklist

- ☐ Orientation activity—getting to know the online class environment:
  - ○ Give a tour
  - ○ Create a scavenger hunt
  - ○ Create a syllabus quiz
  - ○ Have students create a "class success plan" that requires them to read the syllabus and summarize what they'll need to do, along with ideas for how to be a successful online student
- ☐ Get to know one another:
  - ○ Introduce themselves
  - ○ Share interests and goals for the class
- ☐ Create a class community space:
  - ○ Create a space where students can share information and connect with one another to form interest groups or study groups
- ☐ Class activities to define the learning community:
  - ○ Students work together with you to define the desired class community (e.g., how much interaction do they think is reasonable? Should people turn on cameras? What are some policies you can create together as a class?)
  - ○ Students brainstorm and discuss what it means to be a good learner online; identify strategies they can use to be successful in online learning; share ideas for how they can set themselves up for success—organizing their personal space to focus on learning; participating in live sessions or discussions; group work; etc.

Other strategies instructors have used to build community online include ideas such as the following adapted from Gunawardena et al. (2019):

Checklist of Ideas for Building Community Online

- ☐ *Cybercafe:* Create a dedicated space for students to be able to meet and talk informally/socially. Perhaps this is open for 10 minutes before class or for 30 minutes after class. Students can help you decide what they prefer as well.
- ☐ *Create peer support groups:* In the first week, establish small groups of three to four students each that will be their go-to group for any questions

or support outside of class. You can let them create their own groups or create groups for them. Many LMSs have a Group tool that lets you create dedicated group spaces that you can check in on.

☐ *Create an open space for class questions:* Students often have questions that every other student may be wondering about as well. Discussion boards and other tools can be good spaces for students to post questions where you can answer them when you have time but in a forum where others can see your answers as well. If you create this option, be sure you set aside time each week to check back on this space.

In each instance, students may be reticent or feel unsure about using spaces or may not realize they can drive conversations and take initiative without you. Explicitly communicate to students what the spaces are for and emphasize any that are for them to use on their own.

Communications Throughout the Course: Feedback and Responsiveness

Feedback

One of the most important types of communication in your online class is feedback. How feedback is integrated and managed in an online class is one of the most important variables in student learning and perceptions of the online experience. Feedback should happen consistently, reliably, and throughout your entire class, as one of the most important forms of interaction and communication in any learning environment. In online learning in particular, it is essential to helping you establish teaching presence and social presence.

Student dissatisfaction with online learning frequently mentions lack of feedback from the teacher. Conversely, student satisfaction with online learning frequently mentions how responsive and timely the instructor is and how helpful the feedback is. Frequency, timeliness, and quality are all essential characteristics of feedback in an effective online learning experience. When feedback and interactions are low, infrequent, not timely, or otherwise unreliable or insubstantial, students start to feel a sense of isolation and become dissatisfied with the online learning experience. Imagine if students came into a classroom but the teacher never made eye contact, never addressed the students, and never talked with them, and then when they submitted work they didn't receive any feedback or received it weeks later with just a few minor comments. We want to think similarly about how our students in the online class would feel if we didn't engage with them and support their learning directly through interactions and feedback.

Treating feedback as a form of interaction and identifying various ways you can integrate feedback into your online teaching can transform your own experience as an online teacher. Specifically, baking in opportunities for formative feedback throughout your class is a strategy that can address a lot of the concerns or complaints about online learning. This may mean rethinking some class assignments or projects to consider how students can submit interim deliverables that provide you more opportunities for formative feedback on their assignment or project as it evolves. For example, if you want students to complete a paper, perhaps have them submit a proposal for their topic early on, an outline and summary a few weeks later, then a draft, and then the final paper. This helps lower overreliance on single high-stakes assessments and can also help build students' confidence and motivation throughout a class.

Using strategy-focused feedback instead of error-focused feedback can also help students develop self-efficacy and self-regulation skills. For example, rather than simply noting what a student did wrong or highlighting misspelled words and typos, tell students what they can do to improve their work and also emphasize what they are doing well and should keep doing. This helps them better understand what is working for them and where they can make improvements.

How you approach assessments in your class and how you communicate with students about their performance contribute significantly to class culture and can also help address concerns about cheating. Lang (2013) explored what leads to cheating and what class features create conditions for cheating, as well as features that decrease cheating behaviors. Table 10.3 summarizes instructional features that contribute to and decrease cheating behaviors. Many of the strategies that decrease cheating behaviors have the added benefit of facilitating learning and self-efficacy for learners. Feedback opportunities and the type of feedback provided play a central role in what type of class culture assessment practices contribute to.

Table 10.3 Conditions That Encourage or Discourage Cheating

Focus	Conditions that encourage cheating	Conditions that discourage cheating
Class emphasis	Strong emphasis on a single outcome or a limited number of outcomes, such as one test or paper or just a few tests/papers	Emphasize mastery of learning and the learning process, including improvement over time, rather than performance at a fixed point in time
Stakes	Extremely high stakes: a lot is riding on few performances	Create lower, more frequent stakes throughout the class (but take care to avoid "death by a thousand cuts" from too many small-point items)
Motivation	Extrinsic motivation: a reward or threat of punishment is associated with performance rather than the joy of learning or improving, what Lang (2013) describes as a focus on what happens after the performance rather than the performance itself	Foster intrinsic motivation: place more emphasis on the learning process, provide strategy-focused feedback with opportunity to apply and improve over time
Self-efficacy	Low self-efficacy: learners lack confidence in their ability to complete a task successfully	Help learners develop higher self-efficacy: use authentic assessments and real problems relevant to the real world, provide ongoing strategy-focused feedback to help them develop confidence

It may be helpful to visualize what formative feedback looks like throughout your class (for an example, see Figure 10.5). Identify points in time throughout your class when you can provide learners constructive feedback. This may be opportunities for quizzes where you bake feedback into the quiz, or submission of drafts or other artifacts for quick feedback and turnaround as they work on something. In a math class, you could have students record themselves working out problems that you review, and give them feedback not just on right or wrong answers but on their process and methods. In an English arts or and humanities class, this could be drafts, proposals, or journals throughout. For group projects or science experiments, students could submit plans that you provide feedback on, and then document their work at different stages and a draft report before a final report is due.

Figure 10.5 Formative assessment and feedback integrated throughout a course.

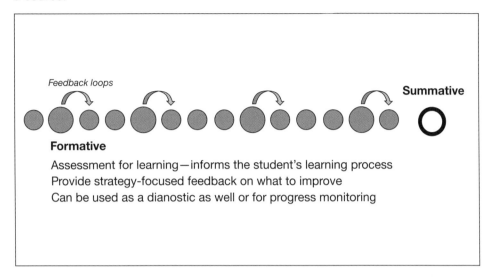

Feedback loops

Summative

Formative
Assessment for learning—informs the student's learning process
Provide strategy-focused feedback on what to improve
Can be used as a dianostic as well or for progress monitoring

Responsiveness and Timeliness

Regardless of how many opportunities for feedback and formative assessment you integrate into a class, online students are sensitive to how responsive their teacher is and how timely communications are. When a teacher seems to "disappear" for a time or takes too long to return work with feedback, this increases students' sense of distance and isolation online. Nearly every rubric for effective online learning will mention responsiveness to students and timeliness of grading or responses as key ingredients.

One way you can support yourself for timeliness and responsiveness is to use your calendar both to block off time and to create reminders or prompts throughout your week. Both of us create appointments on our calendars for our classes each week that remind us to check on specific discussions, send weekly emails, or other communication tasks. Stephanie also takes time at the start of a year or quarter to put all assignments on her calendar, with a reminder to grade the assignment that also blocks off a chunk of time for grading and student feedback. Generally, a target of one or two weeks for getting all things graded and returned with feedback keeps students feeling like they are getting timely feedback and support. It is also good to communicate to students about how long you anticipate it will take you to grade and return, especially if you think it may take more than a week or if you have some unusual events (e.g., travel) that may mean it will take you longer than usual. Both your feedback to students on their work and any communications you send to students about grading—whether it's housekeeping-type updates or summaries of observations for the entire class—also contribute to a sense of teaching presence and structure in your online class.

Summary

In preparing to implement and deliver your course, two ideas are central for planning: organization and communication. For organization, create a user-friendly course environment that is easy to navigate and uncluttered, with a clear sequencing of information for learners. Additionally, having clear goals that you share with students is one way to provide organization and help them focus and self-regulate their learning.

Tools that are helpful for organization include a course matrix or table that summarizes the weekly structure for students, including what readings they will be doing, any discussions or activities, and assignment due dates. A detailed syllabus that includes the course matrix along with other course information like contact information, description and objectives, links to resources, assessment and grading breakdown, and other supportive information provides learners a lot of clarity around expectations. These also help learners know how to structure and manage their time for their learning. Additionally, rubrics are a tool that simultaneously provide organization and structure for learners and help communicate expectations.

These can be key both to supporting learners as they work on projects and to supporting you in the grading or feedback process. Organizing your course with a home page and weekly overview pages in the LMS helps students identify key information they need on Day 1 or throughout the course on the home page and focus on what they need each week in the weekly overviews. You can "flatten" the structure of your course by using one landing page for each week that links to everything students should access for the week and provides them an overview (written, video, or both).

A great deal of communication happens through course organization, but additional types of communication are also important in online learning. We organized these types into communications about the startup and structure of the course, community building communications (especially that help set the tone in Week 1), and communications throughout the course with a specific emphasis on feedback. Students and their families need communications in advance to help them prepare. Like open houses for schools before the first day, online open houses and orientations in advance of the first day can help everyone become more comfortable with the environment and start to build relationships early. Virtual "meet the teacher" events and online "scavenger hunts" that help students use the tools they will use in class can help lessen their stress and improve their orientation and navigation. Developing a communication plan can help you identify and implement ideas. In Week 1 you can also start to create a learning community online through a number of strategies: orientation activities, discussions to get to know one another, a class community space for students to connect, and activities with the class to define the class community and expectations and even brainstorm and discuss strategies for success as online learners.

Feedback is one of the most important strategies you have as an online instructor. Used strategically, feedback is a critical form of ongoing communication that supports learners in their learning and also creates a sense of teaching presence that is essential in an online class. Identifying opportunities for feedback and creating reminders to check on discussions and set aside time for grading can help you create consistent, reliable, and timely substantive communication loops with your students.

As you implement your class, Table 10.4 provides an implementation checklist with some key reminders for organization and communication strategies throughout your course delivery.

Table 10.4 Implementation Checklist: Keys to a Successful Course Experience

Get students oriented	Give clear instructions
☐ Create a video or link to an orientation that students can access before the first day of class. ☐ Send a welcome email one week in advance to give students time to prepare and gather what they need.	☐ Write an overview for each weekly module that includes clear instructions on what to do that week and when, along with links for where to submit anything due or quick access to a tool or discussion. ☐ Provide written email updates and post announcements for your class as necessary.
Give timely responses	**Give timely feedback**
☐ Set aside time on your calendar, like an appointment, to regularly check discussions and reply, respond to emails, and write and send weekly summary emails.	☐ Put all assignment due dates on your calendar, with a reminder to set time aside for grading.

Be You!

☐ Imagine you are talking to a student sitting in a chair right next to you as you write replies and emails.

☐ If you make jokes, use cues like emojis or indicators (e.g., {smile}) to communicate the subtle cues you would send in-person.

☐ Authenticity matters, so be you and don't be afraid to be human. If a dog barks during a session or your child comes strolling in, roll with it—your students will appreciate that you are a human with a life too.

Chapter 11

Removing Barriers and Creating Intentional Supports

The leadership in the Applewood district and the planning team coordinating their online initiative felt really proud of all the front-end work. They were excited by teachers' ideas for their online classes that would lead to effective, engaging online learning. However, some teachers were starting to express concerns about whether certain resources were available or whether they would run afoul of some school, district, or even state or federal policies. The leadership team really wanted to support their teachers, but they needed a more organized way to think about how they were going to support this initiative beyond just providing tools and training on tools. What were the various things that might pose potential barriers and could be turned around into supports? Should some policies be revised, or perhaps even new policies developed to guide the use of new tools and systems? Was training or professional development really necessary, or did teachers simply need new or different resources to do their jobs better? How could they build a system of support that helped their teachers in their jobs?

Although the main emphasis of the book is on quality online instruction, we want to ensure we address critical system-level planning considerations and excellence at the leadership level. As organizational and human performance experts Rummler and Brache (2012, p. 13) said, "If you pit a good performer against a bad system, the system will win almost every time." Effective online educators, learners, and their families need the support of a system around them that supports them in being and doing the best they can. Research also demonstrates time and again that many online learning efforts struggle because they lack important system-level ingredients. This chapter discusses those ingredients for institution-level excellence in leading and coordinating online initiatives.

To structure the elements involved in macrolevel planning, we use the concept of a *performance support system* (PSS): systemic elements that work together to support effective performance (for individuals and for the school, district, or institution). The following elements are important to supporting online teachers and learners (or can serve as barriers to performance): resources and support tools, policies, skills and knowledge, job or task expectations and clarifications, communications and feedback loops, and rewards and incentives. A PSS provides those who are involved in planning and evaluating an online initiative a way to identify disparate elements that can influence performance and outcomes and to generate an organized plan that aligns systems features, instructional decisions, and desired outcomes. We also discuss characteristics of excellence that have been identified in case studies on effective online programs, and how districts or schools—or the virtual schools within them—can build better systems of support. For each of these PSS elements, we provide examples as well as questions for decision makers to address parts of the PSS as necessary.

A Vision of Administrative Excellence for Online Programs

Since online learning has existed for some time, there are research studies, case studies, and standards that can inform a vision of what excellence in leadership looks like for online and blended learning initiatives. Figure 11.1 summarizes characteristics of institutional excellence that have been identified across research on leadership of online learning initiatives. These characteristics are also reflected in standards for administration of online programs developed by the Online Learning Consortium (OLC), an organization that was established in 1999 and has created one often-used set of standards for online instructional and leadership quality.

If you have been developing your plan for online learning as you've read through this book, then you may already have a clearly articulated vision for online learning that is aligned with your district's or institution's strategic plan (see Chapters 1–3). You may also have a well-formulated vision for the community as an educational ecosystem that is affording different possibilities as well as strategies for building community in online courses and programs (see Chapter 5). The next step for administration and leadership is to then to provide support for these visions and

Figure 11.1 Characteristics of excellence for administration of online programs.

Vision & Mission for Online	• Clearly articulated rationale for why online and what the strategic value is of that for the institution and stakeholders
Supports Institution's Mission, Values, and Strategic Plan	• Online learning is positioned strategically within the district's or institution's overall organizational structure and clearly tied to its mission, values, and strategic plan
Community Definition	• Underscore that online students are equal members of your learning community/family (not separate or unequal in any way)
Governance Structure	• Intentional shared decision making related to online education; ongoing review for continuous improvement
Aligned Policies	• New policies that may be necessary to support online are developed in collaboration with stakeholders; existing policies are revised jointly with stakeholders to better support new expectations
Sufficiently Resourced	• Established and clear process for planning and resource allocation for online programs, including financial planning; sufficient resources to effectively support online programs and activities critical for success (e.g., outreach/marketing)
Community of Practice	• Opportunities for educators and students to share ideas, test ideas together (e.g., a sandbox), and collaborate

strategies with policies, resourcing, communication and decision-making infrastructure, and a community of practice that supports knowledge, skill, and creative ideas, as well as other key system supports. These supports are reflected in planning and administration of online programs in two ways: coordination between instructional and systems planning, and building a PSS that fosters coordination and excellence.

Building a Performance Support System

In addition to strategic planning and articulating a strong vision and strategic objectives, leadership plays a crucial role in supporting educators and the district through thoughtful operational planning. To identify the necessary systemic supports that will help both your team and your district's system perform optimally, we must first unpack limitations to the most common solution used for supporting individuals: training and professional development (PD). Training and PD should be understood as a specific type of solution that addresses a specific type of gap: a knowledge and skills gap. Training or PD assumes that the root cause of performance gaps is lack of knowledge or skills among the individuals who carry out tasks. There are times when individuals do have gaps in knowledge or skills, in which case training or PD is the right solution to address the root cause. However, it turns out that individuals' knowledge and skills gaps account for only about 10–20% of the problem space. Thus, addressing them may be a part of the solution set, but they cannot address even a majority of the problem space on their own. The remaining root causes are systemic in nature and require systemic supports or interventions. The quote above from Rummler and Brache about pitting good performers against bad systems is essential to understanding how desired performance starts with systems planning and design. More than half a century of research on human performance repeatedly shows that focusing on individuals' skills and knowledge misses about 80–90% of the actual root causes that lead to performance gaps. In reviewing the research on human performance, Triner et al. (1996, p. 61) observed that "a training intervention is only required in one out of five performance problems." That number is routinely corroborated by other learning and performance researchers (Clark, 1994; Deming, 1986; Spitzer, 1990).

Training may certainly be part of a solution set, so we cover it as an important support to consider. But no amount of training can overcome other systemic barriers, which is really the essence of the Rummler and Brache quote. Individuals who have the requisite knowledge and skills but lack the resources or are incentivized differently by policies or reward structures will usually perform the way a system incentivizes or resources them. This is true generally for all different types of performance; here, we focus on how different systemic barriers and supports can be addressed specifically as they relate to quality online learning. The more comprehensive and robust your planning is to support all individuals who use, rely, or act on different aspects of the online learning system, the better you can support everyone in their roles and build a high-quality online learning initiative.

A System for Support

If training alone is not a sufficient support for success, then what are the additional supports that should be in place? Figure 11.2 summarizes the remaining 80–90% of the supports—or barriers—that impact performance. Our task as leaders is to turn what may be barriers into supports.

Figure 11.2 Supports for human performance within an organization or system.

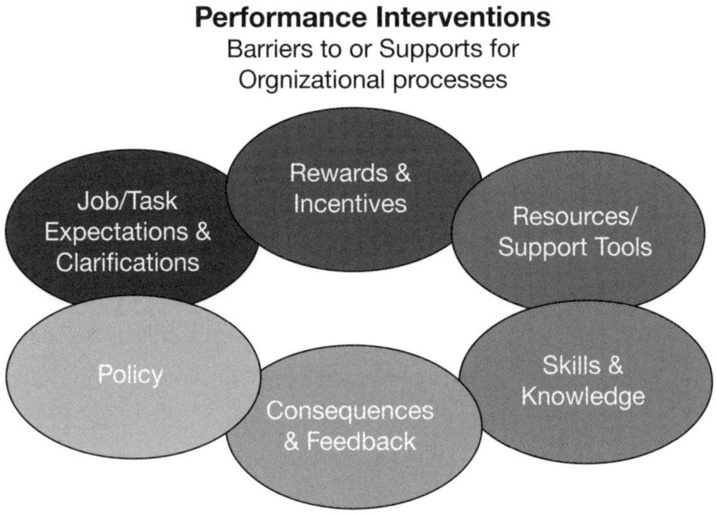

Performance Interventions
Barriers to or Supports for
Orgnizational processes

(Job/Task Expectations & Clarifications, Rewards & Incentives, Resources/Support Tools, Policy, Consequences & Feedback, Skills & Knowledge)

Resources and Support Tools

One of the most commonly cited reasons people feel they aren't able to do a job well is lack of resources or support tools. Conversely, adequate resourcing is a common reason people cite if they feel supported in their work and able to do their jobs. Resources—or lack of resources—can be both physical and abstract. For example, for online teaching, lack of time and more time required to do it well are cited as common factors. Instructors often state that teaching online requires more work and more time than in-person, with that time focused on grading, feedback, facilitating interactions, responding to emails and discussions, and other teaching activities in online learning. Physical resources are also important, such as the tools to do their job. This includes more than just the learning management system. Online educators must have an adequately resourced workspace and equipment to do their online work, including peripherals such as video cameras, microphones, and document cameras or tablets that allow them to display items or show work (whether recorded or in real time), as well as the software that supports their ability to present, interact, and provide content—live or recorded. Additionally, they need a dedicated workspace where they can listen to students or videos, record videos for students, host live discussions, and host private meetings with students to discuss their work and performance. This involves dedicated space for teaching online where the teacher can manage other noises and distractions and also maintain privacy and confidentiality with students and families for sensitive conversations.

Instruction will also be shaped by how educators are resourced in terms of both the technology ecosystem procured and the support systems provided to instructors and staff who support the online learning ecosystem. As discussed in Chapter 3, different tools reflect different definitions and philosophies of online learning. Some emphasize a limited vision of online learning as purely content delivery and do not support interactions or students' ability to exert autonomy in the learning system. Others will have some features that specifically support interactions and allow the system to be implemented flexibly, so that groups and student organizations can be created in addition to classes. It is extremely difficult to reengineer a system that doesn't have features supporting your vision for online learning, and it is time-consuming to migrate from one system to another. Creating a map or matrix of requirements and desirable features in advance helps you get the right resources in place to support the vision and standards you're aiming for. Additionally, review these systems for flexibility and interoperability—this will be key to supporting a range of instructional activities and strategies that can vary across grade levels and across domain areas. For example, the same suite of resources that may support humanities content areas well will probably lack some features that would support STEM areas well. Educators may be able to use one core set of technologies for most tasks, but outside of that subset of tasks, they will need different technologies for different tasks. This is why thinking of your technology infrastructure as an ecosystem is important—a single learning management system will not fill all the needs, just most of the core needs.

Start by generally mapping out what information, job aids, and resources the different stakeholders will need. Your planning should include resources for instructors, students, parents/families, staff, administrators, and any others.

Checklist: Some Planning Questions to Ask Related to Resources

- [ ] What resources or tools does your district currently have that would support online teaching and learning?
- [ ] What tools do you have in your online ecosystem to support different types of interaction, different types of assessment, and different content delivery formats?
- [ ] What should happen for you to have an effective technology infrastructure? How can you engage both faculty and students in helping identify needs and gaps?
- [ ] What resources or tools should you procure to better support effective online learning?

☐ How can you create more time for faculty developing and
teaching online?

☐ Is there dedicated space that meets teachers' needs for online teaching that
is quiet, where they can have confidential conversations or record videos?

Below we summarize questions that can help identify resources for instructors'
and staff members various needs (Table 11.1) and to identify resources for students
and parents (omitting instructional planning, because they are not involved in that
process; see Table 11.2).

Table 11.1 Identifying Resources for Instructors and Staff

Stakeholder group	Instruction and assessment planning	Interaction and community	Instructional materials
Instructors	• What hardware and software will help them do their job? • What time should be allocated for planning and delivery, and how is this integrated into their school-day schedules? • What workspace is necessary to support them?	• How do instructors want students to interact with one another, and how do they want to interact with students? What tools do instructors need to interact with students? (e.g., discussion boards, Zoom, Google Docs) • How do instructors want students interacting with content? What tools do instructors need to deliver content that will also allow for discussion and interaction on the content such as feedback and assessment?	• Do instructors have resources to develop materials such as videos, simulations, or other multimedia materials? If not, could that be procured? If so, how can you ensure they know the resources exist? • Do instructors have access to existing material repositories? If so, do they know where and how to access these?
Staff	• What hardware and software will help them do their jobs? • What time should be allocated? • What workspace is necessary?	• Do support staff have access to the same resources as educators?	• Do support staff have access to the same resources as educators?

Table 11.2 Identifying Resources for Students and Parents or Families

Stakeholder group	Interaction and community	Instructional materials
Students	• Do students need certain tools to interact with the content? For example, in STEM disciplines they may need tablets, cameras for demonstrating their work, or some way of scanning/recording problems they work out and submit. • Do students need additional resources the school should provide such as specific equipment or hotspots for connectivity?	• What may pose barriers to accessing instructional materials? How can those barriers be removed or diminished?
Parents/ Families	• What resources do parents/families need to support their students?	• What may pose barriers to accessing instructional materials? How can those barriers be removed or diminished?

Policies

Policies often lead to the other types of gaps. For example, policies can create incentive structures or establish rules that relate to resourcing. As a result, they are one of the other commonly cited barriers to performance. You may have a clear vision for online learning and invest in the technology and other resources, but then a policy or set of policies may motivate different behaviors or decisions. These may be school, district, state, or even federal policies that shape the behaviors and motivations of those within the system. Where possible, identify policies that may run contrary to creating a quality online initiative or inadvertently disincentivize people to support quality online learning.

Some Planning Questions to Ask Related to Policies and Online Learning

☐ What are some policies that limit the desired performance (e.g., promotion or performance evaluation policies)?

☐ How could those policies be adapted?

☐ By not adapting those policies, what could be the potential cost to your online initiative?

☐ What policies should be developed to support desired performance? For example, does your district need a policy on data collection and rights to privacy?

☐ Who can you involve in developing and approving these policies?

☐ What other parts of the system should be modified to support these new policies?

☐ What processes will you use for revising, creating, or updating policies?

Specifically for online instruction, consider the following policy-related evaluations for instructional and assessment planning, interaction, and materials:

Checklist: Policy-Related Evaluations Specifically for Online Teachers

☐ What policies, such as establishment of quality standards or lack of such standards, might drive instructional and assessment practices? How are they driving instructional and assessment decisions?

☐ Are there any policies on load or planning time that support or limit online teachers in their ability to dedicate adequate time to planning and delivery?

☐ Do any particular policies or reward/incentive structures motivate instructors to spend less time on interactions that support learning? If so, how and where might these policies be adjusted?

☐ What policies might interfere with instructors' ability to create or select materials? For example, is there a policy limiting them to certain repositories or resources? Are there policies that restrict their time for instructional development (intentionally or unintentionally)?

☐ Are there clear institutional policies on copyright, accessibility, affordability, or other considerations?

Policy review and revisions can be applied at the curriculum and course level as well. For example, policies on attendance and grading often drive particular behaviors among students. Changes to these policies and practices can dramatically change the learning environment and culture. Consider the following questions:

Checklist: Policy-Related Evaluations Specifically for Online Students

☐ Do any particular class or school policies or incentive structures (e.g., grading policies or practices) motivate students to focus solely on grades rather than interactions with peers and/or interaction with instructors through feedback and continual improvement? If so, how and where might these be adjusted?

☐ Do any particular class or school policies limit the ability to create flexible options for students who may need more flexible approaches for any variety of reasons?

☐ Do any particular class or school policies incentivize students to behave in ways that would be detrimental to their health and well-being? (This may happen more in-person, such as attendance policies that motivate students to attend even if they are sick, thus spreading illness and not allowing them the rest and recuperation they need.)

A formal policy review can help identify places where existing policies may create friction with desired performance or outcomes. Additionally, surveying teachers and other school personnel for feedback on any policies that they feel either pose limitations or should be developed can help identify policy-related barriers and gaps that might be readily addressed through revisions, removal, or additions.

Skills and Knowledge Development

Although a gap in skills and knowledge may not be the only barrier to performance, it can be a common one, especially early in an online initiative. One of the challenges with the mass move to online modalities during the COVID-19 pandemic was that many instructors lacked foundational skills and knowledge for how to design and deliver effective online instruction. We certainly hope a book like this one helps address the knowledge and skills gap. Even individuals who have been teaching online for some time may not have had access to many resources that help them reflect on their practices and learn new evidence-based strategies (Moore & Hong, 2022). For established programs, considering PD or book clubs with this book can support not only those who are new to online learning but also those who have been engaged with it for some time.

Checklist: Some Preliminary Questions to Help Identify Training and Professional Development Needs

☐ Have your instructors received any formal training, education, PD, or certification in online teaching and online course design? What training or classes (e.g., from a local university) might they take to learn?

  ○ How many people (employees, teachers, principals, staff members, others) have received some form of training related to online teaching and learning?

○ What entity might you partner with (internal or external) to develop or provide training or education on online teaching and learning?

○ Who will receive that training or education? What are your expected outcomes from that training or education?

○ How will you know if people are putting their new knowledge and skills to work?

☐ What training or PD can they take that is offered online so they have an opportunity to experience the role of the online learner and engage in some metacognition and reflection about their experiences (both adopting the good and designing differently to avoid the bad)?

☐ How can training or PD be sequenced so that participants are not overwhelmed by too much information at the start? (What can be covered prior to an initiative, in Year 1, in Year 2, and so on?)

○ For example, in this book, we cover instructional strategies and assessment, interactions, and multimedia learning materials. Preliminary training and PD could focus on strategies and assessment with some emphasis on interactions. Year 1 could continue an emphasis on online interactions and community building. Year 2 could emphasize learning principles for designing online materials and evaluating existing materials, during which teachers reevaluate or redesign some materials. Year 3 could emphasize increasing interaction and further building community, as well as revising some additional materials.

☐ What are key points in the year when instructors, students, or others carry out specific tasks? For example, when do they use the gradebook or submit grades?

○ What parts of the process could be supported through job aids or just-in-time supports (e.g., videos embedded in the system or in reminder emails at key points), instead of yet another training session that participants must remember months later? Where might knowledge and information be offloaded to the environment for just-in-time reminders and quick tutorials?

☐ How will you identify ongoing needs for training or PD? How will you distinguish when a lack of knowledge and skills is the actual barrier versus other barriers that may inhibit people regardless of their knowledge and skills?

In addition to PD or training, we strongly encourage you to create a community of knowledge and a community of practice around your online initiative. This can include knowledge and idea sharing across educators as well as across students and their families. Students and families who are more seasoned in online learning, especially in your district's version of it, can be of great support to others who are new to it. We often foster these communities for in-person learning through school events and other structures around the school, but most online learning planning doesn't consider how important these informal networks of knowledge and information are to ensuring success for people. The checklist below offers some detailed questions and considerations for a range of knowledge and skills gaps that you may need to address in planning for your online initiative.

Checklist: Knowledge and Skills Gaps to Consider in Planning for Your Online Initiative

- ☐ What training or PD do the following groups need for teaching online or supporting online or blended instruction?
  - ○ Instructors:
  - ○ Staff:
  - ○ Administrators:
  - ○ Others:
- ☐ How will students and families or other required users receive orientation to the online system and courses, the same way they would for face-to-face courses and school buildings?
  - ○ Who will develop and deliver these orientations? When will they occur? How can students and families develop familiarity and comfort with the systems and tools prior to Day 1 of classes?
- ☐ How will you create a community of knowledge that values knowledge sharing among online educators? Among students? Among students families?
  - ○ What are some opportunities for sharing ideas and collective brainstorming, either within groups or among these groups?
  - ○ How can your online learning ecosystem be leveraged to support knowledge communities, not just class sites?
- ☐ What times for individual reflection on practice can be created so online teachers have an opportunity to be reflective about their online practices?

Job/Task Expectations and Clarifications

Job and task expectations and clarifications define what is expected of individuals in their roles in the system. These often take the form of job descriptions and annual priorities for any employees including educators, administrators, support staff, and others. This can also include vendors and the expectations that are outlined for them in their scopes of work. Depending on how jobs and expectations are defined, people will perform according to what they perceive is and is not part of their job and the priorities communicated to them both formally and informally. If a job or task is poorly defined, or if a job description does not include certain features, then an individual may view something as "not my job." This arises sometimes in relation to online learning when individuals argue that they were not hired to teach online or that conducting online workshops or providing support online was not part of what they agreed to as part of the terms of their job description.

Additionally, individuals may often have job tasks and expectations that already fill their time, or they may not have the credentials or expertise to take on new roles as part of their job. In situations like this, you may be looking to hire someone or a team of individuals with new skill sets to better support new initiatives like online learning. Individuals and teams that support online learning often have skills, knowledge, and credentials in developing and teaching online learning, managing learning management systems and learning technologies, and developing multimedia content. It may be necessary or desirable to write new job descriptions and hire individuals specifically for these new roles or tasks, to better support an online learning initiative, and expectations specifically relating to online and blended learning can be detailed explicitly in those new job descriptions and expectations. We encourage such job descriptions—new or revised—to reflect principles and practices found throughout this book. Hiring an individual who may have the technical skills to develop multimedia, for example, but does not have a grounding in learning sciences that informs design and development guarantees the effort is not starting from the strongest possible point and may lead to materials that interfere with learning rather than facilitate comprehension and interaction.

During the planning process for online and blended learning, it is good to review tasks and expectations for all employees who will be involved and determine whether any revisions or additions are in order.

**Checklist: Some Questions to Help Guide Planning
in Online Tasks and Expectations**

☐ Do any roles or jobs for any team members lack tasks or priorities associated with the performance we want to see relative to online or blended learning?

☐ Are any individuals expressing reluctance because their tasks already consume their time or they feel new initiatives or tasks are not part of their job expectations?

☐ What job descriptions or priorities should change to adjust priorities and expectations?

☐ What new tasks should be identified and added for all key individuals?

☐ Should any new jobs be created to take on newly identified tasks and expectations? If so, how can those job descriptions be written to reflect both clear expectations and effective practices related to online and blended learning?

Idea Sparks: Multilingual Systems to Support Parent/Caretaker Engagement and Communication

When students aren't in school, we're really thinking through how we are communicating. Who's going to speak Spanish on the tech support line? How do we provide support to and connect with parents who don't speak English? Why are we making it more difficult to connect with parents if what we really want is their participation?

—Mark Benigni, Meriden Public Schools Superintendent, quoted in *Learning Accelerator* (2020)

Meriden Public Schools in Connecticut has a large Spanish-speaking student and parent population. In response to clear needs magnified by the pandemic, the system hired bilingual staff to offer technology support and to be available for parents and caretakers to call for questions on devices, learning management systems, and other online tools and resources. The school system also shifted all parent–teacher conferences to online, which has dramatically increased attendance and access.

As you develop your communication plan, consider potential barriers to access, such as language, and how those can be addressed through different resourcing and supports.

Feedback Loops and Communication

Feedback loops are primarily about the information gathered (or not) in a system and how that information is relayed or communicated (or not) throughout the system and to people. Feedback loops can be quite difficult to see in a system because often they are invisible elements. Sometimes feedback occurs through visible structures, like a system that documents technical issues and allows an information technology team to track issues from first notice through troubleshooting and resolution (such as a ticket tracking system). Often, though, it can be hard to see where data is picked up and where it is getting lost, or there may be delays in the data making it to the right people who can act on it, or they may receive too much data, leading to a backup and long delays. Feedback loops are essential to stability, but they can also contribute to "stuckness." Meadows (2008) describes two types of feedback loops: balancing and reinforcing. Generically, neither of these is more or less desirable than the other. Some balancing, or stabilizing, feedback loops provide important stability, but in some cases a reinforcing (or runaway) feedback loop—like interest on savings—is more desirable. A savings account that is stabilizing (seeks to maintain a status quo with minimal fluctuation) may be a desirable segment of an investment portfolio but is not a recipe for building a successful investment portfolio. In a balancing feedback loop, Meadows (2008, p. 112) explains, "not much changes, despite outside forces pushing the system. . . . This is a great structure if you are trying to maintain your body temperature . . . but some behavior patterns that persist over long periods of time are undesirable . . . [and] the system seems intractably stuck."

In human systems, feedback loops work to maintain status quo, but sometimes maintaining the status quo requires disruption. We see this quite often where existing inequities or negative impacts are maintained and perpetuated. Intractable stuckness is an indication of a problematic feedback loop in which information is not being gathered, is getting lost, or is going nowhere. For some number of reasons, the system is not acting on that information. In schools, the emphasis on "return to normal" is a good example of the system attempting a reset back to a status quo. Chapter 1 discusses system resilience and how the systems that are most resilient are those that are able to learn, grow, and evolve, not just maintain a stable status quo. Integrating online and blended learning strategically and meaningfully into a district's educational system is one way of growing, learning, and evolving instead of staying stuck in the same status quo that created and exacerbated many inequities in 2020 and 2021.

At a more operational and tactical level, asking questions about what the status quo is, how is that perpetuated or supported, and what seems to be getting reinforced may help identify feedback loops in the system. Systems are very hard to see when they work well, but they are very easy to see when they are not working well. Evaluate *what* is *not* working and identify *for whom* the system is not working. This can be accomplished by intentionally creating feedback loops and continuous evaluation and improvement loops. Ways to gather information about what is working and what is not, and for whom is it working or not, include anonymous feedback; periodic interviews, observations, and focus groups; and data dashboards with performance analytics.

Communication emphasizes that it is not sufficient to gather the data—that data has to be turned into information that can inform decision-making, and that information has to be communicated to those who can make decisions (see Figure 11.3). That communication also needs to be timely, so identify who are different audiences, what information those audiences want, and when. These are key to mapping out what data and information should be gathered, how, and how often. The checklist below offers some questions that can help you identify and redesign feedback loops that are not supported desired performance or outcomes.

Figure 11.3 Move from data to information that supports decision-making.

Checklist: Some Questions to Help Identify and Redesign Feedback Loops

☐ What are some places where the system appears to not be working? This could be based on observations or feedback.

☐ What are the indicators that the system appears to be working or not?

☐ Who is providing feedback? Frame your investigation to identify not a problem with the individual but, rather, what specifically is not working for them and what may be an explanation besides human error.

☐ Are there any backups in the system? What might help that spot in the system better manage the backup?

☐ What seems to be getting better or worse over time? What seems to be perpetuating the improving or worsening condition? (Is there another barrier, such as lack of resources, that is an additional root cause for a reinforcing feedback loop in the system?)

☐ How can you intentionally gather feedback from individuals and stakeholder groups?

☐ When and how should data and information be gathered and communicated out to different groups or passed along for action?

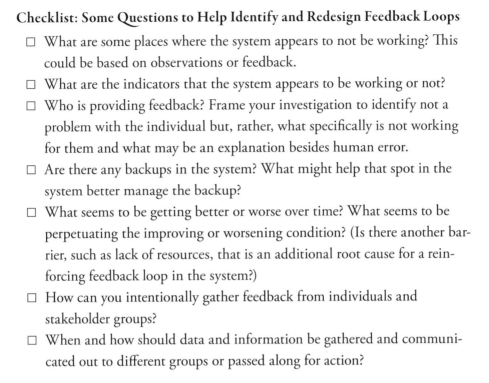

Learning Analytics and Data Repositories: Additional Considerations

One of the most common data repositories in online learning is learning management systems, many of which now offer data and data dashboards. These can track a wide range of behaviors, including how many times individuals log in, when, and for how long; what materials are accessed, when, and for how long; assessment results for students within and across classes; numbers of posts or interactions for teachers and students within a class; and myriad other data points.

While many of these are useful and can help support decision-making and adjustments, there are a number of additional considerations related to how data is collected, stored, and used. Ethical and legal concerns relate to data rights and privacy, and other legal concerns may arise from how that data is used to inform decision-making. Additionally, data dashboards can lead to "data myopia" (Harris, 2012), where decision makers begin to hyperfocus on the things for which data can easily be collected rather than the actual problems or questions they need to answer. Data collection and learning analytics practices can also foster a culture of distrust, depending on how the data is used and communicated.

Although there are many ways data collection and use can lead to negative consequences, there are also many ways in which it can lead to positive impacts, and the collection and use of data can reflect community ideals. Just like online learning can be designed effectively or ineffectively, learning analytics and data in education should be situated in a context of careful, intentional planning and design. The following practices can help you navigate the collection and use of data to better support learners and other people impacted by data practices:

- Explicitly articulate the questions you need to answer as a decision maker. Then identify the data you need to help you answer that question and how you will gather it. (Put the horse and cart in the right order.)

- Create a governance structure for data collection, and use to involve teachers, students, and others in developing processes and policies. This is critical for creating a culture of trust, driving the use of data in desirable directions, and creating communication and feedback loops.

Scholes (2016) provides a number of suggestions for minimizing potential harms and maximizing potential benefits of learning analytics. She recommends starting any learning analytics planning with the question of how students are perceived and treated in one's vision for learning analytics: Are they treated as individuals with rights, and are they treated as agents in the learning process?

- Learning analytics should support students as individuals, not just as members of a group. Its use should afford individual assessment and inform the individual in a way that supports their learning development (rather than categorizing them and excluding them from access to learning opportunities).

- Students should be afforded agency throughout the process. They should know what data is being gathered, have the opportunity to opt in or opt out, and be involved in individual conversations about their data and decision-making based on that.

Scholes (2016) also recommends using factors and data points that include more focus on individual choices, efforts, and achievements. For example, if students who complete an online study timetable prior to starting their courses are less likely to drop out of online learning, then design an orientation activity for students to complete the timetable and incorporate that as a data point in the learning analytics dashboard. She also recommends carefully distinguishing between factors that are static versus dynamic (i.e., changeable through an intervention). Often, learner characteristics that are actually changeable are treated as static. For example, in online learning, "readiness" and self-regulation are treated as static characteristics when in fact they can be developed through orientations and other strategies that can be integrated into the online learning environment (Moore, 2021b).

Scholes (2016) urges that data should be made available to students as a form of learning support and self-assessment. Teachers or other designers can support this, for example, by allowing students to see their own data and also see correlations between the amount of time they spent at a course site and their test or assignment scores. Activities such as self-checks and self-assessment or self-reflection based on the data can help students better understand their learning processes and needs and develop self-assessment and self-regulation skills.

Consequences, Rewards, and Incentives

An individual can have the knowledge and skills, be well resourced, and have clear job expectations or tasks and yet still not engage—or not engage optimally—in those expectations and tasks because of perceived or actual consequences and disincentives to do the work. For example, in a higher education context, a major disincentive to teaching online stems from the policies and processes of tenure and promotion. Often, these create expectations for what is prioritized or valued more, driving how individuals spend their time. Designing effective online learning takes time, and instructors may feel they are taking some risks in trying to be innovative, risks that may lead to lower student evaluations and take time away from other priorities. This can create a strong disincentive for instructors to invest the time required for quality online instruction. In some cases institutions have revised their rubrics for teaching evaluation to encourage innovation and risk taking and to minimize the use of student evaluations (for a number of reasons, including issues of reliability and bias). Other times, comments from leadership that express a devaluation of online or blended learning disincentivize people to focus their time and effort in these areas. Comments, policies, and other actions from leadership that express placing a lower value on online learning conveys that this is not where efforts or successes will be valued. Why would an individual want to invest deeply in something that isn't valued?

Consequences, rewards, and incentives focus on how leaders establish value for an activity in the system and communicate that value in all directions. Lack of consequences or rewards can send the same message as words and actions that actively devalue online and blended learning and teaching. If the intent is to promote a quality online effort and support your team, then the focus here is on considering how to convey that your team's efforts are valued and are worthwhile. Often, penalties or negative consequences can be inadvert. For example, if designing and delivering quality online teaching takes more time than in-person class prep, but teachers are not given any additional time for teaching online, then a penalty is levied on their time, thus creating a disincentive.

There are a number of ways to convey that efforts in teaching online are valued and to actually value those efforts—tangible and abstract, for example, creating awards that recognize online or blended teaching; showcasing online teaching in faculty meetings and newsletters; creating a day for teachers to network and brainstorm together to create a "marketplace of ideas" where their creative solutions are also celebrating; and adapting or developing policies (as discussed earlier) that better reflect how online learning is valued and supported. Additionally, aligning expectations with annual performance reviews and identifying supports for ongoing improvement help establish clear consequences (negative or positive) for desired performance.

Turning consequences, rewards, and incentives from negatives into positive is a key way you can shape your organizational culture. If you seek to create a culture where individuals feel free to take risks, be creative, and view failure as a part of the learning and development process, then you have to change how consequences and incentives are driving your school's or district's culture. The following questions can be helpful for a planning process that includes identifying where consequences, rewards, and incentives can be adjusted.

Checklist: Identifying Consequences

☐ Do teachers express concern over negative consequences if they try something new? If so, what do they identify as the root of that concern—where is that stemming from? (E.g., perhaps a policy creates this impression?)

☐ Do teachers express concern over negative consequences if they try something new and it doesn't work well? If so, what do they identify as the root of that concern?

☐ What do you think should be the consequence for someone who improves or delivers on their desired performance? Does this actually happen?

☐ What do you think should be the consequence when someone does *not* improve or deliver on desired performance? Is there an opportunity here to reframe consequences into opportunities for support and development?

Checklist: Identifying Rewards and Incentives

☐ Are there any possible disincentives for teaching online? (For example, if teachers are refusing, what are their reasons?)

  ○ If so, how can you address those disincentives?

  ○ Rather than interpreting these reasons as reflective of individuals, how can you unpack them to better understand possible systemic causes?

☐ Could an educator be penalized, however inadvertently, for teaching online?

  ○ If so, how can you address the root cause that's creating the penalty?

☐ Are there any ways in which innovative practices can hurt an educator, staff member, or others? (For example, if a teacher gets lower evaluations because they tried something that didn't work so well, will they be penalized for that?)

  ○ What policies or practices should be adjusted so that "learning from failures" is supported and attempts to innovate are celebrated?

☐ How will you recognize innovation and outstanding work?

The Performance Support System: A Solution Set

Again, we want to emphasize that supporting performance is not a matter of picking one of these issues to address. Instead, often a mix of factors impacts performance, and a good solution is often a solution *set* where interventions are mapped to actual root causes. Training, for example, will not address problematic policies, nor will adapting policies address gaps in skills or knowledge. Often, we must develop a solution set—aka a performance support system (PSS)—comprising a number of supports or interventions. This also involves considering when a change in one issue or area might necessitate a change elsewhere. For example, a change in the technology infrastructure or a change in policy might also necessitate new training or resourcing. Surveys and interviews that explicitly ask participants about resources, policies, rewards/incentives, communication, feedback loops, job requirements and expectations, and skills or knowledge can be very helpful to highlight both gaps and supports that are present.

Appendix B provides a sample survey, which can be easily adapted to your context, that allows you to calculate a gap (or difference) between "what is" and "what should be," adapted from Kaufman's (1996, 1997, 2000a, 2000b) work on gap and needs analysis. Another option is the "force field analysis" tool developed by Chevalier (2014) that can be adapted to any performance context. (For full information on these sources, see the references list at the end of the book.)

Summary

In this chapter, we covered indicators of administrative excellence for online programs. Successful online learning initiatives do not arise from quality courses and curricula alone. They require a host of supports and commitments from leadership. Administrative excellence is reflected in a clear vision and mission for online learning that aligns with the district's or institution's strategic plan. Strong leaders also ensure that online learning is seen as part of the entire educational ecosystem and that online learners are treated as equal members of the learning community. They also create opportunities for shared governance and communication that allow teachers, students, families, staff, and others to have direct input into decisions, policies, and other decisions. They also align policies to support online learning and direct it toward desirable outcomes and impacts—both learning and other impacts such as equity, privacy, accessibility, and other considerations. Successful online learning initiatives are also sufficiently resourced, and the district or institution fosters a community of practice around online that facilitates idea sharing and supports innovation and ongoing learning.

To accomplish this vision of excellence for administration of online learning, we introduced the idea of the performance support system (PSS), which reflects a systemic approach to identifying features in a system that can either hinder or support performance and then turn any barriers into supports. The most common types of barriers or supports include resources/support tools, policies, skills and knowledge development, job/task expectations and clarifications, feedback loops and communication, and consequences, rewards, and incentive structures. We discussed specific ways leaders can examine each of these areas to better align elements in their organization to support quality online learning systems and experiences.

Chapter 12

Coordinating Instructional and Macro Choices

Often, it's difficult to connect the dots when planning and development are occur-
ring at two or more levels for an initiative. While leaders and teachers alike in the
Applewood district were feeling excited and ready for online learning, they still felt
like things were falling through the cracks and some aspects of planning weren't connecting. They needed a way to connect instructional- and district-level planning so
that the two aligned better. Teachers felt unclear about some of the standards or
even expressed no awareness of standards. Some also were frustrated that their fan-
tastic instructional plans wouldn't be possible because they didn't have the tools, and
the district sounded like it planned to purchase tools they didn't really need. How
could they connect the parts and better align instructional needs and strategic or
operational planning?

This book has been structured with instructional design and decision-making for
online learning (Chapters 4–10), bookended by chapters on macrolevel leadership
and planning for online learning (Chapters 1–3 and 11). This bookending is an
important message, as it underscores that successful online learning initiatives
require research-anchored instructional practices that are situated in a supportive
system provided by leadership. These two sides of the planning, design, and delivery
stages of online learning are essential. However, it is not enough for the people in
these separate roles to simply do their planning, design, development, and imple-

mentation in their silos. There is important space between these two where strong coordination can build important bridges between instructional and macroplanning.

In previous chapters, we raised the concept of "handshakes"—such as how a district's vision for online learning can and should influence instructional decisions, and how instructional decisions can and should influence systemic planning like resources and procurement. For example, for instructional needs, if you include the ability to record explanations with visuals and audio narration, then system-level planning should include procuring software and hardware that support that capability. If instructional needs include the ability to evaluate learning through active assessments such as drag-and-drop or sorting, or the ability for students to work in groups and collaborate, then system-level planning should review technologies based on whether they support those instructional features. Likewise, the standards for quality and excellence and the vision for online learning established as a part of school- or district-level planning should inform instructional decisions and development. We want to conclude with a focus on ways the instructional and macro levels of planning can be bridged to create effective handshakes between the two.

In this chapter, we provide job aids to facilitate that coordination process. Many of the prompts on the left and right side of the tables we provide to support coordination include details you may have already mapped out in previous sections. The tables in this chapter can serve as support tools for meetings that help align instructional decisions with planning and coordination decisions. We will cover handshakes on:

- instructional strategies and methods,
- interactions and community,
- digital content selection and production,
- assessment methods and tools,
- technology selection and procurement,
- development, and
- implementation and evaluation.

Handshakes on Instructional Strategies
In Figure 12.1, we have depicted an outline for instructional planning around instructional strategies on the left side and macrolevel planning and coordination tasks or needs on the right side. In between is the space where these two require

coordination. Figure 12.1 provides an example where instructors have specific instructional needs that should inform school or district planning (hence the directional arrow towards Planning & Coordination). Additionally, assuming the school or district has established a vision and standards for online, those should be coordinated and aligned down into instructional decisions.

Figure 12.1 Handshakes to support coordination on instructional strategies and methods.

Instructional Decisions	Handshake	Planning & Coordination
Strategies and Methods for Instructions and Assessment		
What is the learning objective? **Type of Objective:** ☐ Knowledge/Comprehension ☐ Application ☐ Analysis ☐ Synthesis ☐ Evaluation Presentation Strategy: Generative Strategies (Practice/Activities): Assessment:	**Presentation Needs and Tools (circle or add):** Ability to record explanations that include visuals with audio narration; Examples that include pictures, visuals, and/or videos Other: **Practice and Assessment Needs and Tools (circle or add):** Knowledge checks (quizzes and tests); Drag and drop/sorting activities; Wiki/GoogleDoc Other: Alignment with standards Review what resources are available that supports teh desired instruction; identify gaps for potential procurement (or alternatives)	Established strategic objectives and school/district/organizational vision Adopt/adapt/establish clear standards for online and blended instruction ☐ Addresses both design as well as delivery/implementation Integrate instructional needs into technology evaluation and procurement critera ☐ Develop a matrix for educational technology procurement that includes instructional needs as well as other factors like integration, accessibility, etc. Student Orientation: Develop and provide an introduction or orientation to prepare students for success in online courses/programs Create a sandbox and/or communication process to help test and communicate out new possibilities to instructors

Notice how the Presentation Needs and Tools in the center space have an impact on system-level planning—especially technology evaluation and procurement criteria. This could also inform revisions to a district's strategic objectives and vision or standards for online and blended instruction as educators conceive innovative ideas, or learn more from ongoing education or professional development and want to implement principles they are learning. Additionally, the shape of instruction will influence student and parent orientations, both the nature of it and the content covered in orientations. Instructors' ideas may also suggest the need for a sandbox space and opportunities to test and explore.

On the planning and coordination side of the handshake, the first two elements are (1) establishing strategic objectives and a school/district/organizational vision. and (2) adopting, adapting, or establishing clear standards for online and blended instruction. Both of these should be completed prior to any instructional planning, so they can flow into instructional planning (see Chapters 1–3). These elements can then be applied to further systems planning, such as technology evaluation and procurement (see Figure 11.2).

Figure 12.2 Alignment of vision and standards for excellence in online learning with instructional planning and systems planning.

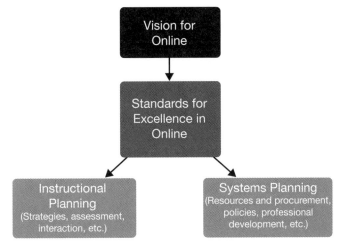

Figures 12.3 and 12.4 provide additional coordination tools with prompts and empty space for handshakes that you can fill in as a team. These figures incorporate the system elements covered in Chapter 11 as prompts to consider throughout. Note that the elements on the left side (policy, resources, etc.) are not intended to suggest that those items align only with that instructional consideration. In the free and open planning guide, developed by Stephanie and available through her university (http://digitalrepository.unm.edu/ulls_fsp/154), you will see that the items along the left span all of the different instructional considerations. As you discuss different types of objectives or other instructional decisions and needs, you should continually consider whether any planning or revisions are necessary related to resources/support tools, skills and knowledge development, feedback loops and consequences, rewards and incentives, job/task expectations, and policies.

Figure 12.3 Coordinating tool for planning the alignment between instructional strategies and system-level planning.

What is the learning objective? **Type of Objective** ☐ Knowledge/Comprehension ☐ Application ☐ Analysis ☐ Synthesis ☐ Evaluation Presentation Strategy: Generative Strategies (Practice/Activities): Assessment:	**Presentation Needs and Tools:** **Practice and Assessment Needs and Tools:**	**Resources/Support Tools:** What information, job aids, and resources do the following stakeholder groups need? Instructors: Students: Parents: Staff: Administrators: Others:
What is the learning objective? **Type of Objective** ☐ Knowledge/Comprehension ☐ Application ☐ Analysis ☐ Synthesis ☐ Evaluation Presentation Strategy: Generative Strategies (Practice/Activities): Assessment:	**Presentation Needs and Tools:** **Practice and Assessment Needs and Tools:**	**Skills & Knowledge Development:** What training or PD do the following groups need for teaching/supporting online or blended instruction? Instructors: Staff: Administrators: Others: **Feedback Loops and Consequences:** How will you communicate information out to students, parents, and teachers? How will you build a (hard and soft) data cycle to inform your process and how things are going?

Figure 12.4 Coordinating tool for planning the alignment between instructional strategies and system-level planning.

Type of Objective: Affective Seeing examples, role-playing, case studies, simulations, and diverse teams are all possible strategies (that can be used independently or in conjunction with each other) for affective learning objectives. Note your ideas here. Examples (demonstrating the model): Role-playing: Case studies or scenarios: Simulation: Diverse teams (consider what sort of diversity is central to your objective—disciplinary, cultural, skills/capabilities, racial, geographic, etc.):	**Presenation Needs and Tools:** **Collaboration/Interaction Needs and Tools:**	**Rewards and Incentives:** Are there any possible disincentives? If so, how can you address those? How will you recognize innovation and outstanding work? How will you nurture interested teachers and students? Are there any ways in which innovative practices can hurt a teacher that you will account for? (e.g. student evaluations often dip in early stages of new practices—how can you support iteration and "learning from failures") **Job/Task Expectations:** Should ay job requirements or definitions be rewritten? Are there any new roles and responsibilities that will require new positions? How can you incorporate instructional needs and system support needs in to those job descriptions?

In Figure 12.5, coordination space is provided for any objectives or learning activities related to collaboration or teamwork.

Figure 12.5 Coordinating instructional decisions on collaboration or teamwork with system-level planning.

Type of Objective: Collaboration/Teamwork	Presentation Needs and Tools:	Policies:
Specify the nature of the teamwork (this may be the same as what you indicate under Student-Student interaction)		Are there specific policy implications that should be discussed and tended to?
Type of collaboration/teamwork:		*For example:*
☐ Group work on single product		• Tenure and promotion policies
		• Student privacy and data policies
☐ Individual work that is peer reviewed	Collaboration/Interaction Needs and Tools:	• Load policies
		• Establishment of quality standards
☐ Other: _____		
How will the group work happen:		What process(es) will you use for revising/creating/updating policies?
☐ Synchronous meetings for work required?		
☐ Asynchronous sharing and discussion required?		
☐ Real-time messaging to peers desired?		
☐ Other: _____		
Scaffolding for Team:		
☐ Team planning document (roles, responsibilities, etc.)		
☐ Team member feedback (e.g. CATME)		
☐ Designated collaboration space and communication tools		
☐ Other: _____		

Handshakes on Interactions and Community

Given the importance of interactions and community in online learning, efforts to facilitate interaction and community through instructional decisions should be similarly supported by system-level planning and coordination. Figures 12.6 and 12.7 provide prompts for Instructional Decisions related to student–instructor and student–student interaction possibilities on the left and Planning and Coordination on the right (using the same PSS structure to organize prompts for considerations). The column in the middle is space for your planning team to take notes for coordinating desired interactions with system-level planning. Note that the prompts under Resources, etc., are specific to facilitating interactions in online learning.

Figure 12.6 Student–instructor instructional and systems planning handshakes.

Types of Interaction—Student Engagement with You, Each Other, and the Class Material		
Types of interaction identified in research: Student-Content, Student–Instructor, and Student–Student		
In this section, you will map out your plan for engagement using these three types of interaction as a structure.		
Type of Interaction: **Student–Content** *Student-content interaction is facilitated by the instructional strategies and methods that you select. Those are articulated above in strategies that align with different types of objectives.* **Type of Interaction:** **Student–Instructor** ☐ Virtual Office Hours ☐ Live synchronous sessions—optional ☐ Live synchronsu sessions —required ☐ Asycrhonous forum/discussion board discussions ☐ One-on-one Q&A and support ☐ One-to-many message/information distribution ☐ Formative feedback on student work as they develop it ☐ Summative feedback on student work after they complete and submit it ☐ _____ ☐ _____	*Align: Resources, Policies, Rewards/Incentives, etc.*	**Resources:** Do instructors and students have the tools they need to interact with each other? *Students:* Do students need certain tools to interact with the content? For example, in STEM disciplines they may need tablets, cameras for demonstrating their work, or some way of scanning/recording problems they work out and submit. Do all students have internet access? If not, can they access the content via a mobile device? If that's not feasible, what are alternatives (phone, mail, radio, television) that may be more accessible for your learners? (Return to your rapid front-end analysis—ideally your decisions at this point are grounded in that rapid analysis.) *Instructors:* What tools do instructors need to interact with students? (e.g. discussion boards, listservs, live video conferences like Zoom, Connect, Skype, MS Teams, etc.) What tools do instructors need to deliver content that will also allow for discussion and interaction on the content such as feedback and assessment? (e.g. an LMS like Canvas, Desire2Learn, Blackboard, Moodle, Google Classroom, or others)

Figure 12.7 Student–student instructional and systems planning handshakes.

Type of Interaction: Student–Student	Align: Resources, Policies, Rewards/Incentives, etc.	Support staff:
Type of Interaction: **Student–Student** Select the desired types of student–student interaction (and add additional ideas) ☐ Discussion on asynchronous forum/discussion boards ☐ Construction of a single artifact/product by more than one individual ☐ Ability to share draft and final documents/products with each other ☐ Group work on joint project—syncrhonous ☐ Group work on joint project—asynchronous ☐ Peer review on individual work—synchronous ☐ Peer review on individual work—asynchronous ☐ Self-organized student meeting groups—asynchronous ☐ Self-organized student meeting groups—synchronous ☐ Real-time messaging to peers for Q&A ☐ _____ ☐ _____	*Align: Resources, Policies, Rewards/Incentives, etc.*	*Support staff:* Do support staff have access to the same resources? **Related Skills & Knowledge:** Do students, instructors, and staff require any training to learn the tools? **Policies and Rewards/Incentives:** Do any particular policies or rewards/incentives structures (such as tenure and promotion) incentivize instructors to spend less time on interactions? If so, how and where might these be adjusted? Do any particular policies or incentive structures (such as grading policies or practices incentivize students to focus solely on grades rather than interactions with peers and/or interaction with instructors through feedback and continual improvement? If so, how and where might these be adjusted?

Handshakes on Digital Content Selection and Production

Coordination on instructional materials and content often relates to whether educators have the resources and skills to develop new digital content or access and incorporate existing digital content. Policies may also greatly impact what educators can or cannot use, as well as influence their considerations of existing digital content. For example, copyright laws and institutional policies should inform materials that instructors select. Figure 12.8 focuses on the creation of new digital content for online learning with instructional considerations on the left, planning and coordination on the right, and space between to align system and instructional decisions. You may also want to detail here what materials you plan to create and what tools or software you will need to create those materials.

Figure 12.8 Instructional materials handshakes.

Instructional Materials—Selection and Production		
Materials: New - Multimedia (where to invest multimedia development time and effort) What are the 3–5 main concepts that, if students leave knowing anything from your instruction, these are the main things they understand: 1. _____ 2. _____ 3. _____ 4. _____ 5. _____ Sequence these in order of most importance. If you need to wait until future iterations to develop one or some of these, which one(s) could wait?	*Align: Resources, Policies, and Rewards/ Incentives*	**Resources:** Do instructors have resources to develop materials such as videos or other multimedia materials? If not, could that be procured? If so, how can you ensure they know the resources exist? Do instructors have access to existing material repositories? If so, do they know where and how to access these? **Policies:** What policies might interfere with instructors' ability to create or select materials? For example, should they be allocated more time, even if temporarily, to create or identify sources? Are instructors aware of any institutional policies on copyright? **Skills & Knowledge Development:** What training or PD do instructors need to use tools or access existing materials?

For the use of existing digital content, the following questions will help coordinate instructional decisions on selection and use of existing materials or resources along with system-level considerations as well. For each existing material you are considering, work through the following questions to help guide selection.

- Is the content accurate?
- Is the content aligned with an instructional objective? (If yes, which one?)
- Does the video/handout/product design reflect multimedia learning principles (how humans process information; Mayer et al.) such that it will facilitate comprehension and retention?

- What instruction, explanation, or guidance needs to be provided to situate this material in the appropriate instructional context?
- Are there any misunderstandings that might arise? How will you assess for them?
- Is there an additional cost for using the material?
- Would use of it violate copyright or fair use?
- Is it accessible for learners with disabilities? If not, how can you differentiate the materials or instruction to ensure full access to the learning?
- Are there any representations of characters (e.g., in simulations) that could perpetuate stereotypes or discrimination?

Handshakes on Assessment Methods and Tools

As noted in Chapter 9, assessment is one of the major drivers in every educational system, so you are likely to run into significant areas where instructional decisions around assessment need to be aligned with programmatic/institutional resources, policies, and other barriers or supports. At a basic level, assessment needs across different domains should be supported by infrastructure for those assessment methods. For example, in addition to quizzing, teachers often use strategies such as editing a document or completing a virtual lab or a field experiment. Identify supports instructors may need to better understand how to assess different learning outcomes differently, and what tools (resources) will support implementation of higher-order and authentic assessments that go beyond tests and quizzes. Creating a map of assessment strategies across the curriculum can highlight areas of overlap where some technologies may help with a large portion of needs and other areas where specific tools may be necessary to assess learning in a particular domain. Sandbox communities to share ideas can also help educators identify possible uses of tools in other domains, thereby impacting both the feasibility of a particular tool and the instructional possibilities in other domains. Continue asking similar questions as we discussed above about the PSS and alignment of resources, policies, and rewards or incentives in particular as you evaluate both strategies and technologies for assessment. Additional needs around skills and knowledge, job or task definitions and clarification, and feedback loops and communication needs may also emerge.

For assessment methods and tools, it is also important to identify the possible negative impacts, especially for online and remote proctoring tools. While these may seem like a simple fix for assessment needs, they can greatly impact the nature of a learning community. Students may feel the use of these conveys distrust, and they may also feel their personal privacy and dignity are violated. The mass move to online during the pandemic also ushered in increased use of these tools (Flaherty, 2020; Young, 2021), but along with that came problems and legal challenges. For example, concerns over discrimination plague online and remote proctoring tools (Indiana University, n.d.; Harwell, 2019), and to date there is no research evidence to suggest that these tools cut down on cheating instances or contribute to improved learning or performance outcomes. Some legal challenges included invasion of privacy, such as one case in which a court agreed with a student that the feature that scans a room is a violation of students' Fourth Amendment rights protecting citizens from "unreasonable searches and seizures" (Bowman, 2022). Other situations have highlighted how ethical principles such as dignity and privacy may be violated by implementation of these types of technologies (Chin, 2021; Glass, 2021). Simply mapping assessment methods to technologies can easily overlook important ethical and legal considerations that should inform both system and instructional planning.

Activity 1: Agreements

Pick one technology you are using or consider using. Read the "End Users Licensing Agreement," or EULA. Rewrite this in a way your students and their families can understand. What options do they have for opting out or in? How will those choices be communicated as well?

Activity 2: Creating Governance Structures for Data Rights and Privacy

Create a stakeholder map of everyone impacted by or using a particular technology. Create a committee with representatives. Start by articulating different needs and concerns. Based on these needs and concerns, draft policies and criteria that will govern evaluation, procurement, data collection and management, accessibility, and other identified needs.

To better evaluate undesired impacts, consider involving stakeholders in a process of review and discussion, and consider policies that address data rights and privacy, dignity, accessibility, and other considerations. Developing policies as a community around student data rights and privacy can engender trust and create a healthier community. That policy can also then be folded into procurement requirements and process. Questions that often arise around online learning and use of online systems include the following:

- How will access to end-of-course assessment data be handled?
- Who stores and manages that data, and who has access to it?
- How will that data be used? How will students and parents have a say in what data is stored or retained and how it is used?
- What sort of opt-in or opt-out policies should protect these rights? How will that be communicated regularly to students and families in a way they understand?
- What policies and procedures may need to be in place to ensure you foster a culture of trust—with students and with educators?

Handshakes on Technology Selection and Procurement

Procurement is perhaps one of the best levers in a system for delivering desired results and impacts. These considerations should go beyond what is procured to how needs and policies are treated as constraints and requirements in the procurement process. As you identify the various needs and concerns, translate these into procurement parameters—constraints and requirements that are incorporated into documentation or processes used for procuring new technologies. Having a committee or working group help with this can ensure that multiple stakeholders are involved in the process (e.g., instructors, staff, students, administration).

As new technologies and resources are procured, continue asking similar questions as discussed above about the PSS and alignment of resources, policies, and rewards or incentives in particular as you evaluate both strategies and technologies for assessment. Additional needs around skills and knowledge, job or task definitions and clarification, and feedback loops and communication needs may also emerge. For example, once you've selected technologies, how will you help everyone come up to speed on the necessary skills/knowledge? What feedback loops will be helpful to have, such as are the tools working/suitable to the tasks? How will you evaluate your technology infrastructure on an ongoing basis?

Handshakes on Development

By the time an online initiative is at the development stage, much of the planning and procurement should be completed and as well aligned as possible. Unfortunately, too many initiatives related to technology start here, and this is where those initiatives go awry and lead to wastes of time, resources, and energy. A core emphasis in this book is avoiding this scenario. Assuming you have been following a planful process as outlined in this book, alignment at this stages means that teachers and staff are receiving support to help them get everything into the learning management system, get it organized, set dates, set up the gradebook and other features, and have an extra set of eyes to review for readiness before Day 1 delivery. In addition to people resources, process supports like a development checklist such as those found in Chapter 10 or in some of the rubrics we mentioned in Chapter 3 can help everyone keep track of details and communicate needs during the development phase. Some jobs or tasks may need revision or clarification to ensure that staff you believe should support educators are clear on those expectations. In some instances, new positions may also be created with new job descriptions for these roles. If the district is reassigning existing personnel or resources to support the online initiative, these individuals may also require additional training and personal development to help them develop any new skills or knowledge to meet adjusted expectations.

Handshakes on Implementation and Evaluation

Although most of the planning and development process should be completed by this point, this marks the beginning of the teaching and ongoing improvement process for instructors and students. Continue asking similar questions as discussed above about the PSS and alignment of resources, policies, and rewards or incentives in particular as you evaluate both strategies and technologies for assessment. Additional needs around skills and knowledge, job or task definitions, and clarification, and feedback loops and communication needs may also emerge.

One common question that arises relative to implementation and ongoing evaluation relates to rewards and incentives and policies. Instructors who are implementing something new or innovative often experience a dip in their evaluations and kick up more areas for improvements in their course designs. This can be a serious disincentive for instructors to try new things. What policies might be helpful in encouraging innovation and experimentation rather than discouraging it? How will you handle any possible dips in student evaluations or feedback that evidences frustration with new or innovative ideas? If an instructor appears to struggle online, what will be your support infrastructure and communications/feedback loops? How can you focus those on support and improvement rather than punishment?

Summary

In this chapter, we discussed how planning at the instructional level should coordinate with planning at the system (school/district/institution) level. There are several key points in the online planning and development process where instructional decisions and administrative decisions impact each other. For example, the vision and standards of excellence established during broader district- or institutional-level planning should cascade down into instructional decisions and planning, and instructional decisions and strategies should flow back up to shape administrative decisions such as technology procurement. The major "handshakes" that we discussed are instructional strategies, interactions & community, digital content selection and production, assessment methods and tools, technology selection and procurement, development, and implementation and evaluation.

Building a successful online learning initiative that is part of an educational ecosystem can be an important strategic direction both for meeting the needs of diverse learners and needs in your district and for creating a more resilient system that better withstands adversities. Accomplishing this is no small or light task, and we hope the big ideas presented in this book—an educational ecosystem, instruction anchored in research and effective online practices, and systems of support that coordinate instructional and system-level planning—help you feel you are able to make better-informed choices and decisions to create online learning worthy of all the individuals working on and impacted by that system.

APPENDIX A

Checklist for Successful Online Learning

☐ The choice to develop an online learning initiative is clearly aligned with addressing a problem, need, or gap that online learning is well suited to solve.

☐ A vision for online learning has been articulated and is aligned with broader district or institutional strategic plan and goals.

☐ There is a clear understanding of different varieties of online learning and purposeful selection of a variety or mix of varieties that align with the type of educational experience the district or institution wishes to facilitate.

☐ The district or institution develops an online learning ecosystem that includes access to important resources and supports for learners, not just online courses and curricula.

☐ The district or institution develops a performance support system to support the online learning ecosystem that aligns policies, resources and infrastructure, job expectations, knowledge and skills development (training and professional development), incentives and rewards, and communication and feedback loops to support educators, staff, and students toward success in online learning.

    ○ Policies are revised, removed, or added to support effective online teaching as well as ethical and legal considerations such as privacy, dignity, and accessibility.

    ○ Technology selection and procurement and other resourcing decisions (e.g., time, work space, equipment) are aligned instructional planning.

○ Job expectations are clarified with revised job descriptions for those who will either teach online or support the online learning ecosystem. Where necessary and possible, new jobs are created to support online learning and learners.

○ Training and professional development focus on effective online instruction and facilitating interactions and community, not just tools (i.e., how to teach effectively using the tools, not just how to use the tools).

○ Teaching online is not an inadvertent additional burden, which would disincentivize effort. This and other barriers that would disincentivize have been lowered or removed.

○ Purposeful communication and feedback loops are established and followed, including technical issues and fixes, clear and consistent communications with parents and staff as well as with teachers and students, easy access to information through course sites, and ongoing evaluation that created a continuous feedback loop of improvement.

☐ Effective online learning is a result of intentional instructional and system design decisions stemming from purposeful planning that is anchored in research evidence of what works and in what conditions.

☐ In addition to preparing and delivering online content, educators and leaders have designed instruction and implemented technology infrastructure and resources to support formal and informal learning interactions— both between instructors and students and among students.

☐ Learner diversity is an assumed default characteristic of learner populations in any modality, and resources and supports in the online learning ecosystem reflect a commitment to supporting all learners.

☐ The online learning team engages in a process of continual improvement where information and data are gathered on system performance and used to make improvements, not to target or blame.

☐ The online learning team ensures that ethical and legal considerations are incorporated throughout the entire planning and design processes, including how technologies are evaluated and addressed systemically through policies, resourcing, skills and knowledge development, and other system supports.

Analysis Worksheet to Identify Gaps in Your Performance Support System

ROOT CAUSE ANALYSIS WORKSHEET TO SUPPORT ONLINE LEARNING

FACTORS	DRIVING FORCES					RESTRAINING FORCES			
EXAMPLES	+4	+3	+2	+1	0	-1	-2	-3	-4
Clear expectations	·	⊙	·	·		·	·	·	·
Time	·	·	·	·		·	·	·	⊙
INFORMATION									
Clear expectations	·	·	·	·		·	·	·	·
Clear standards	·	·	·	·		·	·	·	·
Relevant feedback	·	·	·	·		·	·	·	·
Data / learning analytics systems	·	·	·	·		·	·	·	·

Adapted from Roger Chevalier, "Improving Workplace Performance," Performance Improvement, vol. 53, no. 5, May/June 2014. © 2014 International Society for Performance Improvement. Published online in Wiley Online Library (wileyonlinelibrary.com) • DOI: 10.1002/pfi.21410

RESOURCES

Materials and tools   •   •   •   •   •   •   •   •

Time   •   •   •   •   •   •   •   •

Clear processes /
procedures   •   •   •   •   •   •   •   •

Dedicated environment   •   •   •   •   •   •   •   •

INCENTIVES

Financial   •   •   •   •   •   •   •   •

Other incentives: _____ •   •   •   •   •   •   •   •

Enriched jobs /
work valued   •   •   •   •   •   •   •   •

Positive work environment /
culture   •   •   •   •   •   •   •   •

KNOWLEDGE AND SKILLS

Necessary knowledge   •   •   •   •   •   •   •   •

Necessary skills   •   •   •   •   •   •   •   •

Proper placement   •   •   •   •   •   •   •   •

POLICIES

Policies are present   •   •   •   •   •   •   •   •

Policies are aligned   •   •   •   •   •   •   •   •

Expectations are realistic •   •   •   •   •   •   •   •

CAPACITY & INFRASTRUCTURE (EXCELLENCE)

Clear vision and
mission for online   •   •   •   •   •   •   •   •

Strategic plan for online •   •   •   •   •   •   •   •

Shared governance
structure   •   •   •   •   •   •   •   •

Community of practice   •   •   •   •   •   •   •   •

Recruit / select the
right people   •   •   •   •   •   •   •   •

Resources for Ethical and Other Issues Related to Online Learning

We have primarily focused on instructional and planning considerations in this book. However, there are additional considerations such as accessibility, privacy, and security. We have curated a quick-start list of resources on a range of topics that can be good additional resources. Moore and Tillberg-Webb's text (2023) has a more exhaustive list of references, but these are a good starter set.

Privacy & Safety

Quintel, D. F. & York, A. (Eds.). (2023). *Privacy and safety in online learning.* Middle Tennessee Open Press. Available as an open source at https://mtsu.pressbooks.pub/privacyandsafetyinonlinelearning/

Accessibility & UDL

CAST Remote Learning Resources: https://www.cast.org/our-work/remote-online-environments

Comprehensive Accessibility Resource List: https://docs.google.com/document/d/18xma_O3Yerz4qR1YmuEYaXwkGtEfibeaDijSMTBy4Yg/edit

Universal Design for Learning: Presuming competence by design. A tutorial for systems, environment, curricular and materials design in learning systems. http://www.hyperformer.com/UDL_tutorial/

Broad Coverage of a Range of Topics

This resources covers many topics, including the digital equity/digital divide; learning analytics and AI ethics; cultural considerations; diverse learners; accessibility and inclusive design; data privacy and security; OER and fair use.

Moore, S. & Tillberg-Webb, H. (2023). *Ethics and educational technology: Reflection, interrogation, and design as a framework for practice.* Routledge.

References

Anderson, L. W. (Ed.), Krathwohl, D.R. (Ed.), Airasian, P. W., Cruikshank, K.A., Mayer, R. E., Pintrich, P. R., Raths, J., & Wittrock, M. C. (2001). *A taxonomy for learning, teaching, and assessing: A revision of Bloom's Taxonomy of Educational Objectives* (Complete edition). Longman.

Anderson, T. (2003). Getting the mix right again: An updated and theoretical rationale for interaction. *International Review of Research in Open and Distributed Learning, 4*(2). https://doi.org/10.19173/irrodl.v4i2.149

Anderson, T., Rourke, L., Garrison, D. R., & Archer, W. (2001). Assessing teaching presence in a computer conferencing environment. *Journal of Asynchronous Learning Networks, 5*(2), 1–17. http://dx.doi.org/10.24059/olj.v5i2.1875

Apgar, D., & Cadmus, T. (2021). Using mixed methods to assess the coping and self-regulation skills of undergraduate social work students impacted by COVID-19. *Clinical Social Work Journal, 50*, 1–12. https://doi.org/10.1007/s10615-021-00790-3

Asanov, I., Flores, F. McKenzie, D., Mensmann, M., & Schulte, M. (2021). Remote-learning, time-use, and mental health of Ecuadorian high-school students during the COVID-19 quarantine. *World Development, 138*. https://doi.org/10.1016/j.worlddev.2020.105225

Asimow, M. (1962). *Introduction to design*. Prentice-Hall.

Barbour, M. K. (2007). What are they doing and how are they doing it? Rural student experiences in virtual schooling. Unpublished PhD dissertation, University of Georgia, Athens, GA.

Barbour, M. K. (2019). The landscape of K–12 online learning: Examining the state of the field. In M. G. Moore & W. C. Diehl (Eds.), *Handbook of distance education* (4th ed.; pp. 521–542). Routledge.

Bartuseviciene, I., Pazaver, A., & Kitada, M. (2021). Building a resilient university: Ensuring academic continuity—transition from face-to-face to online in the COVID-19 pandemic. *WMU Journal of Maritime Affairs, 20,* 151–172. https://doi.org/10.1007/s13437-021-00239-x

Baxi, K., Del Campo, M., Masoud, F., Cheng, R., Donovan, E., Smith, C., Tomlin, D., Cayer, A., Mellis, D., Tayob, H., Erdoğdu, G. P. S., Pevzner, N., Tremblay-McGaw, R., & Fleming. B. (2020, April). Field notes on pandemic teaching: 6. *Places Journal.* https://placesjournal.org/article/field-notes-on-pandemic-teaching-6/

Beabout, B. (2014). Community leadership: Seeking social justice while re-creating public schools in post-Katrina New Orleans. In I. Bogotch and C. M. Shields (Eds.), *International Handbook of Educational Leadership* (pp. 543–570). Springer. https://doi.org/0.1007/978-94-007-6555-9_30

Becker, S. P., Breaux, R., Cusick, C. N., Dvorsky, M. R., Marsh, N. P., Sciberras, E., & Langberg, J. M. (2020). Remote learning during COVID-19: Examining school practices, service continuation, and difficulties for adolescents with ADHD. The *Journal of Adolescent Health, 67*(6), 769–777. https://doi.org/10.1016/j.jadohealth.2020.09.002

Berge, Z. L. (1995). Facilitating computer conferencing: Recommendations from the field. *Educational Technology, 35*(1) 22–30. https://courses.dcs.wisc.edu/design-teaching/FacilitationManagement _Spring2016/facilitation-module/1_Online_Instructor_Roles/resources/ roi_Berge-Role%20of%20the%20Online%20Instructorr.pdf

Bernard, R. M., Abrami, P. C., Lou, Y., Borokhovski, E., Wade, A., Wozney, L., Wallet, P. A., Fiset, M., & Huang, B. (2004). How does distance education compare with classroom instruction? A meta-analysis of the empirical literature. *Review of Educational Research, 74*(3), 379–439.

Bernard, R. M., Abrami, P. C., Borokhovski, E., Wade, A., Tamim, R., Surkes, M., & Bethel, E. C. (2009). A meta-analysis of three interaction treatments in distance education. *Review of Educational Research, 79*(3), 1243–1289.

Biber, D. D., Melton, B., & Czech, D. R. (2020). The impact of COVID-19 on college anxiety, optimism, gratitude, and course satisfaction. *Journal of American College Health, 70*(7), 1–6. https://doi.org/10.1080/07448481.2020.1842424

Blau, I., Shamir-Inbal, T., & Avdiel, O. (2020). How does the pedagogical design of a technology-enhanced collaborative academic course promote digital literacies, self-regulation, and perceived learning of students? *The Internet and Higher Education, 45*. https://doi.org/10.1016/j.iheduc.2019.100722

Borup, J. (2016). Teacher perceptions of learner-learner engagement at a cyber high school. *International Review of Research in Open and Distributed Learning, 17*(3), 231–250. https://doi.org/10.19173/irrodl.v17i3.2361

Borup, J., Chambers, C. B., & Stimson, R. (2018, September 20). *Helping online students be successful: Student perceptions of online teacher and on-site mentor facilitation support*. Michigan Virtual University. https://mvlri.org/research/publications/helping-online-students-be-successful-student-perceptions-of-support/

Borup, J., Chambers, C. B., & Stimson, R. (2019). K–12 Student perceptions of online teacher and on-site facilitator support in supplemental online courses. *Online Learning, 23*(4), 253–280. https://olj.onlinelearning consortium.org/index.php/olj/article/view/1565

Borup, J., Graham, C. R., & Davies, R. S. (2013). The nature of adolescent learner interaction in a virtual high school setting. *Journal of Computer Assisted Learning, 29*(2), 153–167. https://doi.org/10.1111/j.1365-2729.2012.00479.x

Borup, J., Graham, C. R., & Drysdale, J. S. (2014a). The nature of teacher engagement at an online high school. *British Journal of Educational Technology, 45*(5), 793–806. https://doi.org/10.1111/bjet.12089

Borup, J., Graham, C. R., West, R. E., Archambault, L., & Spring, K. J. (2020). Academic communities of engagement: An expansive lens for examining support structures in blended and online learning. *Educational Technology Research and Development, 68*(2), 807–832. https://doi.org/10.1007/s11423-020-09744-x

Borup, J., West, R. E., Graham, C. R., & Davies, R. S. (2014b). The Adolescent Community of Engagement: A framework for research on adolescent online learning. *Journal of Technology and Teacher Education, 22*(1), 107–129. https://www.learntechlib.org/p/112371/

Bowman, E. (2022, August 26). Scanning students' rooms during remote tests is unconstitutional, judge rules. *National Public Radio*. https://www.npr.org/2022/08/25/1119337956/test-proctoring-room-scans-unconstitutional-cleveland-state-university

Brown, J. S., Collins, A., & Duguid, P. (1989). Situated cognition and the culture of learning. *Educational Researcher, 18*(1), 32–42. https://doi.org/10.3102/0013189X018001032

Burnham, B. R., & Walden, B. (1997). Interactions in distance education: A report from the other side. In R. E. Nolan & H. Chelesvig (Eds.), *Annual Adult Education Research Conference Proceedings* (pp. 49–54). Oklahoma State University, Stillwater, School of Occupational and Adult Education. https://files.eric.ed.gov/fulltext/ED409460.pdf

Caldwell, J. (2020, June 18). Spoiled for choice: Virtual labs for science education. BCcampus News. https://bccampus.ca/2020/06/18/spoiled-for-choice-virtual-labs-for-science-education/

Chappuis, J., & Stiggins, R. S. (2016). *An introduction to student-involved assessment FOR learning* (7th ed.). Pearson.

Chaturvedi, K., Vishwakarma, D., & Singh, N. (2021). COVID-19 and its impact on education, social life and mental health of students: A survey. *Children and Youth Services Review, 121.* https://doi.org/10.1016/j.childyouth.2020.105866

Chevalier, R. (2014). Improving workplace performance. *Performance Improvement, 53*(5), 6–19. https://doi.org/10.1002/pfi.21410

Chin, M. (2021, May 5). College student sues Proctorio after source code copyright claim. *The Verge.* https://www.theverge.com/2021/4/22/22397499/proctorio-lawsuit-electronic-frontier-foundation-test-proctoring-software

Cho, M.-H., & Shen, D. (2013). Self-regulation in online learning. *Distance Education, 34*(3), 290–301. https://doi.org/10.1080/01587919.2013.835770

Clark, R., & Mayer, R. (2016). *e-Learning and the science of instruction: Proven guidelines for consumers and designers of multimedia learning* (4th ed.). Wiley.

Clark, R. C. (1994). Hang up your training hat. *Training and Development, 48*(9), 61.

Cleland, E. (2011). Biodiversity and ecosystem stability. *Nature Education Knowledge 3*(10), 14.

Collins, A., Brown, J. S., & Newman, S. E. (1987). *Cognitive apprenticeship: Teaching the craft of reading, writing and mathematics* (Technical Report No. 403). BBN Laboratories.

Cowan, N. (2010). The magical mystery four: How is working memory capacity limited, and why? *Current Directions in Psychological Science, 19*(1): 51–57. https://doi.org/10.1177/0963721409359277

Davis, N. E., Demiraslan, Y., Charania, A., Compton, L., & Correia, A. (2007a, February). *Teacher education goes into virtual schooling* [Paper]. Fund for the Improvement of Postsecondary Education (FIPSE) Comprehensive Conference, Washington, D.C.

Davis, N. E., Roblyer, M. D., Charania, A., Ferdig, R., Harms, C., Compton, L. K. L., & Cho, M. O. (2007b). Illustrating the "virtual" in virtual schooling: Challenges and strategies for creating real tools to prepare virtual teachers. *Internet and Higher Education, 10*(1), 27–39. https://doi.org/10.1016/j.iheduc.2006.11.001

Deming, E. (1986). *Out of the crisis* (2nd ed.). MIT Press.

Dickson, W. P. (2005). *Toward a deeper understanding of student performance in virtual high school courses: Using quantitative analyses and data visualization to inform decision making.* Learning Point Associates.

Digital Learning Collaborative. (2020). *Snapshot 2020: A review of K–12 online, blended, and digital learning.* https://static1.squarespace.com/static/5a98496696d4556b01f86662/t/5e61341d879e630db4481a01/1583428708513/DLC-KP-Snapshot2020.pdf/

DiPietro, M. (2010). Virtual school pedagogy: The instructional practices of K–12 virtual school teachers. *Journal of Educational Computing Research, 42*(3), 327–354.

DiPietro, M., Ferdig, R. E., Black, E. W., & Preston, M. (2008). Best practices in teaching K–12 online: Lessons learned from Michigan Virtual School teachers. *Journal of Interactive Online Learning, 7*(1), 10–38. https://www.ncolr.org/jiol/issues/pdf/7.1.2.pdf

Donaldson, E. (2021, February 10). Denton among the first Texas school districts planning to keep virtual education for the long haul. *Dallas Morning News.* https://www.dallasnews.com/news/education/2021/02/10/denton-among-the-first-texas-school-districts-planning-to-keep-virtual-education-for-the-long-haul/

Fawns, T., & Ross, J. (2020, June 3). Spotlight on alternative assessment methods: Alternatives to exams. *Teaching Matters Blog.* https://www.teaching-matters-blog.ed.ac.uk/spotlight-on-alternative-assessment-methods-alternatives-to-exams/

Fedesco, H. N. (2020). *Leading synchronous online discussions.* Vanderbilt University Course Development Resources. https://www.vanderbilt.edu/cdr/module-2/leading-synchronous-online-discussions/

Ferdig, R., Cavanaugh, C., DiPietro, M., Black, E., & Dawson, K. (2009). Virtual schooling standards and best practices for teacher education. *Journal of Technology and Teacher Education, 17*(4), 479–503. https://www.learntechlib.org/p/30481/

Fiorella, L., & Mayer, R. E. (2016). Eight ways to promote generative learning. *Educational Psychology Review, 28*(4), 717–741. https://doi.org/10.1007/s10648-015-9348-9

Fischer, C., McPartlan, P., Orona, G., Yu, R., Xu, D., & Warschauer, M. (2022). Salient syllabi: Examining design characteristics of science online courses in higher education. *PLoS ONE*, *17*(11): e0276839. https://doi.org/10.1371/journal.pone.0276839

Fisher, M., & Root, T. (2021, August 30). In hardest slam since Katrina, New Orleans's levees stand firm. *Washington Post*. https://www.washingtonpost.com/climate-environment/climate-solutions/in-hardest-slam-since-katrina-new-orleanss-levees-stand-firm/2021/08/30/4ca6322e-09b0-11ec-a6dd-296ba7fb2dce_story.html

Flaherty, C. (2020, May 11). Big Proctor. *Inside Higher Ed*. https://www.insidehighered.com/news/2020/05/11/online-proctoring-surging-during-covid-19

Garrison, D. R. (1989). *Understanding distance education: A framework for the future*. Routledge.

Garrison, D. R., Anderson, T., & Archer, W. (2000). Critical inquiry in a text-based environment: Computer conferencing in higher education. *The Internet and Higher Education*, *2*(2–3), 87–105. https://doi.org/10.1016/S1096-7516(00)00016-6

Glass, I. (producer). (2021, October 1). 749: My bad (audio podcast transcript). *This American Life*. https://www.thisamericanlife.org/749/transcript

Gunawardena, C. N., Frechette, C., & Layne, L. (2019). *Culturally inclusive instructional design: A framework and guide to building online wisdom communities*. Routledge.

Gusman, M. S, Grimm, K. J., Cohen. A. B., & Doane, L. D. (2021). Stress and sleep across the onset of the novel coronavirus disease 2019 pandemic: Impact of distance learning on US college students' health trajectories. *Sleep*, *44*(12), 1–13. https://doi.org/10.1093/sleep/zsab193

Halverson, L. R., & Graham, C. R. (2019). Learner engagement in blended learning environments: A conceptual framework. *Online Learning*, *23*(2), 145–178. https://doi.org/10.24059/olj.v23i2.1481

Hanke, U. (2012). Generative learning. In N. M. Seel (Ed.), *Encyclopedia of the Sciences of Learning*. Springer. https://doi.org/10.1007/978-1-4419-1428-6_171

Harris, J. (2012, March 20). Data myopia and business relativity. *OCDQ Blog*. http://www.ocdqblog.com/home/data-myopia-and-business-relativity.html.

Harwell, D. (2019, December 19). Federal study confirms racial bias of many facial-recognition systems, casts doubt on expanding their use. *Washington Post*. https://www.washingtonpost.com/technology/2019/12/19/federal-study-confirms-racial-bias-many-facial-recognition-systems-casts-doubt-their-expanding-use/

Haughey, M., & Muirhead, W. (1999). *On-line learning: Best practices for Alberta school jurisdictions*. Government of Alberta. https://eric.ed.gov/?id=ED438798

Hawkins, A., Barbour, M. K., & Graham, C. R. (2011). Strictly business: Teacher perceptions of interaction in virtual schooling. *International Journal of E-Learning and Distance Education*, *25*(2). https://www.ijede.ca/index.php/jde/article/view/726

Heinemann, M. H. (2005). Teacher-student interaction and learning in on-line theological education. Part I: Concepts and concerns. *Christian Higher Education*, *4*(3), 183–209. https://doi.org/10.1080/15363750590959995

Hill, P. (2021, July 28). Colleges that prospered during the pandemic. *Chronicle of Higher Education*. https://www.chronicle.com/article/the-colleges-that-prospered-during-the-pandemic

Hillman, D. C., Willis, D. J., & Gunawardena, C. N. (1994). Learner-interface interaction in distance education: An extension of contemporary models and strategies for practitioners. *American Journal of Distance Education*, *8*(2), 30–42. https://doi.org/10.1080/08923649409526853

Hodges, C. B., & Barbour, M. K. (2021). Assessing learning during emergency remote education. *Italian Journal of Educational Technology*, *29*(2), 85–98. https://doi.org/10.17471/2499-4324/1208

Hodges, C., Moore, S., Lockee, B., Bond, A., & Jewett, A. (2021). An instructional design process for emergency remote teaching. In A. Tlili, D. Burgos, & A. Tabacco (Eds.), *Education in crisis context: COVID-19 as an opportunity for global learning* (pp. 37–51). Springer. https://doi.org/10.1007/978-981-15-7869-4_3

Hodges, C., Moore, S., Lockee, B., Trust, T., & Bond., A. (2020, March 27). The difference between emergency remote teaching and online learning. *Educause Review*. https://er.educause.edu/articles/2020/3/the-difference-between-emergency-remote-teaching-and-online-learning

Holmes, D. (2021, October 14). Designing for change. *World Landscape Architecture*. https://worldlandscapearchitect.com/designing-for-change/#.Y4d3Y3bMKbg

Hung, J. L., Hsu, Y. C., & Rice, K. (2012a). Integrating data mining in program evaluation of K–12 online education. *Journal of Educational Technology and Society*, *15*(3), 27–41.

Hung, J. L., Rice, K., & Saba, A. (2012b). An educational data mining model for online teaching and learning. *Journal of Educational Technology Development and Exchange, 5*(2), 77–93. https://dx.doi.org/10.18785/jetde.0502.06

Indiana University. (n.d.). Proctoring and equity. Retrieved November 18, 2022, from.https://citl.indiana.edu/teaching-resources/diversity-inclusion/proctoring/index.html

Jekielek, S. M., Moore, K. A., Hair, E. C., & Scarupa, H. J. (2002, February). Mentoring: A promising strategy for youth development (Research Brief). Child Trends. https://oclawin.org/wp-content/uploads/2015/08/jekielek-mentoring.pdf

Jones, J. C. (1966). *Design methods reviewed*. Springer.

Kaufman, R. (1996). Needs assessment: Internal and external. In D. Ely & T. Plomp (Eds.), *Classic writings on instructional technology* (pp. 111–118). Libraries Unlimited.

Kaufman, R. (1997). A new reality for organizational success: Two bottom lines. *Performance Improvement, 38*(8), 3.

Kaufman, R. (2000a). Education past, present and future: From how to what to why. *International Journal of Educational Reform, 9*(1), 2–8.

Kaufman, R. (2000b). *Mega planning: Practical tools for organizational success*. Sage.

Keller, J. (1987). Development and use of the ARCS model of instructional design. *Journal of Instructional Development, 10*, 2. https://link.springer.com/article/10.1007/BF02905780

Kennedy, V., Twilley, R., Kleypas, J., Cowan, J., & Hare, S. (2002). Coastal and marine ecosystems and global climate change: Potential effects on U.S. resources. Pew Center on Global Climate Change. https://www.c2es.org/wp-content/uploads/2002/08/marine_ecosystems.pdf

Khazan, O. (2018, April 11). The myth of "learning styles." *Atlantic*. https://www.theatlantic.com/science/archive/2018/04/the-myth-of-learning-styles/557687/

Lang, J. (2013). *Cheating lessons: Learning from academic dishonesty*. Harvard University Press.

Lehrer-Small, A. (2022, November 14). Virtual school enrollment kept climbing even as COVID receded, new data reveal. *The 74 Million*. https://www.the74million.org/article/virtual-school-enrollment-kept-climbing-even-as-covid-receded-new-data-reveal/

Lockee, B., Moore, M., & Burton, J. (2001). Old concerns with new distance education research. *Educause Quarterly, 24*(2), 60–68.

Lohr, L. (2007). *Creating graphics for learning and performance: Lessons in visual literacy* (2nd ed.). Pearson College Division.

Lynch, R., & Dembo, M. (2004). The relationship between self-regulation and online learning in a blended learning context. *International Review of Research in Open and Distributed Learning, 5*(2). https://doi.org/10.19173/irrodl.v5i2.189

Mathur, P. (1978). Re-modelling Panchayati Raj institutions in India. *Indian Journal of Public Administration, 24*(3), 592–616. https://doi.org/10.1177/0019556119780304

May, C. (2018, May 29). The problem with "learning styles." *Scientific American.* https://www.scientificamerican.com/article/the-problem-with-learning-styles/

Mayer, R. E. (2008). Applying the science of learning: Evidence-based principles for the design of multimedia instruction. *American Psychologist, 63*(8), 760–769.

Mayer, R. (2020). *Multimedia learning* (3rd ed.). Cambridge University Press.

McQuate, S. (2021, September 2). UW engineer explains how the redesigned levee system in New Orleans helped mitigate the impact of Hurricane Ida. *UW News.* https://www.washington.edu/news/2021/09/02/uw-engineer-explains-how-redesigned-levee-system-new-orleans-helped-mitigate-hurricane-ida/

Meadows, D. (2008). *Thinking in systems: A primer.* Chelsea Green.

Means, B., Bakia, M., & Murphy, R. (2014). *Learning online: What research tells us about whether, when, and how.* New York: Routledge.

Milman, N. & Wessmiller, J. (2016). Motivating the online learner using Keller's ARCS Model. *Distance Learning, 17*(4), 33–37.

Moore, M. G. (1983). The individual adult learner. In M. Tight (Ed.), *Adult learning and education* (pp. 153–168). Croom Helm.

Moore, M. G. (1989). Editorial: Three types of interaction. *American Journal of Distance Education, 3*(2), 1–7. https://doi.org/10.1080/08923648909526659

Moore, M.G. (1990). Recent contributions to the theory of distance education. *Open Learning, 5*(3), 10–15.

Moore, M. G., & Kearsley, G. (1995). *Distance education: A systems view.* Wadsworth.

Moore, S. (2021a). The design models we have are not the design models we need. *Journal of Applied Instructional Design, 10*(4). https://dx.doi.org/10.51869/104/smo

Moore, S. (2021b). *SEL at a Distance.* Norton.

Moore, S. (2022). The joyous paradox of making the multitude the norm: Blended learning as a reconstructive act. In R. C. Li, S. K. S. Cheung, P. H. F. Ng, L.-P. Wong, & F. L. Wang (Eds.), *ICBL 2022: Blended learning:*

Engaging students in the new normal era (conference proceedings; pp. 20–34). Springer. https://doi.org/10.1007/978-3-031-08939-8_3

Moore, S., & Hill, P. (2020, April 28). Planning for resilience, not resistance. *PhilOnEd-Tech* (blog). https://philonedtech.com/planning-for-resilience-not-resistance/

Moore, S., & Hong, J. (2022). Designing a virtual practicum to prepare teachers for online instruction: Developing confidence and competence through an online field experience. *International Journal of Designs for Learning, 13*(2), 70–86. https://scholarworks.iu.edu/journals/index.php/ijdl/article/view/33417

Moore, S., & Piety, P. (2022). Online learning ecosystems: Comprehensive planning and support for distance learners. *Distance Education, 43*(2), 179–203. https://doi.org/10.1080/01587919.2022.2064820

Moore, S. L., & Tillberg-Webb, H. (2023). *Ethics and educational technology: Reflection, interrogation, and design as a framework for practice.* Routledge/Taylor & Francis.

Moore, S., Veletsianos, G., & Barbour, M. (2022). A synthesis of research on mental health and remote learning: How pandemic grief haunts claims of causality. *OTESSA Journal, 2*(1). https://journal.otessa.org/index.php/oj/article/view/36

Morrison, G., Ross, S., Kalman, H., & Kemp, J. (2013). *Designing effective instruction* (6th ed.). Wiley.

Mulcahy, D. M., Dibbon, D., & Norberg, C. (2008). *An investigation into the nature of education in a rural and remote region of Newfoundland and Labrador: The Straits.* Harris Centre, Memorial University of Newfoundland. https://research.library.mun.ca/214/1/investigation_into_the_nature_of_education.pdf

Nippard, E., & Murphy, E. (2007). Social presence in the web-based synchronous secondary classroom. *Canadian Journal of Learning and Technology, 33*(1). https://cjlt.ca/index.php/cjlt/article/view/26460

Page, H. (1966). *Principles of Aerial Design.* Van Nostrand.

Parker, J., & Herrington, J. (2015). Setting the climate in an authentic online community of learning. Paper presented at the Annual Meeting of the Australian Association for Research in Education (AARE), Freemantle, Western Australia, November 29–December 3.

Patton, A. (2013, July 12). Oklahoma tornado prompts discussions on surviving, rebuilding. *Government Technology.* https://www.govtech.com/recovery/devastating-oklahoma-tornado-surviving-rebuilding.html

Pérez-Gómez, A., & Parcell, S. (2011). *Chora 6: Intervals in the philosophy of architecture*. McGill-Queen's University Press.

Racine, N., McArthur, B., Cooke, J., Eirich, R., Zhu, J., & Madigan, S. (2021). Global prevalence of depressive and anxiety symptoms in children and adolescents during COVID-19. *JAMA Pediatrics, 175*(11), 1142-1150. https://doi.org/10.1001/jamapediatrics.2021.2482

Reigeluth, C. M. (1993). Principles of educational systems design. *International Journal of Educational Research, 19*(2), 117–131.

Reigeluth, C., Karnopp, J., Sommer, B., Namba, N., Jaeger, P., & Sherwood, L. (2020). *Vision and action: Reinventing schools through personalized competency-based education*. Marzano Resources.

Reigeluth, C. M., & Stinson, D. (2007). The Decatur story: Reinvention of a school corporation—mission and values for Decatur's school transformation. *Indiana School Boards Association Journal, 53*(1), 17–19.

Rice, K. (2012). *Making the move to K–12 online teaching: Research-based strategies and practices*. Pearson Education.

Rice, M. (2022). Special education teachers' use of technologies during the COVID-19 era. *TechTrends, 66*(2), 310-326.

Richman, T. (2021, January 10). Even after COVID-19, North Texas districts expect a demand for some virtual learning options. *Dallas Morning News*. https://www.dallasnews.com/news/education/2021/01/10/even-after-covid-19-north-texas-districts-expect-a-demand-for-some-virtual-learning-options/

Rittel, H. W. J., & Webber, M. M. (1973). Dilemmas in a general theory of planning. *Policy Sciences, 4*(2), 155–169. https://doi.org/10.1007/bf01405730

Roblyer, M. D. (2006). Virtually successful: Defeating the dropout problem through online school programs. *Phi Delta Kappan, 88*(1), 31–36. https://doi.org/10.1177/003172170608800107

Rose, D., & Meyer, A. (2002). *Teaching every student in the digital age: Universal design for learning*. Association for Supervision and Curriculum Development.

Rose, D., & Meyer, A. (2013). *Universal design for learning: Theory and practice*. CAST.

Rourke, L., Anderson, T., Garrison, D. R., & Archer, W. (1999). Assessing social presence in asynchronous text-based computer conference. *Journal of Distance Education, 14*(2), 51–70. https://www.ijede.ca/index.php/jde/article/view/153

Rummler, G. A., & Brache, A. P. (2012). *Improving performance: How to manage the white space in the organization chart* (2nd ed.). Jossey-Bass.

Sapolin, A. (2022, August 22). Cleveland State student wins federal lawsuit against university on break of Fourth Amendment. *Cleveland 19 News.* https://www.cleveland19.com/2022/08/23/cleveland-state-student-wins-federal-lawsuit-against-university-breach-fourth-amendment/

Scholes, V. (2016). The ethics of using learning analytics to categorize students on risk. *Educational Technology Research and Development, 64*(5), 939–955. https://doi.org/10.1007/s11423-016-9458-1

Schwartz, H., Grant, D., Diliberti, M., Hunter, G., & Setodji, C. (2020). Remote learning is here to stay: Results from the first American school district panel survey. RAND Corporation. https://doi.org/10.7249/RRA956-1

Short, J., Williams, E., & Christie, B. (1976). *The social psychology of telecommunication.* Wiley.

Simon, H. A. (1969). *Sciences of the artificial.* MIT Press.

Singer, N. (2021, April 12). Online schools are here to stay, even after the pandemic. *The New York Times.*

Skylar, A. A. (2009). A comparison of asynchronous online text-based lectures and synchronous interactive web conferencing lectures. *Issues in Teacher Education, 18*(2), 69-84.

Sotola, L. K., & Crede, M. (2021). Regarding class quizzes: A meta-analytic synthesis of studies on the relationship between frequent low-stakes testing and class performance. *Educational Psychology Review, 33,* 407–421. https://doi.org/10.1007/s10648-020-09563-9

Spitzer, D. (1990). Confessions of a performance technologist. *Educational Technology, 30*(5), 12–15.

Stiggins, R. J., & Conklin, N. 1992. *In teachers' hands: Investigating the practice of classroom assessment.* SUNY Press.

Sturgis, C., & Casey, K. (2018). *Quality principles for competency-based education.* iNACOL. https://aurora-institute.org/wp-content/uploads/Quality-Principles-Book.pdf

Surry, D., & Ensminger, D. (2001). What's wrong with media comparison studies? *Educational Technology, 41*(4), 32–35.

Sutton, L. A. (2001). The principle of vicarious interaction in computer-mediated communications. *International Journal of Educational Telecommunications, 7*(3), 223–242. https://www.learntechlib.org/primary/p/9534/

Svihla, V. (2020). Problem framing. In J. K. McDonald & R. E. West

(Eds.), *Design for learning: Principles, processes, and praxis.* EdTech Books. https://edtechbooks.org/id/problem_framing

Thackaberry, A. (2017). Competency-based education models: An emerging taxonomy. Unpublished PhD dissertation, Kent State University. https://etd.ohiolink.edu/apexprod/rws_etd/send_file/send?accession=kent1491776906336325&disposition=inline

Triner, D., Greenberry, A., & & Watkins, R. (1996). Training needs assessment: A contradiction of terms. *Educational Technology, 36*(6), 51–55.

U.S. Department of Education. (2009). *Evaluation of evidence-based practices in online learning: A meta-analysis and review of online learning studies.* U.S. Department of Education.

Vygotsky, L. S. (1962). *Thought and language* (E. Hanfmann & G. Vakar, Trans.). MIT Press.

Vygotsky, L. S. (1978). *Mind in society: The development of higher psychologist processes.* Harvard University Press.

Weiner, C. (2003). Key ingredients to online learning: Adolescent students study in cyberspace—The nature of the study. *International Journal of E-Learning, 2*(3), 44–50. https://www.learntechlib.org/p/14497/

Weller, M. (2018, July). Twenty years of edtech. *Educause Review.* https://er.educause.edu/articles/2018/7/twenty-years-of-edtech

Williams, R. (2014). *The non-designer's design book,* (4th ed). Peachpit Press.

Wolcott, L. L. (1995). The distance teacher as reflective practitioner. *Educational Technology, 35*(1), 39–43.

Young, J. R. (2021, November 19). Automated proctoring swept in during pandemic. *EdSurge.* https://www.edsurge.com/news/2021-11-19-automated-proctoring-swept-in-during-pandemic-it-s-likely-to-stick-around-despite-concerns

Zhao, Y., Lei, J., Yan, B., Lai, C., & Tan, H. S. (2005). What makes a difference? A practical analysis of research on the effectiveness of distance education. *Teachers College Record, 107*(8), 1836–1884.

Zimmerman, B. J. (2002). Becoming a self-regulated learner: An overview. *Theory into Practice, 41*(2), 64–70. https://doi.org/10.1207/s15430421tip4102_2

Zimmerman, B. J., & Schunk, D. H. (2011). Self-regulated learning and performance: An introduction and an overview. In B. J. Zimmerman & D. H. Schunk (Eds.), *Handbook of self-regulation of learning and performance* (pp. 1–12). Routledge.

Index

In this index, *f* and *t* stand for figure and table, respectively.

About the Authors

Stephanie L. Moore is an assistant professor of organization, information, and learning sciences at the University of New Mexico. Prior to that role, she spent over two decades designing and delivering award-winning online learning programs across a wide range of contexts. She is also the author of *SEL at a Distance,* part of the SEL series at Norton, and *Ethics and Educational Technology*, the first text that explores critical ethical issues around educational technologies.

Michael K. Barbour is a professor of instructional design for the College of Education and Health Sciences at Touro University California. For over two decades his research has focused on the effective design, delivery, and support of K–12 distance, online, and blended learning, as well as how regulation, governance, and policy can impact that effectiveness. Michael's background and expertise has resulted in testimony before legislative committees and as an expert witness in several U.S. states, across Canada, and in New Zealand. Additionally, he has also consulted on research and development projects in Australia, South Korea, Saudi Arabia, and Sweden.